The Game of my Life

Jack Mahon

in conversation with

The Giants of the GAA Past and Present

BLACKWATER PRESS

Printed in Ireland at the press of the publishers 1993

Broomhill Business Park,
Broomhill Road,
Tallaght,
Dublin 24.

ISBN: 0 86121 4137

Design and Layout
Paddy Barrett

Contents

Acknowledgements

When I retired from teaching at the end of January 1993, I sold the idea of this book to Blackwater Press publisher, John O'Connor, and set off on a journey down the "Highways and Byeways" of Ireland meeting the household names of the G.A.A. in their own homes and enjoying the experience. That took a fair amount of organisation but I met the finest group of people one could hope to encounter. All so humble, so welcoming and so thrilled to be included in this book. My gratitude to one and all of them and their very hospitable families. My thanks too, to Paddy and Florrie Barrett for their patience and unflagging dedication and to Anna O'Donovan and all at Blackwater Press, who were so helpful.

Jack Mahon - October 1993

Chapter 1

Martin Carney

Donegal and Mayo

There are few more enthusiastic lovers of the game of Gaelic football than Castlebar based teacher Martin Carney whose fresh and infectious approach to the game is as vibrant today as it was when I met him first as a student in U.C.G. over twenty years ago. Then he was an inseparable pal of another Gaelic football devotee Tony Regan, known in U.C.G. circles as "The Horse". Martin, who was born in Bundoran and brought up in Allingham's Ballyshannon was quite chuffed to be included in this galaxy of stars. In fact he was the first interviewee.

Who first sowed the seeds of love for the game in you?

"It began with my father Owen Carney, a brother of Jackie Carney, one of the stars of Mayo's wonderful team of the '30's. The family hailed from Lahardane outside Ballina and were steeped in football. So my father bred a love for the game in me from the beginning. As I got older, there was a very vibrant G.A.A. club in the town of Ballyshannon named AODH RUADH, where we also were very lucky to have the influence of the De La Salle Brothers, in particular Br. Kieran and Br. Raphael. One special memory is of being brought to Croke Park for the first time as a seven-year-old in 1959 by my father to see the All-Ireland semi-final between Dublin and Kerry and I remember the excitement of that occasion generated an added interest and an enthusiasm to go and play football. Getting back to that first visit to Croke Park, the cathedral of football, there was a wild excitement and exuberance about the place that made me instantly love it and gave me a desire to play the game which allowed people to play there. Funny, it was years before I was in Croke Park again as I went to boarding school in St. Eunan's College, Letterkenny where a man named Michael Cullen gave day in day out attention to the boys who played Gaelic football. I played for Eunan's for three years in the McRory Cup. We won a McLarnon Cup in my Inter Cert year. My years in St. Eunan's were 1965-1970. Some players from my college days who went on to greater things were Mikey Sweeney and Hughie McClafferty."

University days in U.C.G. were to be very meaningful to the Ballyshannon teenager.

"Of all the days that I played football, my University days were the most enjoyable. After coming from a protected and controlled boarding school environment, I was let loose then into the free University life. Here I was thrown in with an awful lot of footballers from different parts of the country, lads like Ger O'Keeffe and Paudie Mahoney of Kerry. Tony Regan was there a year or two before me. We lost three Sigerson Cup finals in my time there. The loss to U.C.C. in 1972 by 5-6 to 3-8 in O'Toole Park, Dublin is memorable. That Cork team had Moss Keane, the Lynch brothers, Paudie and Brendan, Seamus Looney and Simon Murphy, Dan Kavanagh and Richie Bambury. I loved playing Sigerson. There was a great sense of abandon to the way we played. A camaraderie grew up because of the way we trained and socialised together. We lived in each other's pockets more or less for months. The U.C.D. team of then was a team of All-Stars - lads like Paddy Kerr, Kevin Kilmurray, John O'Keeffe, Ogie Moran, Oliver Leddy, J.P. Kane. Sigerson was on a par with county football then. Perhaps it's a bit more difficult now with such an emphasis on the academic side of University life. In our days at College you seemed to be able to have time to enjoy yourself and play football."

While you were attending U.C.G. I remember seeing you participating in a Galway County Senior Final against Dunmore MacHales. Were you annoyed to find almost the whole county against U.C.G.?

"Not at all. My memory of it really is of sharing an apartment in The Bronx and getting a phonecall on the Wednesday night that the county final, which had been brought forward, was on a Sunday. Tony Regan and myself paid our own way from New York to play in it. I played midfield against Pat Donnellan and hardly got a kick of the ball as I remember. It saddens me now not to see U.C.G. involved in club competition in Galway."

Martin Carney represents a pretty unique band of players who played for two counties and two provinces. In fact Martin also won a Railway Cup medal with the Combined

Universities. So it was relatively easy to prevail on him to reminisce on his early Donegal days.

"I first played for Donegal in November 1970 and broke my collar bone in my first full National Football League game against Armagh in Ballyshannon, having made my debut as a substitute against Tyrone. So I didn't play again until the spring of 1971 and my first Senior Football Championship game was against Down in Newry. 1972 was special in so many ways. It started off with a difficult assignment against Down in the first round and we beat them 1-8 to 0-8 in Ballybofey. At the time they had Sean O'Neill, Dan McCartan, Colm McAlarney and a huge number of the 1968 All-Ireland winning team. We then beat Cavan after a replay in Clones. The drawn game in Irvinestown was saved for us with a marvellous Joe Winston equaliser. The Final was played on a very wet day. It bucketed rain. I cannot remember the score but I'll never forget one of the goals, a shot from a long way out by Seamus Bonner. Tyrone were our opponents in this Donegal's first ever Ulster title win. The aftermath is hazy now but I remember the beforehand in the Hibernian Hotel. Frankie McFeely, our midfielder, was captain, I remember him lying down and trying to sleep. He was in his thirties, and I was then in my late teens. I found the whole thing very strange. Clones is a very special place on Ulster Final Day. I'd like it better if you could get out of it quickly afterwards but the traffic jams are always colossal. From the point of view of the game itself Clones has a unique effect. Brian McEniff had a tremendous game. I was marked out of it myself by a small little player called Mickey Hughes. The memory of the homecoming to Donegal Town is hazy too because I had an unusual kind of set up at the time in the sense that I was flown home from the U.S. for all the games and went back the day after the Ulster Final. Two years later we won in Ulster again but of the two teams the 1972 team was the better and we were unlucky not to have Neilly Gallagher and Mickey McLoone, both out with injury in 1972."

Who were the Donegal players who impressed you most?

"Mickey McLoone was my boyhood hero in Ballyshannon. I loved his style. Sean Ferritter as a midfielder was great too. I remember seeing Donegal in the first Ulster Final they ever contested in 1963. We had a team in the minor final and I have one pretty daft memory of the whole occasion - that of the Donegal minor goalkeeper Willie McNeilis swinging like a monkey off the crossbar every time the ball went over the bar. It was a sweltering July day and I remember my Dad carrying me out on his shoulders from the game in Breffni Park, Cavan. Down hammered Donegal that day."

Were Donegal overawed when they travelled to Croke Park for the first time to meet Offaly and Galway in 1972 and 1974 respectively?

"I was very relaxed about 1972, flying in from the U.S. on the Thursday beforehand. Yes, we felt we had a reasonable chance. Against Galway in 1974 I was more hopeful of winning if we played well. That was conditioned of course, by the fact that I lived in Galway at the time and knew my opponents well from club games in Galway. John Tobin was brilliant for Galway that day scoring in all 2-6."

How did the association with Mayo begin?

"I got a teaching job in Mayo in 1975 and started playing football there in 1979. A lot of the old Donegal guard had been dropped or let go controversially. Brian McEniff in particular, had been very harshly done by and dismissed in 1976 and I had become disillusioned with the whole approach."

What was the big difference in the style of play of both counties?

"In Mayo the emphasis was very much on catching and kicking, high fielding, good quality kicking of the ball, not nearly the same emphasis on the combined play as in Donegal. Donegal football, even twenty years ago, was much shorter."

Have you any interesting stories to tell?

"The hero of my first ever Croke Park game was Mick O'Connell and I remember meeting him for the first time in Galway as a student. Mick was doing a Sea Skipper's course in Galway and you, yourself, Jack, asked Tony Regan to get a couple of fellows to train with Mick out in Pearse Stadium. So I remember that night, we duly went out to find Micko already training. We climbed in over the wall, Tony Regan, Tony Conboy and myself and I remember Micko running around the Stadium in a pair of sawn off wellingtons. He took off the wellingtons and put on the football boots and we had a fine training session together. The wellingtons were of course heavier and it must have been a huge relief to wear football boots afterwards. Travelling during all my Donegal playing career with Brian McEniff is another special memory. There was always great steel in the man and I'm thrilled he saw his dream come true in 1992."

Your greatest opponents?

"The greatest player I met was Paudie Lynch of Kerry and U.C.C. You could have played him anywhere. In fact he played for Kerry at full back, centre half forward, midfield, and in later games at corner back. Unfortunately, I never saw Sean Purcell or Christy Ring in action. I'd love to have seen Ring on a hurling field. As team-mates I'd include Brian McEniff and Seamie Granaghan. In Sigerson, Tony Regan was outstanding. Jimmy Langan, bother of Joe, of Mayo fame was a fine Sigerson player."

Your medal collection is very imposing too.

"Six Donegal Senior Football Championship medals with St. Joseph's (an amalgam of Bundoran and Ballyshannon), two Mayo Senior Football Championship medals with Castlebar Mitchel's, one McLarnon Cup medal in 1968 (College), Ulster Senior Football Championship medals in 1972 and 1974, two Ulster Senior Football Club medals with St. Joseph's in 1968 and 1976. Actually the 1968 one was unofficial and we played and beat your own club team Dunmore MacHales in a two-legged final in Tuam and Ballyshannon. I came on as a substitute in both games and I remember yourself at the end of your career coming on as a substitute in Ballyshannon and scoring a point just after coming on. I won one Railway Cup medal with the Combined Universities in 1973 - my only medal. I played for Ulster in 1975 and remember it as Sean O'Neill's last game for Ulster. Jimmy Barry Murphy scored 4 -1 in that game from five kicks at the ball. Jimmy had played the day before in a Senior Hurling Club final for the 'Barrs against Johnstown and I remember meeting him that night and, let's put it this way, he was enjoying himself. I lost three Railway Cup finals in all and played for Connacht both as a forward and as a back - a corner man each time."

How did you find the change from corner forward to corner back in your latter years with Mayo?

"I often feel I should have given up the game when I stopped being able to play as a forward because I was more at ease in attack. I lost my speed around 1983 and in 1985

Liam O'Neill, the Mayo manager, asked me to try out corner back. Most of my University days I played as a halfback or a midfielder. So I found the adjustment very simple and had three very enjoyable years as corner back 1985-1987. The main thing about the backs was you never had to depend on anyone else to play you into the game. Having been a forward gave you an extra creative dimension. The reverse situation, back to forward, takes more adjusting. I won four Connacht Senior Football Championship medals with Mayo, the last one as a substitute in 1989. I had the honour of captaining Mayo to a Connacht title win in 1981."

Who are the players you admire most today?

"Peter Butler (Mayo) and his team-mate T.J. Kilgallon; Martin McHugh of Donegal; Bernard Flynn of Meath, a wonderful corner forward and Robbie O'Malley, a gifted corner back; Larry Tompkins, for his total dedication."

The greatest footballer you ever saw?

"Mikey Sheehy for complete and absolute artistry, Tommy Drumm for gifted defensive work and as a midfielder I'd have Brian Mullins before his car accident. He had extremely delicate feet for a big man, and tremendous ability to place his man and bring others into play. For fielding ability Willie Joe Padden was hard to beat."

Was it hard to quit?

"I should have retired after Galway beat us in the Connacht final of 1987. In all I played county football for twenty-one years, November 1970 to March 1990."

> *Then Martin turned to team-management looking after the Mayo minors in 1991 bringing them to an All-Ireland Final and staying in the job through 1992. Now he is Mayo's U-21 team-manager.*

How does team management compare with playing?

"Playing was always hugely enjoyable and from a health point of view you'd lose an awful lot of nervous tension. As a team manager you tend to bottle that up. The lead up to a match is something I like to get over."

Martin thinks the Railway Cup has no future. The club scene has taken over. Martin never won an All Star award but was on three U.S. trips as a replacement. Standards of fitness are higher now. Standards of sportsmanship may not be as high as they were. Donegal's winning of the All-Ireland showed you didn't need to have a team of six footers with big strong muscular bodies to win an All-Ireland, and you can win with a bit of artistry. The whole business of standards has levelled off in your opinion without dropping appreciably. The G.A.A. he hopes will never die but the organisation needs more people to give their time just to working with young people, former players willing to put something back on Saturday and Sunday mornings. Golf is a factor of course but there is much more interest nowadays in leisure pursuits.

What was the game of your life?

"From the spectator's point of view, there are two. The 1977 All-Ireland semi-final between Kerry and Dublin was a wonderful game, - so absorbing. The two teams were like gladiators at each other's throats for three years previously. This was the final real confrontation between the two. The second half of the Ulster Final of 1992 is the second. I've never seen such a sustained bout of brilliance from so many players on the same day. On the playing side there was the first round of the Ulster Senior Football Championship against Tyrone in Omagh in 1974. I must put that in context. First we beat Tyrone in the Ulster Final of 1972 and lost the first round in Ballybofey in a very controversial torrid affair in 1973. Tyrone won that day so in 1974 we were drawn against them once again in Omagh. Brian McEniff selected me at midfield to play on Frank McGuigan. I could run forever then and I scored three points from midfield in an eighty minute game before going into full forward at the end. We won it by a few points. The second game is a first round Connacht Senior Football Championship game against Leitrim in 1985. That was the time my career was finished as a forward and Liam O'Neill coaxed me to try corner back. It launched a few extra years to my career. But in the heel of the hunt that game in Omagh has to be numero uno."

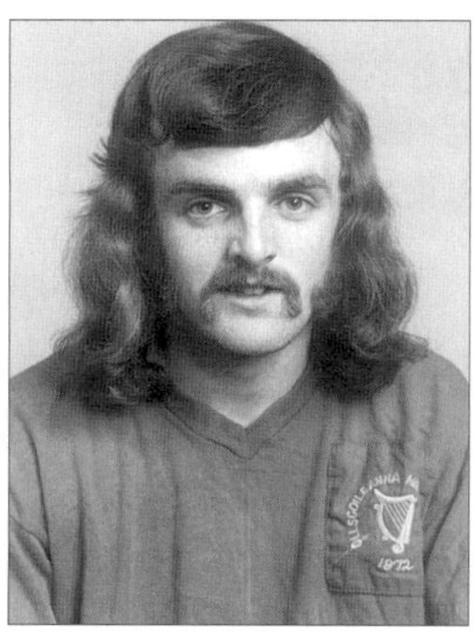

Left:
Martin in his student days in 1972

Right:
Brian McEniff -'there was always great steel in the man'

Receiving the J. J. Nestor Cup (Connacht Senior Championship) in 1981 from the then President of the Connacht Council, Dr Mickey Loftus.

Chapter 2

Johnny Geraghty

Goalkeeper Extraordinary

Pádhraic O'Foghlú, "P.F." as he signed himself, the doyen of Provincial scribes and whose columns in "The Kerryman" were unique in their time, was an old friend. In the sixties, in a personal letter, he described Johnny Geraghty as a goalkeeper of rare talent, his favourite of Galway's 3-in-a-row days. He knew his football. The retired Galway based secondary teacher is a near neighbour of mine in Salthill. I didn't dally about asking him what was the game of his life?

"If there is one I will never want to forget, it would be my first All-Ireland Final against Kerry in 1964. I think myself that my finest hour was in the first game in New York against New York in the 1965 National Football League final. It gets so deeply engrained in you - the 1964 final - that I remember all the details from it. Like going up on the Friday evening on the back of a motor-bike. I had a tartan duffel bag. Bags weren't sponsored at this stage. We were held back at the turnstiles going in and the Kerry fellows were at the next turnstile to us - O'Connell, O'Dwyer and company - I had never seen them before only in the papers."

When did you first show interest in becoming a goalkeeper?

"When I was a kid we always played in our own field on Sundays and every evening. The field was at the back of our house in Kilkerrin (North Galway). I went to the Monastery and it was like mini-All-Irelands the matches we used to have at lunch-time there every day. I was always very small and I ended up in goal in all those games. Then on to St. Jarlath's College where Fr. Brendan Kavanagh was to have a big bearing on my football life. When you went there the first things you saw were the goalposts. It was an academy of football. Study was something you did between matches. Fr. Kavanagh taught you to think about the game. I used to play outfield at the start. I played mostly in the forwards, had a good left and right and could take frees with both feet. It looked ominous that I'd never get on a team being too small. I was only about nine stone and in fourth year Fr. Kavanagh tried me out for the juniors in goal. That was the start of it."

What was it like being a footballer in Jarlath's?

"A privilege, really. When I was a first year in the college, I could tell you the senior team off by heart. They were the elite. There was no All-Ireland that year but Jarlath's won out in Connacht. They had players like John Ollie Moran, Mattie Ryder, a beautiful free taker and John Biesty. In my third year, 1958, we won the All-Ireland Colleges title. They had lads like Jimmy Walsh, T.J. O'Connor, Kevin McMorrow, Michael 'Tansey' Lyons and Theo Joyce on the team."

Did you win the Hogan Cup in your final year?

"We did. We had a powerful team. Our midfield was Pat Donnellan and John Morley. Pat Sheridan was captain and freetaker, Seamus Leydon was on it. Enda Colleran too. Sheridan was the real general, freetaker, captain. Many of those lads won All-Ireland minor medals with me later that year of 1960. We had a fabulous year beating St. Enda's, St. Joseph's (The Bish), then Garbally who had Cyril Dunne and finally St. Nathy's for whom my old primary school colleague Christy Tyrrell played. Later we easily beat St. Colman's Newry in the semi-final in Croke Park. The final then was the official opening of the St. Kieran's G.A.A. field in Athlone. We beat St. Finian's College, Mullingar 3-10 to 3-7 in a fine game on May 1st."

Did you ever suffer from the elements while playing in goal?

"When I played, it was unheard of for a goalkeeper to wear a track suit and I remember once in a National Football League game in Tullamore playing in a light blue track suit. John Dunne didn't like the idea but it was an extremely cold day. I always got a rub before a match, too. In my time the goalie never took the kickout and I never did and that was a lack."

Johnny was the first goalkeeper I ever saw to direct operations from that position and to place his clearances to advantageous colleagues. What did he see as his role here?

"The traditional goalkeeper before my time was in the Jack Mangan style. Mangan and Aidan Brady used to come thundering out and they were afraid of no one and they would drive the ball over sixty yards. I had a very short kick and I remember talking to your good self, Jack, after my second ever game for Galway against Wicklow in the National Football League in Tuam. I was doing my teaching practice in Fr. Griffin Road Technical School at the time and your critical eye chastised me for kicking away possession twice. After that I used to look up, and try to find a man. You never crossed your goal - John Dunne would kill you. Usually I would find the wing half backs. I'll never forget the 1967 Railway Cup Final getting a ball on the goal line, avoiding an advancing Ulster forward, and drop-kicking a ball all the way to Kearins who gave it to Leydon for a quick point."

Is the former Galway schoolteacher interested in all sports?

"Cricket I can't wear or horse-racing but I love all sports and watch them a lot. Basketball is one of my favourites."

His general comments on sports writers and commentators are enthralling.

"With the Gaelic people my favourite has to be Paddy Downey. He was always fair and he saw more angles to it than others. I loved the colourful features that Pádhraic Puirséal used to write in his time. I loved the old 'Gaelic Weekly'. Nowadays, I like Colm O'Rourke's writing enormously. He is very good and fair. He isn't as critical as Liam Hayes and does not seem to have any axes to grind. Vincent Hogan, I can take in small doses. I taught Martin Breheny, while teaching in Glenamaddy and had great admiration for him. I love the style of David Walsh. His articles on cycling are very well written. Dunphy's analysis is good but I don't like the fact that he is so hyper-critical, that he literally takes the bones and the character almost from the player. It's a bit like the media sticking the microphone inside one's skin and that's really going too far and invading one's privacy. I think you have to sit well back and analyse it and put it in context and ultimately do justice to the player."

What commentators, as distinct from sports writers, impressed him?

"Micheál Ó Muircheartaigh would have to be my favourite. I love his colour and his descriptions. Even the 'caipín cosanta' for a helmet is so expressive. His description of

Donie Nealon wearing an overcoat during the heat of a Munster final is unforgettable."

The great sporting books he read?

"*The Great Bike Race* written by Geoffrey Nicholson on the Tour de France. One of the best pieces of sporting journalism I've ever read. The first book I ever read in the library in Jarlath's was the *Tommy Doyle Story* by Raymond Smith. I've read most of the Lions Tours books and James Hunt's autobiography. Frank Stapleton's was one of the least I enjoyed. The Barry John story was superb. Great passion. John was a man of the people, the ordinary home-spun hero who just had a talent for football. It wasn't a wild talent like that of Gazza or Georgie Best."

When Geraghty was in his prime, it was rumoured that some English soccer club was interested in him.

"In 1964 Galway played Dublin in the Wembley Tournament on a Saturday and I had the best game I ever had, on that hallowed sod. Nothing could beat me and we won it 0-10 to 0-4. Some English man, who said he was an agent for Manchester United, rang me in the hotel that night. I wasn't interested as I had an idea I was too small to make it. The smallest English International goalkeeper ever was Ron Springett at 5'9" and I was only 5'7". I played soccer in Galway for a year with Bohemians in 1970-1971. It is a totally different game. You don't get any shots as such to save. It's all about nipping out, knowing when to move off your line, throwing the ball and that."

Who first encouraged the young Geraghty boy to play?

"Gaelic football was all around me. You either played at the cross of Park, Gowran's Cross or the Paddock. Farming all the week and football in the evenings and at the weekends."

What other goalkeepers impressed you and was there a special bond between goalkeepers?

"Aidan Brady always impressed me. Big and strong. Andy Phillips of Wicklow - I think I modelled myself on him. He was a small neat blondy-haired fellow and he always played in the Railway Cup. I used to get Charlie Buchan's Soccer Monthly while in St. Jarlath's and became a fan of Gordon Banks and before him Ron Springett. In fact the lads at home used to call me Gordie. After games you would always make your way to meet the rival goalkeeper and, if you missed him, he would usually be on his way to you."

You took a shot at refereeing. How did that happen?

"When training school teams I used to referee the training games and liked it. Bad refereeing always annoyed me and I felt I could do better myself. So I started with some under-age games. Took it very seriously, then on to club level and the inter-county panel. The previous Galwayman to referee an All-Ireland Final was Patsy Geraghty from Ballinasloe in the 1950's and secretly I wanted to be the next Galwayman to do so - another Geraghty."

I probed him about a game he refereed between Dublin and Kerry in Croke Park which filled the papers at the time with controversy.

"I only sent off one man but he was a Dub - hence the furore. I had been doing Senior Football Championship games in Connacht and some National Football League games but on this particular Sunday in October 1979 all the top referees were on tour in the U.S., organised months in advance by the Referee's Social Committee. So the second string of referees were out and I got the top National Football League game at Croke Park just a few short weeks after the All-Ireland Final - the year of the famous Sheehy goal. So there was great interest in the 'replay'. It was a very tough game. Early on there was an incident out at the sideline between Jimmy Deenihan and Tony Hanahoe and by the time I went over Hanahoe was all blood and Deenihan unscathed. When I checked with the sideline man all he said was, 'I never saw a ting', in strict Dublinese, so I wasn't getting much help there. Anyway, halfway through the first half Deenihan got a ball and came out with it. Anton O'Toole was in front of him and swung around with the elbow and got the Kerryman straight in the face. Deenihan went down. I was only two yards away. It was deliberate striking. I didn't even want to think so I sent him straight off. I got fierce abuse afterwards. It was the first time I was escorted off the pitch by Gardai but then I had broken all the rules in sending off a Dub in Croke Park. Micheál O'Hehir at the time, I was told, described it as a trivial incident so how biased can you be? Now I liked O'Hehir, he was great for atmosphere and all that but he had this weakness for Dublin. But wherever Micheál is I wish him well. He gave absolute pleasure to so many for so long."

What was your greatest save?

"The one that I enjoyed most was in the semi-final against Cork in 1966 - the Niall Fitzgerald game. Out of the blue there were only the two of us inside the thirty yard line and the ball was coming for Fitzgerald all on his owneo, so I hared out and at the moment he got the ball he turned to shoot to an empty net and I was in front of him and I happened to block his kick after diving full length. We were twenty yards out and it was a last chance dive for me which worked."

Who were the greatest players in your own time and today?

"Probably the best player I saw from the point of view of style and all that was Sean Purcell. I was a lot younger and was very impressed. Mick O'Connell impressed me enormously. He had natural ability, talent and style. He could take frees and could catch the ball, kick right and left. I loved the point taking ability of Charlie Gallagher of Cavan. I thought he had a great turn and could put a great curl on a ball. A bit like Mickey Kearins. Of the seventies, I rated Spillane the best of all those Kerry fellows. Some people would say Sheehy was the best and Jacko had the longer innings but Spillane could do everything all over the field. Great work rate and a clean player and he fought back, too, after injury. My favourite player of recent times is Colm O'Rourke. There is 10% of him I wouldn't like - the physical side of him but he epitomised Meath even when he was a young player. He could win ball and took frees when they had no free taker and he got scores. The Down team of the 1960's were a superb team to look at. I remember when they hit Croke Park for the first time for the semi-final of 1959. They were a joy to watch. Doherty I had great regard for more so than O'Neill. He was a very natural footballer and could score from all angles. Donegal of 1992 had a good system. An elderly team that Brian McEniff got the maximum out of. I'm a great fan of Martin McHugh."

On the G.A.A's future the Kilkerrin born retired teacher feels it won't retain the traditional role it had.

"The value of the game in my day was you played the game and enjoyed it. I was never sent off and was booked once. It will survive, will be financially viable and will run its competitions. It has gone too competitive and there is too much emphasis on winning. It has lost a lot of its Puritanism, its strict amateurism. Just witness all the sending off of recent times. A lot of players out there just play to win and management must take the blame. Some of the lads I played against are my best friends but then you read in Liam Hayes's book how the Meath fellows would walk one side of the beach and wouldn't talk to the Cork fellows whom they played against in a few All-Irelands. It's following the way society is going and the way soccer has gone and the way pure rugby is going. It's a social change and I'd be fearful enough of it. It's gone too professional. It's all about winning. It has lost its innocence."

We talked about the status of being an All-Ireland man. Is there such a thing?

"I suppose there is. At funerals, for instance, somebody's mother will introduce you to someone as the All-Ireland man of now almost thirty years ago. If you are ever in Paddy Bawn's pub in Dingle you'll be recognised and Kerry people generally show great recognition for footballers. I remember an incident involving Garry McMahon, Brian's son, and a fine footballer himself, recognising me once here in Galway and being ever so modest about himself."

I put it to Johnny that he took up team-management very successfully for a time and left it there after a short time.

"I managed the Galway minors to All-Ireland success in 1976 and took the job again in 1977. At the time, while convalescing in hospital before training began, I read 'Fundamental Principles of Soccer Coaching' by Eric Batty and it's a great system of training where you use the ball a lot. The first time we came in training I had ten balls and we did all this skill work with the ball - no laps. I quoted from a Gerry Daly press interview - Gerry, the soccer international, and I also brought in my own minor All-Ireland medal won in 1960 and told them of the honour it conferred and the worth in preparing well. They were all eighteen-year-olds and they'd never get the chance again. It worked. They gave me everything. One night there was a clash of training with the seniors, who won the Connacht Senior Football Championship that year too, and it meant we were put on an hour earlier before the seniors trained. This time, as always, we did the usual skill-work with the ball, free taking etc. and the bould 'Tull' Dunne was observing it all. It was the week before the All-Ireland semi-final. When I was finished 'Tull' came up to me and said, 'Is that it now?'. When I said yes he said, 'Look it here, do you know you are in a semi-final? This is what you'll do. Put those balls into that onion bag and go out there and do a few right sprints'."

Finally, I asked him how did the three exercises, playing, refereeing, training or management compare?

"Nothing like playing the game. Playing is what it's all about. Management gave me great satisfaction. Refereeing I did by obligation, trying to put something back, but in retrospect, I didn't enjoy it."

Above, left: P.F's favourite Three-in-a-row man
right: Sean Purcell-'best player I ever saw from the point of view of style'.

Chapter 3

Mickey Kearins

Sligo's Sharpshooter Supreme

Over a long career in Gaelic football the quiet spoken gentleman footballer and cattle dealer from Dromard has a whole list of scoring achievements to his credit. I was privileged to be present in Castlebar and Roscommon for some of his greatest scoring feats. Gifted with two great feet, he had a lovely graceful movement and must be short listed as one of Sligo's greatest ever stars. In Sligo they talk of the Colleran brothers, of John Joe Lavin, Nace O'Dowd of course, but Mickey Kearins is still their pride and joy.

Mickey went to National School in Ballinaleg where Fr. McHugh from the parish was keenly interested in Gaelic football. His father played a lot of club football and played for Sligo a few times, too. Born in 1943 in Dromard which lies between Sligo and Ballina, Mickey, after the primary school days, spent three years in St. Muredach's College in Ballina. It was after he left Muredach's and went to work with his father in the cattle business that he really got the taste for football.

"I got on the Sligo minors in 1960 and we lost to a good minor team from Galway. Galway went on to win the All-Ireland that year with young lads like Noel Tierney, Johnny Geraghty, Seamus Leydon, Christy Tyrrell, Gerry Prendergast, a real star then, and my own midfield opponent Sean Cleary. On our own team, were Peter James Brennan, Sean Gettins and Joe Hannon. I first played Senior Football Championship for Sligo in 1962 and in the Senior Football League in 1961. The first National Football League game was against Cavan in Ballymote, in which I was marked by Gabriel Kelly. I was very excited about playing for my county. The first Senior Football Championship game was against Connacht champions, Roscommon, in Charlestown and it was a humdinger. We lost by one point from a goal scored with the last kick of the game. We had Cathal Cawley, Patrick Kilgannon, Joe Hannon and Bill Shannon on our team."

> *I remember the game most of all for the excitement of seeing the emergence of an unknown star in young Kearins and the great possibility of a shock result as the huge crowd encroached onto the field.*

Who did you look up to in your young days with Sligo?

"Nace O'Dowd, of course, I always admired. Around that time I met Joe Masterson, a great Sligo character, and Mr. G.A.A. in the county."

When did your club St. Patrick's in Dromard become a force in Sligo football?

"In the late 1950's, we were only a junior team, winning the County Junior Football Championship in 1964. There was no Intermediate grade in Sligo so we went automatically to senior in 1965. Our first Senior Football Championship success was in 1968 and I won five titles in all with Dromard. Three of my brothers, James, Peadar and Noel shared in those successes and I managed the team as well. I won two other Sligo Senior Football Championship medals in 1963 and 1964 with Ballisodare. I have nine Sligo medals (seven senior and two junior)."

> *His inter provincial record for Sligo is, of course, unsurpassed in his native county, where representative honours are rare. He played for thirteen consecutive years for Connacht with Dermot Earley, Sean Purcell and Gerry O'Malley having similar lines of achievement in Connacht's white jersey. That Railway Cup career began in 1963 and was to project the dapper Sligo man on to the national consciousness as a footballer of special skills. He gained his one and only All Star in its initial year of 1971, an honour he cherishes still, and feels he might have made it again in 1972 but Paddy Moriarty of Armagh got the nod then. Mickey would like to see the Railway Cup continue.*

"It's a great occasion for players who are with weaker counties who never get the chance to play alongside good players from other counties. When I started in the 1960's, just imagine the thrill it was for me to play in the same forward line as the Galway lads of the three-in-a-row team and they always took me into the game. The

Galway lads were very easy to play with. Whoever was in the best position got the ball. In that thirteen years I won two Railway Cup medals 1967 and 1969."

In all, Mickey played in three forward positions for the black and white of Sligo, or the Magpies, as Joe Masterson used to call them, left half forward, occasionally at centre half forward and full forward in the latter times. His scoring feats were the talk of Ireland. These are the ones he remembers best.

"The one that sticks out most was the drawn Connacht Final against Galway in Castlebar in 1971. I scored fourteen points, five from play and the nine from placed balls included two from forty fives and one sideline kick."

> *I was present that day and regard it as the finest display of scoring artistry I have ever seen. The points from play were scored with both feet. Over the years I have seen marvellous scoring achievements from such as Mikey Sheehy, Paddy Doherty, Larry Tompkins, Tony McTague, Brian Stafford, Cyril Dunne, Martin McHugh and Jimmy Keaveney, but none to cap that one. There are others.*

"Another day in Croke Park, against the Combined Universities in 1973, I scored twelve points all from placed balls. Another day in Hyde Park against the same opposition, I scored thirteen points, but four or five of those were from play. There was another day in Castlebar's McHale Park in a drawn Connacht Senior Football Championship game against Mayo, I got thirteen points, as well."

Did you ever feel like giving it all up after so many defeats and near misses?

"I played inter-county for seventeen years, starting in 1961 and finishing in 1978. Of course, you did feel that way, as you know you have to be winning sometimes to keep your interest alive."

Who were the Sligo players who kept the flame alive so that eventually the county won its second ever Connacht title in 1975?

"The Collearys, Jim and Tom, the Caffreys, Liam and Aidan and Cathal Cawley were all very keen players. You had John Brennan too, who was very good and quite a number of the great Sligo minor team of 1968 came good in 1970 and 1971."

Were your opponents very aggressive and tight marking?

"There were some but I never met many that were really dirty players especially in Connacht, but outside it, you met the odd one."

Who were your greatest opponents?

"Brian McEniff was the tightest man I ever played on. He was a very sticky opponent. John Donnellan too, on his day, could be good. Liam O'Neill was another very sticky player but my ideal right half back would be McEniff. He'd be on my team. Of the Sligo players of my time I suppose Cathal Cawley was the most consistent and Brendan McAuley very good to play with. Every time he got the ball you were sure of getting a good service."

Did you train much?

"In those early years, yes. At least four times a week. I used to train in the mornings often at six or seven o'clock depending on my work. I'd run three or four miles in a field and that serious training lasted for ten years. I never practised much at place kicking. Nor did I take a few pots at the posts before the game started. I trained regularly too with club and county. Superstition didn't bother me. It was vital that you'd get the first free in the game right. Regarding nerves, I was always nervous before a game, knowing that the Sligo team would be depending a fair bit on me. I was fearful of having a bad day with them."

The best players of your own time and now?

"Sean Purcell was the greatest player I ever saw. He could play anywhere. Some players down the years were good at place kicking, or catching or different things. He had the lot. Mick O'Connell's anticipation for fielding was outstanding. John Egan was a great corner forward, strong on the ball and had a good shot too. There aren't too many outstanding players today like Purcell or O'Connell. Tony Boyle is a good forward but I wouldn't rate him as outstanding."

Mickey was very critical of his own Sligo team's worth prior to the 1992 Senior Football Championship. Was he only trying to rouse them into doing well, which they did subsequently against Mayo?

"I knew there were a number of fellows on the team that hadn't any interest in the game. They weren't putting it in at training. I didn't give them a chance against Mayo in Castlebar. They should have done it on the day. I used to work for the manager of the team Paul Clarke for ten years or so and I'm sure he was very annoyed with my remarks."

Mickey doesn't see Sligo succeeding like Donegal in 1992, nor in the near future.

"There are lots of good juveniles but when they become seniors, many of them don't make it. Some of the adult teams, nine times out of ten, play it on the ground. They won't lift the ball and pass it around. In the Sligo Town area there is a huge interest in soccer. Too many are playing soccer in the morning and trying to play Gaelic football in the evening."

Turning to your career as a referee, did you take it up accidentally?

"I meant to take it up and had started refereeing club games before the end of my inter-county career. I wanted to stay in the game at some level. My first major game was the 1978 Sligo county final. My main achievements in that field were refereeing four Connacht finals, a National Football League, two All-Ireland Club and a Railway Cup final plus an All-Ireland Senior Football semi-final."

What was the enjoyment you got out of refereeing by comparison with playing?

"There is nothing to beat the playing scene. You'd know yourself whether you had done a reasonably good job or not and you'd be happy if you did well. I used to train with my club two evenings a week when I was refereeing and it helped to keep the weight down. Having played the game helped my refereeing. You'd know the tricks of the trade."

Were most players sporting in their approach to the game?

"95% or more. There would nearly always be one man to watch in every team."

I then queried him on his controversial sending off of Meath's Colm O'Rourke in a National Football League game. What caused it?

"It was an incident just after half-time and he got a heavy enough shoulder while in possession. It knocked the ball out of his hands but he didn't try to retrieve it but came after me. The play moved away to the other end of the field and he followed me the whole way down, talking 'friendly' to me all the way! I had to send him off."

Subsequently I saw Colm challenge Mickey again as the Sligo man was doing the line in the 1988 All-Ireland Final. What happened then?

"There was a line ball incident and he felt I gave the wrong decision. I know myself now, that I did give the wrong decision after seeing the replay of the incident on television. That final of 1988, he was lucky to stay on the field. He had some very dangerous tackles during the game. He didn't need to do that, he was such a good player. In his last three or four years playing for Meath he was too good for all his opponents. He actually made that Meath forward line. He was the play maker and he made Brian Stafford. Bernard Flynn was good too."

What was the toughest game you ever refereed?

"The All-Ireland semi-final between Dublin and Cork. I sent Keith Barr off that day. He was involved in an incident five minutes earlier and he ran thirty or forty yards to get involved in the second incident. There was an awful lot of off-the-ball stuff that day, and it is very difficult to manage these games. The goal he scored in the 1992 Leinster final against Kildare was the best I have ever seen."

The Sligo man gave up refereeing in disillusionment - why?

"I felt I was getting no backing from the Sligo County Board. The new assessment procedure is very welcome. Now I'm not involved at all and have no interest in team management either. I go to games now purely for pleasure and my son, Karl, who went to St. Jarlath's College, Tuam, plays for the county."

Do you find it hard to watch your son playing?

"I'd enjoy a game better if he wasn't playing. Of course, he suffers from being the son of Mickey Kearins and the comparisons but he doesn't talk about it. We always talk about the games he plays."

Any good stories?

"Just one. I remember my first Railway Cup game was against Leinster in Ballinasloe in 1963. At the start, as I was moving into position before the ball was thrown in, I noticed my direct opponent, Paddy McCormack, digging a hole along the ground with his boot. He said,
'You're young Kearins from Sligo? I presume you expect to go back to Sligo this evening'.
'Hopefully,' I said.
'If you don't pass that mark, you have a fair chance of getting back'.
I passed the mark a few times and managed him well, scoring four points off play."

What was the game of your life?

"That draw with Galway in 1971 was probably the best game I ever played. Another game to remember was against Mayo in Charlestown in 1965. We were nine points down some minutes after half time and we finished up winning by three."

Any other sporting interests?

"Golf is too time consuming. International soccer was a big interest. I often went to Old Trafford and Elland Road to see games. In 1974 I travelled to the European Cup final in Paris to see Johnny Giles especially. Giles, Bobby Charlton and George Best were favourites."

Mickey Kearins

Your greatest thrill?

"Winning my first Sligo Senior Football Championship medal with St. Patrick's, Dromard. Seamie Donegan was one of the great characters of that team. But the man I had most affection for in Sligo, Joe Masterson, has passed away. They erected a lovely memorial to him in his native Tubbercurry - a Town Clock erected in the centre of the town. I was present the day it was unveiled. The clock idea was a typically Irish memorial - you see, the much loved Joe found it hard to be on time for anything."

Mickey Kearins solos through the Mayo defence watched by Connie Moynihan.

Chapter 4

Tony Mac

The Doyen of Roscommon

When I visited Tony McManus, his lovely wife Marie, and their two children Kate and Róisin in their beautiful home just beside the Golf Course in Roscommon, this most loved of all Roscommon forwards was excited about a farewell night being planned for him on the following Friday night in Rockford's, a popular night spot in O'Gara's Royal Hotel, home to Roscommon footballers for years now. They were coming in bus loads from all over the county to honour their hero, who may never have won an All-Ireland medal, though no man ever tried harder. However, he won his way into every Roscommon heart with his courage and bouncy style, epitomised for me by his mastery of scoring points on the run, or what became popularly known as flying points.

Did you stay trying for that All-Ireland too long?

"In hindsight, I think I did. I'd be happier to have 1992 off my football memory, because I spent a lot of the year injured and when you're only half fit, you don't enjoy the game."

Who started you off being interested in the game?

"It was a family tradition. My late father was very keen and he brought me to a lot of matches early on. My eldest brother Pat played football for Roscommon at under-age and senior level and then went on to play for Meath when he was stationed there as a Garda. Eamonn was very keen on it, too, and being the youngest of a family of seven (four boys and three girls), I couldn't but be keen on the game. My national school was Corafulla N.S., but the big influence then was the club in our area, Clan na Gael, where Tony Whyte was vital, being over us at U-12 and U-14 level. With Clan na

Gael, we won U-12, U-14, U-16 and minor up along. So there was a great old spirit all the way and Tony stayed with us en route."

Your Secondary School days were in St. Aloysius College in Athlone, a school as much orientated to soccer as to Gaelic football.You remember particularly Fr. Moran and Michael Phelan for their interest.

"At the time I played a lot of soccer with Athlone Town. My father was very much anti-soccer. They were very keen to get me to play with them and I was playing with Clan at the same time too. But when I went to U.C.D., you had to declare for soccer or Gaelic. There was no wavering with Eugene McGee. So Gaelic was my choice."

Your opinion of Eugene McGee?

"You took him for what he was. He didn't make any pretences. He spoke straight from the heart and at a very early stage took a fondness for me which was obvious. As a lot of the older fellows would say - myself and Colm O'Rourke and Tommy Murphy were his three pets. You see the three of us came in as Freshers together. We haven't met very often since, even though both of us now work in Longford. But that's McGee, he isn't very much of a social person. When he was dealing with you, he either liked you or didn't, but he always did his best for his team."

Was he a good team manager?

"Very good. He was good, because of that aloofness. He kept himself away from the players. He told them what he wanted from them and if they didn't do it, they didn't figure in his plans. No player was too big for him."

Your Sigerson Cup days are worth recalling.

"I went to U.C.D. in 1976 and finished in 1980. We contested the five Sigerson Cup finals while I was there, winning three of them. I captained the winning team of 1979, a really great honour. Captaincy of a College team requires an awful lot of work and McGee would make the captain feel a failure if the team didn't win out. That 1979 team is special to me still. I could name them all, Paddy O'Donoghue from Kildare, Sean O'Doherty, Joe Joe O'Connor from Kerry, P.J. Fennelly, John Caffrey of Dublin,

Colm O'Rourke, Tommy Murphy of Wicklow, another veterinary student like myself, and still a great friend "

What have you to say about Colm O'Rourke?

"O'Rourke was amazing. He was vice-captain to me in 1979. We both contested the captaincy together, when most people felt it was due to me. He believed anything that was worth winning should be contested. We had only four selectors, O'Rourke, McGee, Gerry Dineen and myself. In the 1991 All-Ireland semi-final pre-game parade he walked across to shake my hand. We have great respect for each other and are still great friends. I like his writing in the *Sunday Tribune*. He writes from the heart and says what he has to say and he makes a lot of sense."

You played club, county and representative football at the highest level. How did Sigerson football compare?

"Sigerson, when you're playing it, is the most important thing in your life. It was phenomenal. You could train during the day. It was like professional football. But suddenly, when I was finished with it, it didn't have as much significance."

Let's turn to your club days with Clan na Gael, where, in your time, you built up such an impressive record of titles, apart from the All-Ireland which you craved.

"I won thirteen County Senior Football Championship medals with Clan starting in 1976, right up to 1991. We won eight in a row at one stage and in all six Connacht Senior Football club titles in a row 1984-1989. We beat every team at different stages, such as Nemo Rangers and Burren. We had some very easy wins in Connacht and in All-Ireland semi-finals but then fell at the last hurdle always. I remember the first one we lost to St. Finbarr's in 1986 - a horrendous day of sleeting rain. We lost by three points to a none too great 'Barr's team playing without Dave Barry. Personally, I had one of the worst games I ever played for Clan. If we won that day, we could have gone on to win two or three titles."

They lost five finals altogether, 1984 and four in a row 1987-1990 inclusive. What was it like to lose the fourth in a row?

"It was absolutely devastating. Losing a third was sickening because at that stage a mental block was building up for finals. I remember coming back in 1988 and saying, 'Right, we nearly have enough of it'. And then we lost the last one to Baltinglass, who were up there for the first time. Again we just didn't play that day. Player manager for Baltinglass was my old team mate and friend from Sigerson days in 1979, Tommy Murphy. We met that day of the final and we did exactly the same thing O'Rourke and myself did in 1991 just at the end of the march round."

I have been watching Roscommon football since the days of the Murrays, Kinlough, Keenan, Lynch, Carlos, Boland, Gilmartin, Hoare...on to the days of O'Malley, Brady, Kelly, Jackson...on to the present. Tony McManus built up a very special relationship with Roscommon fans. They loved his courage and will to win. Did he realise he was special to them?

"I do at this stage and it amazes me. I hate being beaten. That means I'm fiercely competitive but I find now that a lot of Roscommon people had great respect for me. There is a retirement function for me next Friday night and the whole county is behind it."

A measure of Tony's popularity down the years can be gauged from his treatment by the local papers, the ***Roscommon Champion*** *and the* ***Herald****.*

"The local papers and indeed *Shannonside* local radio have been more than fair to me. I don't remember them ever turning on me. Indeed I have been asked is it Tony McManus who writes the *Champion*. The *Roscommon Champion* have always been great buddies of mine. It started with Eamonn Sweeney and followed on with Paul Healy and Joe Flaherty. The same goes for Liam Sherlock in the *Herald*. The *Champion* is very much geared towards sport. People are losing interest in reading about court cases so they have taken a right direction in my opinion."

The burning question at the time of the interview was: Would Tony be in Dermot Earley's plans for the 1993 Connacht Senior Football Championship?

"I've certainly retired from the county scene and am very close to doing the same from the club scene. I've had niggling problems with my knees and don't want to finish up a complete crock. No I won't give it all up. I'd like to get involved in the coaching end. I won't jump lightly into anything immediately. In 1993 I'll certainly give time to my family and play some golf."

Tony has become a useful golfer. His handicap has come down quickly to a respectable eleven. Does he play much?

"We play a fair bit around the place. There are a few of us who play a lot of fourballs and we get great crack out of it. I really enjoy it because it is a great social outlet. Last year I got a lot of satisfaction in helping to win the team event in the Artane Boys' Band Competition in Westport."

Does it hurt much not having won an All-Ireland medal?

"It's a big regret. If you set out to do something in life, whatever it is, and if you fail, you'll always be disappointed. I've been a long time trying to win an All-Ireland and, at the end of the day, had to retire without getting it"

The four-in-a-row Connacht title winning team of 1977-1980 should have won an All-Ireland. What went wrong?

"The biggest loss in that great run was the semi-final loss to Dublin in 1979. We had a beautiful forward line, then. We all played instinctively, knew where we were going. In that time you waited your time to make your move and later on in life I had to make so many moves even to get the ball. We had a lot of natural footballers. 'Jigger' was a mighty man for the big occasion, though he'd break your heart in training. John O'Gara was a perfect foil at centre half forward, strong and skilful, not the best scorer, but a creator. Michael Finneran was an absolutely classy player, lovely balance, lovely feet. The pity of it was Mickey Freyne wasn't fully fit at the time and a wee bit younger, because his best days were before we came along. When Dermot Earley went to midfield, he didn't take as much on himself and he laid the ball off. It was great to be a corner forward with Earley at midfield. He hit a tremendous long ball to you on your outside, giving you the chance to win the ball."

The backs were good too?

"We had tremendous backs. Harry Keegan, Pat Lindsay and Tom Heneghan, three of the best backs mentioned always. We had lovely half-backs too, Danny Murray, a sweet footballer, Tom Donlon who didn't get the credit in Roscommon that he deserved, a real player's man."

I queried Tony on his memory of a Connacht Final occasion when the man on the mike in giving the Roscommon lineout, mistakenly gave the name of well known Roscommon official Danny Burke from Castlerea instead of Danny Murray which evoked the cheer of the day?

"I don't remember that, offhand. One has a fine head of hair - the other has none. Danny Burke is a great character. As an under-age player, he was fantastic for us. There's a good story about Danny. In my early days we were playing against Armagh and at that stage if you went down injured, Danny was the man to look after you. Now, things are a lot more sophisticated, with team doctors, masseurs and what not. Anyhow this day, Eamonn, my brother, got a kick into the groin and Danny, then a selector, was in like a flash. He had a look at the prostrate Eamonn, as he knelt on the ground, and said, 'One, two, you're alright, they're still there' and Eamonn looked at him and said, 'Get out'. That's what I mean by Danny, the character."

Then there were the bad years. How did Tony keep going from 1980 to 1990 without winning a Connacht Senior Football Championship medal?

"I had a great relationship with the County Board all along. They looked after me very well when I was in College, giving me extra expenses on the normal and I remember, while in College, going on two All Star trips as a replacement and getting extra cash to help me. That was very fair and I treated them very fairly afterwards. I never put in for expenses in my latter years with Roscommon. About the bad years, the club Clan na Gael were going well and that kept us going."

Tony joined a very select band of Roscommon people, when he won his sixth Connacht Senior Football Championship medal in 1991. Only two others before him, Eamonn Boland, and the late Bill Jackson, had achieved such a record. Was he aware of his achievement in 1991?

"Not really - just heard about it at the time."

What players of other teams impressed you?

"If I have to say one player, who stands out, it has to be Matt Connor. I remember being on a trip to the U.S. with him, once, and saying to myself that surely this is one of the best players I have seen. He was a big man and he had all the attributes of a fine player and a great attitude too. It was so sad what happened to him later. So pure, so balanced. Eugene McGee did well to win the 1982 All-Ireland with that Offaly team but he'd never have done it without Matt. His point scoring was brilliant and after a great score he'd waddle away from the goal as if nothing happened - shyly almost. Mikey Sheehy, the same type of player - tremendous player of balance, skill and brain all thrown in together."

Your greatest opponent?

"I'd say Seamus McHugh of Galway - fair and hard. We didn't have a lot to say to each other and no chawing whatever, which sometimes happens."

The player you respect most today is Maurice Fitzgerald of Kerry?

"A glorious player. One of the few players around I would travel a distance to see in action. He has time on the ball."

> *Tony won an All Star eventually in 1991 but he is a bit sceptical of the All Star award and feels there is too much politics involved, G.A.A. politics, that is. The All Star awardees he feels, should be selected by players.*

Tony McManus

The Game of your life?

"The 1990 League Quarter Final against Dublin in Portlaoise is the one. It was a tight hard match with plenty of physical abuse. We should have won in normal time and this was our best display against the Dubs for some time. Roscommon lost heavily to Down later with Mickey Linden scintillating. Martin McDermott was starting off with the team and he was trying to get them tuned in. They were a wee bit naive and learnt from the experience."

Did you enjoy the aftermath of games?

"There is no player in the country enjoys the morning of a Senior Football Championship game. It is a horrendous feeling and the closer the game comes, the more you feel, what am I getting involved in again? That rotten feeling got worse with the years. I loved the wind down after the game especially after a win. You feel over the moon."

What are your wishes for the G.A.A.?

"The G.A.A. is thriving at the moment. Bigger crowds every year in spite of bad management. The fixture list needs to be re-organised. I'd like the Open Draw for a trial with National Football League games in between Senior Football Championship games. It's possible to have a stinker of a game in the Senior Football Championship, and it would be great to get such a game out of your system in a National Football League game the following Sunday. Most club teams in mid-Summer could play mid-week and on Saturdays."

On Con Houlihan ***(Evening Press)****?*

"An absolutely brilliant writer. He makes anything he writes about so interesting. Anytime we have a big match in Dublin the first thing nearly every player does is to go in and get the *Evening Press* to see what Con has to say. That's the ultimate tribute."

Tony McManus photographed with his wife, Marie and daughter, Kate.

Chapter 5

Jimmy Keaveney

The Darling of the Hill

No man captured the fancy of Heffo's Army more than the St. Vincent's full forward who came back from football oblivion to spearhead "The Dubs" onto the imagination of the public when their epic battles with Kerry captured the nation's sporting headlines. "The Dubs" as they then became popularly known, made the game of Gaelic football in the city fashionable. This had been done in another era when St. Vincent's of Olly Freaney, Kevin Heffernan, Jim Crowley, Mossy Whelan and Snitchy Ferguson fame made sporting headlines and became the talk of the land. "Hill 16" or "The Hill" has always been Dublin's preserve and no one became its darling more than the likeable Keaveney. He could be said to have had two football lives. Jimmy explains:

"I started playing with Dublin in 1964 - Tony Hanahoe and myself. Like all young lads it was always an ambition to play for Dublin and the first success we had was winning the Leinster title in 1965. After that we seemed to go down a bit. The older players who had won an All-Ireland in 1963 such as Des and Lar Foley, Paddy Holden and John Timmons, had all finished playing. I played minor for Dublin 1962 and 1963. St. Vincent's had a great club team and in all I won ten Dublin Senior Football Championship medals starting in 1964 and finishing in 1980."

About the second Football Life.

"What happened was there was really no interest in playing with Dublin at the time. So in 1973 I decided I had enough of it. I finished after we lost to Kildare in the Senior Football Championship in Navan in 1972. I really only missed one year. The whole attitude had changed. Kevin Heffernan had taken over the team. Training was totally different and there was a good buzz."

How did you notice this great buzz?

"At the start of it I saw Dublin play Wexford in the Leinster Senior Football Championship first round game before a National Football League final replay between Roscommon and Kerry. I was on 'The Hill' for the game hoping for the best. Next thing I was called in and it just got better and better."

Your medal collection is impressive.

"In all I won seven Leinster, ten Dublin, and three All-Ireland Senior Football Championship medals but really I'm not overly interested in medals but the most important trophy or medal to me was the All-Ireland Senior Football club medal won with St. Vincent's in 1976."

Your love of St. Vincent's is absolute.

"Vincent's is an amazing club. As someone once said, it's like the Mafia. Once you're in, you don't get out. We solely concentrate on Gaelic games, hurling and football. The kids are coached from a very early age. We are still very successful at juvenile level. A lot of other fellows lose interest when they quit playing but it's different with county men from St. Vincent's. They are all still involved."

Why has the success achievement deteriorated recently at adult level?

"The last seven or eight years we haven't won a Senior Football Championship which was unheard of in my time. As far as we were concerned, we owned the Dublin County Championship. Unfortunately, we have gone through a lean spell. We have a very young team at the moment and they should make an impression soon. Another thing, the Vincent's club was mainly from the Marino area but we pulled players from Marino, Whitehall and Raheny because there was no other club in the area but since Dublin's successes in the 1970's clubs have sprouted up in these areas."

The great influences in your football life began when?

"With my father who was a Belfast man. Basically as a young lad, I played a lot of soccer and dabbled with Gaelic football and hurling. My father had a great interest in Gaelic and then, of course, there was the huge influence of the Dublin team of the 1950's (1955-1959 especially). There was a great buzz around then too, and I followed that team everywhere. Of course, we had the Christian Brothers as well in Marino, who sowed the seeds of G.A.A. interest in us."

You were a very useful hurler too. How did you view hurling as a game?

"I always preferred hurling to football and still do. I loved the game of hurling. I won three Dublin Senior Hurling Championship medals with Vincent's. I don't attach too much significance to medals. In fact one year we won the Dublin title in 1967 and Tony Hanahoe was captain. (I'm talking of football now) and Tony lost the medals. We never got a medal for that year. He lost the whole lot - stolen out of the boot of his car or something but it never bothered us."

How did the modern phenomenon of 'The Dubs' develop?

"The reason for that is that Dublin people in general are great to follow sport and a successful team. Shamrock Rovers used to be the team to follow. They had gone down and were mediocre around the early 1970's. Fortunately, for Gaelic football, this Dublin team started to rise from the ashes and the ordinary Dublin punter decided O.K. they're not a bad side, they play attractive football and they can win an All-Ireland."

You became the darling of 'The Hill'. Did it affect you?

"No it didn't affect me. I always go to 'The Hill' myself. I was there today (February 28th. 1993) for the Galway against Dublin National Football League game. I never knew I was their darling. The majority of those on 'The Hill' come from North Dublin and I'd know a lot of them."

Heffo - how important was he to it all?

"If it wasn't for Kevin Heffernan, we would not have got any success. The amount of work done by Kevin and his helpers, Lorcan Redmond and Donal Colfer in the 1970's was just incredible. A simple little thing, you're training in Parnell Park in June or July for a Leinster Championship game and the pitch gets unbearably hard. In those days Kevin was a member of Clontarf Golf Club, (still is), and they used to have those manual sprinklers for the greens which are just behind Parnell Park. But Kevin, Donal and Lorcan would go up there maybe at twelve o'clock or at lunch-time and haul the sprinklers over the wall and use them on half the pitch to soften the training ground for that night. Little things like that. And I wince nowadays with talk of fellows getting huge money for looking after teams. I know myself that Kevin and the lads never got a penny."

It's a pity that so many of today's coaches have become so mercenary-minded.

"It is a pity. It's a sad thing to see this semi-professionalism coming into Gaelic football. I don't mind if a fellow who had to do a round trip of one hundred and forty miles gets reimbursed, but this thing of managers getting paid or players looking for money for wearing their county jersey, I'd have no time for that."

The great footballers of your time?

"I was fortunate to play with great players like Des and Lar Foley, John Timmons "Snitchy" Ferguson and opponents like Mick O'Connell and Mick O'Dwyer, Martin Newell of Galway whom I always admired. I'm talking of the early days. Probably the greatest player I played against was John O'Keeffe of Kerry. A marvellous full back."

The best of them all?

"People talk about Mick O'Connell and Jack O'Shea. I may be accused of being selfish here but to me Brian Mullins is the man. Maybe not because he played for us in the 1970's but what happened to Brian afterwards when he had that horrific car accident. I saw him with his arm practically stitched to his hip trying to get a skin graft to take for the best part of two weeks in the same position. I'm convinced that but for that car accident Dublin would have won more than one All-Ireland in the early 1980's."

The best around today?

"If any of those players who played for the great Kerry team in the 1980's were playing today you'd go for them. Gaelic football is in a wee bit of a limbo at the moment. Donegal won the 1992 All-Ireland with some marvellous footballers but there is nobody around today like Jack O'Shea or Brian Mullins. You have Eoin Liston back again. Some may say it isn't a good sign but if he can do a job, I'd pick him."

Did football help you in your career?

"Naturally, I'm twenty-five years now with the same company, Tommy and Danny Norton, great G.A.A. people and the man who got me the job first was Paddy Holden. It does open doors for you. You're a named person. You have to have some ability as well. It was a tremendous help to my professional career."

Can you give me an example of Heffernan's meticulous attention to detail?

"When I started back in 1974, Kevin Heffernan introduced this training on a Saturday, which was very unusual for me. A wee bit against the grain because I used to go out for a few pints on a Friday night in our old Vincent's clubhouse up in Raheny and have an ould game of cards and doddle home and take it easy on a Saturday morning. So Kevin decided to introduce this Saturday training, of all times, ten o'clock in the morning. So one night, I was in Vincent's doing my normal thing, when Kevin arrived in and said,
'Obviously, you're not taking this training seriously.'
'Why?' I said.
'What are you doing drinking the night before a training session?'
'Ah, it will be O.K. I'll be there in time,' I replied.
So it happened on three or four occasions. Each Friday night Kevin arrived at the clubhouse, and this Friday night he came and said:
'Look, do me a favour will you? Go home and look after yourself'.
So I thought about it and I realised the work he was putting in and the interest he had in the team. So off I went home, but he still kept coming to Vincent's for another two or three Friday nights checking me out."

Was there much chat between players during games?

"In fairness when we played against Kerry, Galway or Cork you played the game and you never heard any of the slagging you hear about today. One day alright we were playing Offaly in a Leinster Senior Football Championship game in Portlaoise and we were lucky enough to get out of it with a win. Mick Wright was playing for Offaly and he was a fair man to throw himself around. There was a bit of an ould incident in the goal mouth and we ended up getting a penalty. I went to get the ball, Mick had it. 'Ah go away' he said, 'You're only a ....old fish and chip man. That's all that ever came out of that county'. At that stage he was working in Dublin so I said, 'It's still good enough for you to get your living out of it."

The game of his life?

"The biggest thrill I got out of winning any game was two games in 1964 winning the Dublin Senior Hurling Championship and Senior Football Championship just after coming out of minor. Beating Galway in the All-Ireland Final of 1974 meant so much to fellows like Hanahoe, Doherty, Cullen, Driscoll and myself. The amazing thing about it, I remember very little from the game. You're so intense, that everything flies by you. It was a marvellous feeling at the final whistle. I came home after the game actually knackered and remember Bobby Doyle calling to the house. I actually met my father and my wife Angela after the game, then went home and slept for two hours. Then we went to the Dublin celebrations that night."

Your greatest score?

"The 1976 All-Ireland Semi-Final against Galway. It was a bad old game and a dirty old day and we won by the only goal of the game which I scored. It was probably my most important score."

Scoring feats?

"I scored 2-6 in an All-Ireland Final in 1977 against Armagh. It is still a record. You're always on to me about one of the goals I scored that day and did I mean to score it. I meant to score alright. I meant to clip the ball over the bar but it just dipped at the last minute and Brian McAlinden was caught out of the goal and was way off his line and it just went into the corner of the net."

Any managerial ambitions?

"I'm still very much involved with Vincent's club. I've looked after juvenile teams, minor and at the moment I'm looking after the U-21 hurling and football teams. I enjoy it and even when I was playing, I used to look after teams. A funny thing happened on the Saturday morning before the 1976 final. Myself and John Drumgoole were in charge of the U-11 Vincent's team and we were playing Round Towers of Lusk on the Saturday morning. We had played them previously at home and the away team supplies the referee in a double round such as this. Now we had had a bit of trouble with their referee. So I had to referee the game. As I was going in there was a couple of women there and they said, 'Oh God Jimmy the best of luck to you and I hope ye's win the All-Ireland tomorrow'. Obviously, I made a few wrong decisions later while I was refereeing the game. Well the flak I had to take after the game. They were hoping that Kerry would kick the shit out of us the following day."

How important is it for the G.A.A. to be successful in Dublin?

"Very important. People around the country realise that too. The G.A.A. is very strong in Dublin. It's important for Dublin to be winning All-Ireland's every three or four years and we haven't won one now since 1983. The upsurge of Gaelic games in Dublin since the 1970's has been incredible and the number of kids playing them is huge."

Your wishes for the G.A.A.

"I hope to God it stays amateur. I'd be very disappointed if professionalism creeps in. If it does, then a transfer market will be down the end of that road. The loyalty that was built up with your club and county would disappear. The G.A.A. itself is an organisation that has done so much good for this country. If professionalism comes, the G.A.A. as we know it, will disintegrate."

Jimmy would love an Open Draw for all in the Senior Football Championship.

"The Open Draw done properly for the Sam Maguire Cup would be super."

Has winning at all costs become a part of the G.A.A.?

"There have been a few fracas over the past few weeks but we always had that. In fact, it was probably worse when I was young. The rows I saw at club games here in Dublin in football and hurling were worse then. One or two things happen today and they are blown out of all proportion. I saw the Rugby League Final between St. Mary's and Young Munster on telly recently. They beat the shit out of one another for about five minutes and there was nothing said about it."

Your favourite sports writer and commentator?

"Paddy Downey as a writer is something special. I know the man and he is such an interesting man to converse with. My favourite commentator would have to be Micheál Ó Muircheartaigh."

Were Kerry special?

"Yes. The friendship and bond grew and grew. It had to happen from all those games which were all so special. The bond is still there. We all go to the Listowel Races regularly. If they are up to Dublin we meet as well. Kerry people are very decent people and they can never do enough for you. Anywhere a footballer goes in Kerry he is welcome."

Left:
John O'Keeffe - 'a marvellous fullback'.

Right:
Brian Mullins - 'the best of them all'.

Below: Jimmy scoring his greatest goal against Galway in the All-Ireland semi-final of 1976.

Chapter 6

John Connolly

Galway's Prince of Hurlers

For years he carried Galway's hurling hopes on his broad back. Born in Leitir Mór, at a young age he came to reside in famed Castlegar, exactly opposite Ballybrit Racecourse. One of a large family, he quickly showed signs of hurling greatness and was in the van of the Galway hurling resurgence which saw his younger brother Joe lead Galway to All-Ireland success for the first time in fifty-seven years in 1980. A supreme stylist and to this day a superb specimen of manhood, when asked what was it like to be part of a large hurling family like the Cooneys of Sarsfields, the Fennellys, the Cuddys or the Rackards said:

"You grow up with it and when it happens you don't take too much notice of it. In a team situation it probably helped a lot. I was the eldest of the lads in our house, so it was very gradual for me."

Where did you get your craving for the game?

"My father never saw a hurling match until he was about forty and where he got his craving for it, is a bigger question. I remember clearly being carried on the crossbar of his bike as he cycled to the official opening of Pearse Stadium in 1957. To this day I can see the delight and awe in his eyes as he pointed out Joe Salmon, Jim Fives, Jimmy Duggan. I really desired to emulate them that day."

I remember John Connolly as a youngster in Fr. Griffin Road Technical School where I taught and I did my best to make a footballer out of him. Was Gaelic football always a number two sport for the Castlegar youngster?

"I enjoyed playing football but it was always number two and by the time I got to twenty-two, I concentrated on hurling. I played for Galway minor footballers and also at U-21 level for the county."

In my book, "Only The Teachers Grow Old", published in 1992, I referred to the fact that John, Christy O'Connor Jnr., Val O'Brien (Horse Trainer) and Tommy Lally (Soccer) were all in the same class at school. Does you remember those days well?

"I do well and I remember well a day you made a famous statement and in fact three of us, Junior, Val and myself shook hands on a pact and said we'd prove you wrong. I must admit we didn't do a stroke. We were as often as not down at the back of your class hoping you wouldn't call us for anything. You used to take a particular interest in me because I used to play for the school and we often travelled together to games and you often picked on me to see was I working. But one day you looked down at us and said, 'Ye three down there will never become anything', and that's the time we shook hands on it."

Are you still friendly with Christy Junior?

"He's a tremendous bloke. You couldn't find a better ambassador for Galway or Ireland than Junior; the love he has for Galway is unbelievable. I play golf off a handicap of seven myself and get great enjoyment out of it - every Saturday afternoon and Sunday morning. I've had a few games with Christy too and you'd learn a lot from him."

Is there such a thing as the Castlegar hurling spirit?

"I tried to analyse that myself too for a long time. You see I had the two worlds. Tradition and spirit in Castlegar on the one hand that worked for us and the opposite that worked against us for Galway. What is tradition? I found what it meant to me in Castlegar. As a young fellow the local club used to train right in front of our home at the Racecourse in Ballybrit and they'd tog out under the wall and as a young lad I was literally the ball boy hitting the ball back to them from behind the goal. I remember clearly their chat as they togged in about Cups they won and tales like coming back from ten points down to win and this impressed me greatly. Lads like Mick O'Connell, Eddie Abberton, Patsy Kelly, John Corcoran and the Egans who lived next door to our house, under the one roof literally, Paddy, Tommy, Gabriel and John Joe and they were a huge influence, Tommy Broderick too. Against all the odds, they always came out on top. It all subconsciously seeped in to me whereas the opposite became the case with the county team because it was all negative vibes after Mass, at funerals or wherever people met and discussed the county team."

What were your achievements on the field of play?

"Six Galway Senior Hurling Championship medals, one minor and one U-21, one senior club and Senior Hurling Championship All-Ireland in 1980, I can't remember how many Railway Cup medals; two All Stars 1971 and 1979, a Senior All-Ireland Football Vocational Schools title in 1964 and the Texaco award for hurling in 1979, the achievement I hold with greatest pride. Some medals in New York too."

When did you play in New York?

"The years were 1970-1972. I enjoyed Gaelic Park and loved every minute playing there. Before that time the hurling was tough and dirty but at that time there was an abundance of great hurlers there. In 1970 Clare beat Galway in the New York Senior Hurling Championship in a replayed final. That Galway team was as good as any Galway team I ever played on afterwards. Lads like Ken Croke in goal, full backs Paddy Donoghoe and John Maher, a huge man but so agile, the Curtins and Josie Harte from Gort, Paddy Egan, Mick Birmingham, Pádhraic Fahy and Des Coen, all stars really. The days were always fine, the pitch was smaller, great crowds attended and they were so close to you."

When did it first dawn on you that a Galway All-Ireland success was on?

"I started in 1967 and it started with an unfortunate incident. I remember being brought on for the great Jimmy Duggan at left half back against Clare, in a Munster Senior Hurling Championship game. I always had great respect for Jimmy. He was a gentleman on and off the field and for such a small fellow he was a mighty bit of stuff. But I had to go out that day and tell him myself that I was replacing him. Once I got on the team, all I wanted to do was to try and hold my own with the best midfielders of that time. Winning an All-Ireland Final was never on in those early days. Trying to hold your own with the great hurlers of that time was sufficient. In 1972 the U-21's won the All-Ireland with young hurlers like Iggy Clarke, Joe McDonagh, P.J. Molloy on board. That was the start of the whole resurgence. 1975 and the League win proved we were up there with the best and we moved on from there."

Your greatest opponents?

"Mick Roche of Tipperary was a brilliant hurler and a stylist. Frank Cummins of Kilkenny as well as being a great player, was tremendously strong. When he put out his right hand to hold you off, it was like a brick wall. Gerald McCarthy and Justin McCarthy of Cork marvellous hurlers too. If I was to select one as a midfield partner for life it would be Frank Cummins. In club hurling Seamus Murphy from Turloughmore always had a great battle with me."

Funny incidents?

"In the 1971 All-Ireland semi-final in Birr against Tipperary, Mick Roche who was centre half back came out on me in the second half. In the heat of battle we got involved with each other, but like everything else it stopped and finished and I remember chasing the ball into the full forward line and running down the field. I heard Mick coming after me and I knew by his run that it was after me not towards the ball he was going and he bent down and caught my hurl. God, I thought to myself, this fellow is really looking for trouble and he took my hurl and picked this thing off the bas which turned out to be a hairnet. He had this fine big head of black curly hair and to keep it out of his eyes he wore a hairnet. That was before the helmets. In the battle with the hurleys his hairnet got caught in the tin of my hurley. Of course, we shook hands after the game. No matter what kind of battle I had it was always forgotten after the game. One other incident, from a club game against Liam Mellowes, in the County Senior Hurling Championship. I was centre half forward playing on my good friend of many a battle Niall McInerney. We toured the roads of Ireland together for nearly a decade. Anything can happen in a game and in the middle of it all Niall turned to me and said 'I'll never let a Connemara man hurl me', anything to try and upset me. We made it up, of course, afterwards."

You took over as team manager of the Galway senior hurlers just after you retired. How did you like that scene?

"Absolutely different side of things. I went into it in a funny kind of a way in 1982. It's something at which you have to serve your apprenticeship. I went in as coach. I'd have my own ideas how to do it, if I ever went into it again. There has to be a few people involved who know each other very well and think alike. In hindsight it might have been better if I started with a younger age group."

Your opinion of Cyril Farrell?

"He had great enthusiasm and put an awful lot of time and effort into Galway hurling. Towards the late 1980's, when he finished he had improved an awful lot as a manager."

Refereeing - did you have any problems with referees?

"Yes, many. It's one aspect of the game that needs a lot of work done on it. I'd pay referees and grade them. If you did that you'd get a lot more people coming into refereeing. It's terribly important for somebody to be able to control players and have man-management and be able to deal with people. Nowadays, they don't know how to relate to players. They often use this ten yards advantage to show their authority, when often a bit of common-sense would work wonders. Sometimes, of course, it's very necessary when you're dealing with a 'mouth' and the effing and blinding starts but that's a different ball game, but often I only just said 'Aw ref' and had a ten yards penalty against me and that drove me cracked altogether. So few ex-players are involved now."

Have you a favourite referee?

"There was one, Ned O'Brien from Westmeath, in my early days. I would love to meet the man. He was full of common-sense. His psychology was right for me."

The social side?

"It became good enough especially after the start of the All Stars. That was new and big. I remember well going to my first All Star banquet in 1971 and feeling so awkward and inadequate when meeting men like Mick Roche, Jim Treacy, Martin Coogan, Pat Hartigan, Ray Cummins, Eamonn Cregan and 'Babs' Keating. We never really knew each other. The tours helped us too, to get to know each other. In Galway after 1975 we had a marvellous time."

Do you meet your former team-mates often now?

"It's funny we're all around Galway City and county not far from each other but we all go our separate ways. We don't meet formally as such only perhaps at golf Am Am's etc. Maybe we'll do more of that in the future."

Has being John Connolly helped you in business?

"I've no doubt that it has opened doors. Straight away you have the advantage of people knowing you when you walk in. It's important as well the bearing you had on and off the field. On the field behaviour tells you a lot about the person. Being a hurler has helped me in life."

The Connolly Sports Factory - is it doing well?

"It's like everything else. You have to make your own support. You have to have the product and you have to go out and sell it. People will not buy because of your name."

Is the G.A.A. as you knew it from the Racecourse days togging out beside the wall, going to survive?

"I never realised fully, when playing, what hurling means to the ordinary people and their everyday life. The attitude of the players is changing. In our time hurling meant everything to us. Nowadays, the players treat it as a game. Win or lose, they get on with life. The game will prosper. Refereeing I think has got worse. It may go professional and what's wrong with that if the standard is maintained."

Did you ever play with Joe Salmon whom you saw playing as a nine-year-old in 1957?

"No I never played with him. I can still see the neat clean-cut stylish hurler of that day. That image never changed and even to meet him years afterwards he was so friendly and jolly."

The best Galway hurler in your time?

"Very difficult to select from your own team. The one man of my time who always astonished me was Iggy Clarke. The number of times he won balls he had no right to win. He was tremendously strong, a great pair of legs on him, good hands, fine anticipation."

The best hurler around today?

"Joe Cooney is a marvellous hurler. The thing that separates the greats from the nearly greats is their vision. Some people when they get the ball just think of doing one thing with it. Some people can think of five things to do in that split second and pick the right one. He just has time to do things. You have far more time on the ball than people realise but people go at a hundred miles an hour because their mind starts racing and they follow whatever comes into their head. But Joe can be so relaxed. I'd just love to be playing with him."

The Cooney household today must be like what the Connolly one once was?

"I'm sure it is. So many similarities. We seem to have a lot in common. But they would say to you like ourselves you don't think of it as the Connollys or the Cooneys when you're playing. Just another team-mate. It helps spirit of course. Once when we were playing Gort in a tough county Senior Hurling Championship match, Joe was playing on Sylvie Linnane at centre half back and I was at full forward. I had this habit of saying 'Tarraing' when a dropping ball came between Joe and Sylvie. This 'Tarraing, Tarraing' really fooled Sylvie. He had this idea that it was a secret code between us and he probably conjured up this image of me telling Joe to pull on him. The 'Tarraing' was the Irish for 'Pull' and being native speakers we often spoke in Irish."

Where did they all get the love of Irish?

"We came from Leitir Mór to Ballybrit when I was four. We never spoke anything but Irish. My mother always insisted we spoke Irish. I still love the language and my native Leitir Mór and enjoy nothing better than to be back there on a fine Summer's day in Trá Bhán, going through the hills and the bogs and the sand dunes with my great friends and relations. The nearest place to Heaven."

The game of your life?

The All-Ireland semi-final against Tipperary in 1971 in Birr. And the little preparation we had for it. I spent the week in Ballybunion before the game with my friends Tommy Egan and Tommy Glynn. We had no get-togethers then or I wouldn't have missed them. Hurling was everything to me, then. It was the highest point in my hurling life. Other things impinged after that - work, mortgage, family, what not. Hurling had to find its own place. Great to play on Mick Roche and do reasonably well on him. That's the one and the All-Ireland club final which we won with five of us playing and two substitutes. They were Pádhraic, Michael, Joe, Gerry and myself playing and the two gasúrs, Tom and Murt were substitutes. The latter two are still playing for Castlegar. No matter how high or where you play there is something special about playing for your own parish or village, the people you grew up with, the ordinary five-eighths whose life is hurling and the kick you get out of achieving something with your parish - that's the G.A.A. for me."

Left:
John Connolly signing autographs in Eyre Square, Galway.

Right:
Joe Cooney - 'I'd love to be playing with him'.

Below: Two peerless Galway midfielders, the late Joe Salmon, on left, and John Connolly.

Chapter 7

Sean Donnelly of Longford

Youngest County Secretary ever

Longford is a small county with a great football tradition. Its top football college, St. Mel's College in Longford, where Sean is a teacher, has a proud and storied football tradition. Sean Donnelly, while in his prime as a footballer, became the youngest County G.A.A. Secretary ever. He played for his county in three different decades and was one of the county's stars in their one and only Leinster Senior Football Championship title success in 1968.

When did you first get the taste for the game?

"Football has always been the principal game in this county. Hurling is beginning to catch on, but it is still very much second place to football. As long as I can remember, football was big in Longford. Club rivalry has always been keen. The county is small and the clubs meet so often that a great rivalry is built up. In all there were twenty-two adult clubs in my time. My own club is Longford Slashers, a good club with a fine club structure. The great clubs of the 1960's were Clonguish and Granard, who are at a low ebb now. But to address your question, my memory goes back to when I was about ten or eleven and living in Teffia Park in Longford and a neighbour, Joe Hanlon, now Fr. Joe in Dublin, used to organise us young fellows for games in their own field. Unfortunately, all that's left of that field now is the closed up remains of the Hanlon ambulance company. Joe was the eldest of that family and he used to get help from his brother Frank, also a priest."

You teach since 1967 in your old alma mater, St. Mel's College. Is it still the huge football influence it once was?

"Very much so. It supplies footballers to the neighbouring counties as well, especially Leitrim, Roscommon and Westmeath. There were many notable coaches in the college over the years and might I add, St. Jarlath's College in Tuam was always very much respected in St. Mel's for their football tradition. The tradition started with the great Fr. Sean Manning. Everybody is measured against him - he is still very revered. A book has been written about him and an U-21 competition between neighbouring counties to Longford, bears his name. He ended his days as a P.P. in Leitrim where his contribution was also immense. In my own day, we had reasonable teams but not great success. I was on the team in my senior year playing at full forward. The man in charge in my time was Fr. Mick Reid, an Offaly man. After that there was Fr. Gerry McAuley and then Fr. Jimmy McKeown, who had been a protégé of Fr. Manning's and he rekindled much of the Manning spirit with a great run of success in his period. That was the time Dermot Gannon captained Mel's to a Hogan Cup final win over Jarlath's at Ballinasloe. In fact, these schools met in three finals at the time and they were marvellous games. Great names from different eras surfaced like Mick Ryan, Colm Smith and Jim Harold. In my time, Harold was special because in his senior year at school he was also midfield for the county senior team, being on the county minor team also. We are in the process of developing a full sized pitch. We always had three small sized pitches, which we often felt militated against us."

U.C.G. then - was it very meaningful to you?

"I had a marvellous time in U.C.G. from 1959 to 1964. In all I won three Sigersons and lost a final. My best pals at the time were Enda Colleran, Pateen Donnellan, Brianeen Geraghty, Bosco McDermott and Martin Newell. All were to be stars of the future, Christy Tyrrell, Des Feely of Roscommon and Tony Kenny, Johnny Geraghty, Mick Laide, Joe Langan of Mayo, Hugh McGonigle of Sligo, George Glynn and John Stafford-Kelly. It was a marvellous time. At the end of my first year Mattie Glynn became Secretary and he was very important to the organisational side of things. That and the arrival of Paddy McDermott as Chairman. Between the two of them they organised the training and the preparation especially for Sigerson. The biggest effect my time in U.C.G. had, was of seeing the Galway lads, Pateen Donnellan and Enda Colleran training in the closed season on their own, to be fit when they went into training. I used to train a lot with them and realised the commitment that was necessary to go to the top. That was an education. Playing in the early years with Longford, some of the players hardly knew each other and it wasn't possible to have any success under those circumstances."

Who started to change that scene in Longford?

"Although Longford didn't achieve success until the late 1960's, around the early 1960's Liam Hastings, an ex-Mayo player was Chairman of the Longford County Board and he had a tremendous effect on the football scene. He probably laid the seeds for the success afterwards, because he used to call to see me in U.C.G. and constantly graded every footballer in Longford from the start. He got the interest going. My own first game with the seniors was at the end of 1958 against Monaghan in a challenge game and I hadn't even played senior club football at the time. My first Senior Football Championship game was in 1960 and I finished up in 1974."

Who were the others besides Hastings to fashion the upsurge in spirit?

"In 1964 things on a county level had gone pretty low with very poor results. Between Jimmy Flynn, Chairman, Fr. Philip Magee, Central Council delegate and Mattie Fox the Secretary, they organised to get Mick Higgins of Cavan to come as trainer and he was a great bonus. He had a marvellous effect on the team and it coincided with a few good younger players coming on the scene, like Jimmy Hanniffy, Jimmy Flynn, Brendan Gilmore and Tom Mulvihill to complement the lads that were seasoned campaigners."

They won the National Football League in 1966 and the Leinster Senior Football Championship in 1968 before losing gallantly to Kerry. How was it all lost so quickly afterwards?

"I don't admit that it died down at that time, because we were relatively close for many years afterwards, losing in replays in semi-finals against Offaly. We had reasonable success but if you examine the population of Longford you'd be amazed that we ever won out in Leinster. The population is roughly thirty thousand. Add on about two thousand more in the 1960's. Galway City has almost double that population now. Talking of Galway we always had a good record against Galway. The team under John Murphy beat Galway. We were never afraid of Dublin either. But we had our bogey teams too. Horses for courses, if you like. In the early 1980's, we had a very promising team and lost narrowly to Kerry in a play off in the League in Longford. We have enjoyed our successes limited though they are. Football here is far from dead. Emigration hits us sorely. Our best young player of last year, Brian O'Connor has gone to New York and Kieran Gilooley, a full back of a few years back, is starring in London but we still get on with it."

The best Longford player then and now?

"Of my own time the player who led by example and never seemed to have a bad game was Brendan Barden. He was admired far outside Longford as well. He probably was one of the most stylish Longford players ever. He was captain in the glory years and played at right half back. Jimmy Hanniffy too, of course. For any team to win, you need to have one or two special players: Jimmy Hanniffy came on the scene, at the age of nineteen, in 1966 and fresh from College was drafted in as a very light player at midfield. We had seven forwards when Jimmy was at midfield. He was second in command at midfield but he scored as much as any forward. His speciality was when he did get a break, he could come through and score. Himself and Jimmy Flynn could hold their own with any midfield. The best today is Dessie Barry, out and out our best forward of the past few years. One of the best in the country. He rarely lets a game pass without cracking in one or two goals. He is deadly, perhaps not playing as well now as in the past. Dessie is a local postman here and is highly respected."

Your greatest opponent?

"In the early years, I never seemed to get the better of Johnny Egan of Offaly. A very difficult player to play against. I remember him too, scoring a "fifty" in the final seconds against Mel's to put us out of the Leinster Colleges Championship in my final year by a single point. In club football in Longford my toughest opponent was Kevin Doyle of Clonguish and he never played for the county."

The best player in Ireland today?

"I love to see Maurice Fitzgerald of Kerry taking frees. He seems to have no bother from either foot. We'd love to have a freetaker of his calibre in Longford at the moment. I'm disappointed he doesn't achieve more and that Kerry don't achieve more with him. He seems to have the ability but there is a shortfall somewhere. The most dynamic player to come on the scene in recent years is James McCartan of Down. We knew what to expect here in Longford, because he punished St. Mel's when playing for St. Colman's College, Newry in an All-Ireland semi-final. He is a very exciting player to watch."

You went into officialdom at a very early age and became Secretary of the County Board while a player. How did it happen? Was it difficult?

"I was asked to contest the post back in 1967 at the age of twenty-seven and was successful. It wasn't that difficult as Jimmy Flynn was a tremendous Chairman and Fr. Phil Magee seemed to take a lot of responsibility and gave me a lot of assistance particularly since he was team manager of the county team at the time. The thing I disliked most about it was that I seemed to have no real home life as such. Most evenings each week were taken up with the G.A.A. My wife, Anne, will tell you how I often arrived for dates at eleven or twelve o'clock at night, dates that were meant to be much earlier. I was lucky to be Secretary when we won our first and only Leinster Senior Football title. There was so much jubilation at the time. I intended to retire around 1970 but it was just as easy to continue on playing than looking at people playing."

Are you still keen?

"I go to see some game every Sunday. Last Sunday I saw our U-21's bow out of the championship to Meath in Longford. It was a bad beating unfortunately."

Will Longford ever win an All-Ireland in the future - any grade?

"It's easy to be pessimistic at the moment because things aren't too bright. But there is a good effort being made principally under Eugene McGee with a planning programme to span a few years and, hopefully, it will bear some fruit. I'm always very optimistic. Every game I ever played I thought we'd win even though I lost more than I won. In 1964 we were at a very low ebb and yet in 1965 we reached a Leinster Senior Football Final. There is always hope. It's a bit disappointing at the moment though. The local papers in Longford - the *Leader* and the *News* - are very fair. The principal thing in both papers is the G.A.A. Emigration is still hitting us."

Surely Clare and Donegal must have given great hope in 1992?

"Clare certainly gave us hope because we drew with Clare in the B. Final last year and could have won it, losing out in extra time."

Has Gaelic football deteriorated?

"There is a great levelling of standards, but individual skills don't seem to be quite as pronounced as they used to be. We used to go to games to see individuals. Now it is to see a team. My boyhood memories are of going to see players like Packy McGarty of Leitrim, Frankie Stockwell or Sean Purcell of Galway, Kevin Heffernan of Dublin in action. A lot more depends on teamwork today. Donegal were a good example of that."

Anecdotes you have aplenty.

"The first evening I went to Galway as a student I knew nobody but I got my football boots and I was directed down to The Swamp (South Park) for a game. I don't know who the people were or who had the football and we'd go down there every evening. It would gradually build up from five to ten to fifteen to twenty and then we would have a match. I can't remember a lot of the lads who were there, but a regular there was Máirtín Thornton, the former heavyweight boxing champion. He was always pointed out to newcomers as the great Máirtín Thornton. He was crazy on the game and he wouldn't hurt a fly. One time in Galway, while we were out relatively late at a function, Pateen Donnellan got upset at being out so late and it reminded me a bit of Cinderella and the twelve o'clock bell, he decided he'd have to rush home in case 'Tull' Dunne in Ballinasloe would hear he was out after twelve o'clock."

He recalled another incident from a London Senior Football Championship final between his own team, St. Vincent's, and St. Monica's.

"I got a job because of the football, of course, and made a lot of great friends there. The year was 1961. Bobby Burns was on our team too and after about fifteen minutes of the game, Bobby, who was playing great football around that time, got the line and we were down to fourteen men. We had depended on him so much and Monica's were the defending champions. At half-time the instructions were that we were to play football for ten minutes and as it was unlikely that we were going to win, that a row was to start up and everybody was to join in with nobody opting out. The County Board couldn't suspend everybody and there would have to be a replay or there would be no County final. I shivered at the thought of what was going to happen and I played out of my skin to make sure there would be no fisticuffs and we won in the end by five or six points."

The game of your life?

"I enjoyed every game of football that I played. The one I had the biggest influence on was the Leinster Final of 1968, which we won. I was lucky enough to score 2-1 which had a big bearing on our win over Laois. That day too, I had my name taken for the one and only time in my life, early on in the game having clashed with the Laois cornerback, Jim Leonard, who had to be carried off, concussed, but it was an accident. I might have got the line too but John Dowling took my name even though I think John knew it was accidental. For the rest of the game I was the target of a lot of attention but that helped, as I earned a few frees, which were beneficial."

The score you remember best.

"Again from a championship game in London and a fluke too. I was soloing in and lost control of the ball over-kicking it by mistake, as I reached two backs, who collided as they came for me, leaving the way open for me with only the goalie to beat. I shot for the corner of the net and the shot went through his legs. I met a man recently enough in a restaurant in Carlow, who remembers that goal as a comedy of errors or flukes, if you like. But it's a score I like to remember."

Sean Donnelly beats Roscommon's Pat Lindsay to the ball.

Chapter 8

Sean Stack

Of "The Bridge" and Clare

When I walked into the Queen's Hotel in Ennis last March to interview Sean Stack for this book, he had retained much of the youthful vigour he had when I first met him after a Clare hurling win in Tulla, well over fifteen years ago. Now a young forty, Sean could still be out there hurling for Clare as he does regularly for the club he loves, Sixmilebridge or 'The Bridge', as it is known in Clare.

When was your last game prior to the interview?

"Against Kilmallock in the Munster Senior Hurling club final. I'm forty since last August and still play in the same position since day one - centre half back."

The following is a brief resumé of what Sean is at now.

"I'm living in Sixmilebridge and teaching in Shannon Comprehensive School since 1979. I graduated in Maynooth University as an external student in the great hurling days, in the presence of so many student hurlers who became county stars afterwards, the Clarkes, Sean Silke, the Fitzmaurices, Paddy Bollard. We won the Fitzgibbon Cup in 1973 and again later. My Maynooth days lasted from 1973 to 1977."

What happened to Clare hurling since the great days of the 1970's?

"They were never great days, were they? We never won out even in Munster. True we won two National Hurling Leagues. The two league wins were fabulous but we were totally despondent that we didn't add at least a Munster title to them, especially the 1978 one against Cork which never took off."

I was present at that game and felt it didn't even loosen out for Cork until Tom Cashman took the game by the throat and raised his game above everybody else's. How do you remember it?

"He did. I played on him for the first half and he was a new face. I actually enjoyed that first half hour but then I was switched to halfback. He wasn't under the same amount of pressure as the rest, because he was new to the scene. He was a beautiful striker of the ball - really fast. He picked off four points but they were just sharpness of the hands - no extravagant play. I remember one just came to him. He just gave it a little touch of his hurley and bang, first time, over the bar. He got the four points like that - from broken play really. They had the smell of the big day and they knew they were capable of winning all the time. We were convinced we'd win the All-Ireland in 1978, definitely in 1981 and 1986 we were good enough to win it, but we just didn't believe we were going to do it."

You were involved in a controversey with a former team-mate, Sean Hehir, who became team-manager. Is all that cleared up now?

"That's gone and cleared and it's all healthy again."

When I asked him why he wasn't involved himself and why Clare has to go outside its own county for team-managers, he gave this opinion.

"The question I always ask is, why are outsiders taking over a lot of other counties and even more sickening, a lot of clubs? It's fairly typical now in most counties for clubs to go outside their own county for managers. I used to think it was a Clare distinction, that we thought faraway hills were always greener and other guys knew more than us. But most counties have that ailment now."

It works for some counties like John Maughan with the Clare footballers.

"To pick you up on the John Maughan phenomenon. Fabulous man doing a huge amount of work. But if Clare were beaten by Kerry in last year's Munster Final, would he still be involved now? Would all his demands be answered all the time?"

It depends on results really.

"Down the years Kevin Heffernan - home-man - Mick O'Dwyer - homebred-man too - 'Babs' Keating, who transformed Tipperary in 1987 another home-man, Peter McGrath of Down, Brian McEniff of Donegal. They are all home-men and they think a lot of their own and we have them in Clare too."

Where did it all begin for you - this huge interest in hurling?

"It began one hundred yards up the road like every other young lad in the country who lives and dies for the game. After the cows were in every evening it was just hurling, that was it until dark. All this of course, in Sixmilebridge."

Who were the people who helped you on your way?

"There are three people in hurling in my life who influenced me more than anybody else. Dick Barron, when I was a young fellow at home in the Bridge was an enormous influence. He never told us we were any good, or that we played well. But we knew that he was there for us and we wanted to impress him. Our mentor every day, Dick was a farmer who often neglected farm work, maybe loaded fourteen of us into his Hillman Hunter, that was Dick. In our neighbourhood he was Mr Hurling. After that a huge influence would have been Fr. Gerry Meagher in Maynooth College, God rest his soul, and then, of course, the one and only for us was Fr. Harry."

The Fr. Harry, of course, was Fr. Harry Bohan, team manager of Sean's glory years with Clare and a man of great charisma.

"He had a huge influence on all of us. By 'us' I particularly mean the 1974 Clare U-21 team which drastically threw away a Munster title below in Thurles against Waterford."

Was hurling as strong in the Bridge then as it was later?

"I'm talking of 1967. That was the first time I ever pulled on a club jersey. We won two championships that year, U-15 and U-16. I was in the forwards then. So small and light, I usually played way out on the wing because I could hit it and lift it and do all the right things except a fellow could drive me a mile with a shoulder. That was the start of it. Then I went to Sexton St. in Limerick - St. Michael's C.B.S., who won the Harty Cup in 1993 for the first time in many years. I was at school there when it was won by them last."

Were you on that winning team?

"No. I was just a second year student then. It was magic to be there at the time. The names of that team spring to mind immediately - Pat Hartigan, Sean Foley, Eamonn Grimes. They were guys whom we'd creep down to the senior yard at lunchtime just to get a look at. I didn't get on the Harty Cup team until my Leaving Certificate year and we got beaten by Ennis C.B.S."

You were a slow developer in physique as a young lad.

"When I was in Limerick I was only the size of a peanut. Myself and Pat Herbert won a juvenile Colleges title with Sexton Street together and the two of us were sitting down in the front of the picture, dinky size. You'd swear we were mascots. We were small and weedy looking but we were able to do the right things. I was at wing forward and I think Pat was in the corner."

You were lucky to arrive in St. Patrick's College, Maynooth and be part of their greatest ever hurling team.

"I hit it dead on the right time. We had a marvellous team - inter-county hurlers galore. That was as professional a set-up as you could possibly imagine. Paddy Barry from Cork was captain. Paudie Fitzmaurice was captain of one of the Fitzgibbon winning teams. We trained twice a day maybe for six weeks before the Fitzgibbon. Iggy Clarke, his brother Joe, Sean Silke, Paddy Bollard, a great midfielder from Kilkenny. We won out in 1973 and 1974 and were beaten in the final of 1975. Willie Fitzmaurice, another fine midfielder. We won the 1973 final in Pearse Stadium, Salthill and I don't remember the last ten minutes of that at all. About ten minutes before the end, there was a 50-50 ball with a man from Tubber. We just clashed. I was put out cold anyway, so I woke up in hospital. The match was slipping from us at the time I left and we finished up winning by two points."

Then on to Clare and Harry Bohan.

"At that time in Clare you had a right amount of good young players coming from schools and then some very good players like Sean Hehir and Ger Loughnane who had gone to Dublin to St. Patrick's Training College. Now all these hit the scene when we still had good hurlers like Gus Lohan, Jimmy Mac (MacNamara to outsiders!), Jackie O'Gorman and Martin McGeogh at home. Everything blended in really well. So we came from a point defeat in the 1972 Munster U-21 final, to absolutely destroying Tipperary in Cork in 1974, to then go down to Thurles on a torrential night to lose to Waterford. The heavens opened that night and the reason they beat us was, we lost Martin McKeogh, who was a kingpin. Martin was on the Munster team then, and a really great player. Marvellous centre half back. We lost him two weeks before the game with an ankle injury in a challenge game, an injury he never fully recovered from. I suppose I shouldn't be taking it away from Waterford. Then we came along the following Sunday after that loss and Limerick gave us a fourteen point trouncing in the Munster Senior Hurling Championship Final. Fr. Harry had been in charge since the previous October. Two bad successive Sundays for eight of us. That was 1974 and they had to re-think the scene. At that time the word manager was shunned in Clare. There was all sorts of crying opposition to the title of manager and Harry was fighting against the tide but suddenly it all started to happen in 1976. We matured and we still had the anchor men there. In that year, we went through to the National Hurling League undefeated (home and away) and Kilkenny beat us in a final replay. On to 1977 and we did the same thing and beat Kilkenny in the final and lost the Munster final that year to Cork. I still believe that Cork team of 1977 should have beaten us more than they did. In 1978 we beat Kilkenny again in a National Hurling League final (3-10 to 2-10). It was supposed to be a fabulous exhibition of hurling. Suddenly that was the arrival of a great Clare team and an All-Ireland was within our sights. We didn't get carried away with our success. We were definitely good enough to win that 1978 Munster final."

Why then did Clare not win that 1978 final against Cork at Thurles?

"At half time we were on the pig's back. We were only a point behind after playing against a stormer (0-8 to 0-7). In the second half the match just never took off. If Cork got a goal, even. Nothing broke the tension in the match at all. 1978 was devastating."

To Fr. Harry Bohan. How special was he?

"The funny thing about it was, that Harry was realistic enough to know that his knowledge of how to coach or train a team and to speak about hurling was limited, or he thought so anyway. So he didn't get involved in that side of it. Harry came along and convinced us all that we were special. You went home thinking that too. All the players to this day, if Harry asked them to do anything or come anywhere they'd drop all tools and round in."

What was it like for hurling to play second fiddle to Gaelic football in Clare?

"The hurlers aren't in the same orchestra at the moment. They are as enthusiastic as ever - the hurlers - and from talking to them, they are really trying. I still believe the talent is there."

Sean was reluctant to list your achievements.

"One All Star in the wrong year! The year was 1981 and I didn't deserve it, as I had only two good games in the whole year. I was very disappointed not to get one in 1983 - now that may sound arrogant. Consistently in all matches, that was my best year in inter-county fare. Last year, 1992, I won my sixth Clare Senior Hurling Championship medal and the Munster Senior Club title in 1984 - that was definitely one of the highlights of all my years. The biggest kick was winning that Munster club award in 1984, because your 100% loyalty is to your home crowd and your mates and the guys you grew up with, the officers too, and the old men in the parish who appreciate a win like that."

The great Clare hurlers?

"The great ones I heard about before our time, Matt Nugent, Jim Cullinane, a great hurler. I'm going back to 1968 to the first Clare team that I thought were kings. Three matches with Kilkenny to decide the National Hurling League Semi-final in Thurles. Getting beaten in the third one. Like Pat Cronin and Tom Ryan from Tipperary who played with Galway too. Michael Arthurs from Newmarket-on-Fergus was a marvellous hurler and a fantastic athlete but like a lot of us he didn't believe in himself. Pat Cronin was a super hurler. Noel Pyne was as beautiful a sticksman as you'll ever see. I never saw Jimmy Smith really. Saw him in the 1962 County final but I was only seven and I wasn't old enough to appreciate him."

The great ones of your own time?

"To me there were very few better than Jackie O'Gorman. He had everything - the heart of a lion. He could strike it with four guys trying to hook him. Marvellous hands and he used a short little hurley, something it took me a while to realise. He was tough and a leader too."

Your greatest opponents?

"The best forward I've ever seen is Ray Cummins. He was marvellous. He could do things that most fellows only dream about."

The greatest?

"Of the hurlers of my time, Iggy Clarke was king of them all. He was the quietest man I've ever seen on or off a field. But he had physique, speed, marvellous skill, a fabulous free-taker, side line cuts always seventy yards plus and so competitive and the heart of a lion. He had everything. But he never will be heralded as great as he was, because he was so unfortunate the year of the All-Ireland Final of 1980 to miss it through injury. I was lucky enough to be in Maynooth with him."

Is the game of hurling special?

"Oh it is. I've played Gaelic football - a fabulous game - absolutely great enjoyment in it. But I think footballers will have to agree that for a spectator sport nothing can compare with hurling. Now I've seen baseball, American football and basketball all over the States and all the games here at home and nothing gives me a bigger thrill than watching a good hurling match or watching a good dog winning a race!"

Are you fond of dogs?

"I'm stone mad about greyhounds. I have greyhounds at home and since 1987 have got into them big-time. We always had greyhounds in our house down the years."

Are you bitter about how your career ended?

"I was very bitter because I felt I lost three years inter-county hurling and I wanted to stay on and play. That was sore. I don't think you can ever lose the interest. It keeps biting at you. I've been seeing the footballers in the League in the Park here (Cusack Park, Ennis) and 'tis great."

Anecdotes or quirky things?

"We played Blackrock (Cork) two years ago - The Bridge I mean - they were playing against Ballyhea in a Senior Hurling Championship game the following Sunday. So it was a crunch game for them. As it was, we finished up at the venue with thirteen players and we had two that came along, one who had retired some years back and was forty-four then. The other guy is an entertainer and musician and he came along for the 'craic'. The two of them had to play and we beat Blackrock in a right cracker by five points. We went down to their Clubhouse afterwards and our Chairman was talking to one of the prominent officials of Blackrock and I was standing at the other side and the Cork lad said to me, 'Gee that centre back played well tonight - he plays the very same style as his father'. Our Chairman said 'His father is from Kerry, I don't think he ever played hurling' and our Cork friend replied 'Go on, wasn't I watching him all through the 1970's, wasn't his father Sean Stack? His son has the same cut as him'. That was a big insult. Yer man thought I should be retired twenty years ago. The 1970's seemed so long ago to him. It was myself playing centre back, not my son. It was a kind of a compliment too, of course."

Sean Stack

The game of your life?

"The one that gives me the greatest satisfaction still is the 1983 Clare Senior Hurling final. It was the biggest kick I ever got out of a hurling match. We had played Eire Óg (Ennis) in the 1982 final and we knew we had about five titles left behind us. We won in 1977 and 1979. 1980 and 1981 we left them there. Then came 1982 and we drew the final. In the replay Eire Óg beat us narrowly against the run of play. That was a low point. The night before that replay there was a terrible accident in the village and we lost one of our young hurlers in a road accident. I had spent all that night up, down at their house, and the game was totally irrelevant. We went into the Clubhouse before going to the game and I remember a whole bunch of country lads inside all primed in their best physical shape, many of them having slept well not knowing the tragic news. Fr. O'Dowd came in and said a decade of the rosary and I could have seen twenty-five to thirty grown men crying before leaving for Ennis. He was a club minor, just eighteen. He wasn't on the panel but he was always around and on the field and his father was deeply involved. Patrick Quinn was his name. We went up to Ennis and whether it was the shock or what, we played out of our skins to lead by eleven points just five minutes before half-time. Then suddenly our corner back got a bad head injury and had to retire and whatever happened nobody could hit a ball after that. The whole thing suddenly struck us and we lost the final. So we came along in 1983 and the same two teams in the final again. Repeat of 1982, a draw again. They drew with the last puck of the ball. A '21' and Tony Nugent put it away. It was teeming rain and he put it through us for a goal. I came home that night and said 'Not again'.
We came out in the replay and played like we played for the first twenty-five minutes of the replay in 1982 but this time we kept it up. I went out of the Park that evening and I hadn't smoked for about five months and hadn't had a drink for about five weeks. I came up to Considine's and went in and bought ten Majors and a pint of Guinness and I walked up to the Pontoon bridge above in front of the Bank on my own and sat down and had the grandest, most peaceful quarter of an hour of my life. The grandest evening of my life."

Left:
Ray Cummins of Cork - 'the best forward I've ever seen'.

Right:
Iggy Clarke - 'was king of them all'.

Below: Sean Stack in centre, having been presented with a B&I Award with from left: Tadhg Murphy, Jimmy Smyth, former Clare star, Victor Williams B&I, Michael Slattery and Tom Downes.

Chapter 9

Mick Higgins

Of Cavan

He is still a slim whip of a man and when I met him in his comfortable home on the outskirts of Virginia, you'd never think this was the same man who starred in the Polo Grounds All-Ireland Final of 1947. There was never a photograph taken of that team or so Mick said. But then, only for his wife, Margaret, a Meath woman, he wouldn't have kept any newspaper cuttings or photos at all. But life was simpler then, as you'll see from the interview with this lovely Cavan gentleman, who has always been one of my special favourites. I remember the Polo Grounds Final well. The entire student body of St. Jarlath's College, Tuam, huddled together in a corner of the big study hall from 8.30p.m. on as we hung on to Micheál O'Hehir's every word. The names like Batt Garvey, Eddie Dowling and the Lyne brothers from Kerry and of Cavan's Tony Tighe, Peter Donoghoe, Phil "The Gunner" Brady, John Joe O'Reilly, Phil Duke and, of course, Mick, himself still remain. We cheered every score. It was our All-Ireland and it was wrong to export it.

Mick still follows Gaelic football, but his great sporting passion today is the dogs. When did you first wear the Cavan jersey?

"In 1942. It was for the Cavan junior team and my first game was against Monaghan in Cootehill. I didn't play senior until 1943."

Where were you born?

"I was born in New York. Lived for five years there. Came back to live in Kilnaleck, my mother's home place. My father was from Mayo - Kiltimagh to be exact. Spent about three years in Kiltimagh and then back to Kilnaleck and finished my national schooldays there. Peter Donoghoe was at school with me and we had a lot of good footballers in the school. When we started playing club football Tony Tighe from Ballyjamesduff joined us at Mountnugent."

Where did you go after the national schooldays?

"I went to the Marist in Dundalk and spent three years there. We won the McRory Cup there in 1938 and I was on the team - it was their first and I played right three quarter (that is right half forward in Ulster football parlance). The man in charge was Fr. McOsgar."

Who were the great Cavan footballers you looked up to?

"Jack Smallhorn, Big Tom O'Reilly, Paddy Smith of Drumkelly. Big Tom was a big man in every sense."

Your first Senior Football Championship season?

"1943 and my first game was against Monaghan. We won out in Ulster that year and went on to the All-Ireland to lose to Roscommon in a replay. In all I won eight Ulster Senior Football Championship medals between 1943 and 1952, my last one. It was just nearly a matter of form that time for Cavan to win."

Who were the best individual footballers in Ulster outside of Cavan then?

"In Armagh you had Jim McCullagh, John Vallely and Alf Murray. In Monaghan, Vincent Duffy, Eamonn McDonnell and Hughie McKearney. Antrim had Sean Gallagher, Kevin Armstrong, Harry O'Neill, Pat O'Hara and Sean Gibson. The best team we met in Ulster in those days was Antrim. They beat us in the Ulster Final of 1946."

The great Cavan men of your time?

"To win an All-Ireland you must have at least twelve good footballers on the team, I was lucky to come on at that stage. We had a great half back line. P.J. Duke, John Joe O'Reilly, God rest them both and Simon Deignan. That was our strongest line. At midfield we had Phil Brady and Victor Sherlock - two big men, bigger in physique than the present day midfielders. Great catchers both. Sherlock could sail up into a ball. The forwards were so long playing together and we had collective training then so that we knew each other's every move, Tony Tighe, T.P. O'Reilly, Peter Donoghoe, Joe Stafford, Edwin Carolan and John Joe Cassidy."

Who trained the team then and where did this full-time collective training take place?

"Hughie Reilly was our trainer. For two seasons we trained in Ballyjamesduff and stayed in the Percy Ffrench Hotel. In other years we trained in Virginia. We usually trained together for a fortnight. The schedule was like this. You got up at eight o'clock in the morning and the first thing you did was four miles of a roadwalk. Then back for breakfast where you talked football, hung around or maybe played cards until eleven o'clock when you togged and did two hours of physical exercise, sprinting, running etc. Then back in for dinner and we were out at half three. We played football for an hour and a half. Then a half hour's handpassing up and down the field and around in a circle. If you were earning and very few of us were at that time, you were paid £4 a week for loss of wages. Joe Stafford was our highest wage earner then at £4 a week. So he set the standard. Most of the lads were students, clerical and lay and these got £2 a week. There were no free cars or big fees at that time. We then had our evening meal after togging in and at seven o'clock we did ten miles of a walk. At half way, we'd play pitch and toss for half an hour before coming back."

Were there any devils in the pack then?

"Owen Roe McGovern would be the biggest schemer. Paddy Smith, the vet was a great character too. But the whole thing was taken seriously. Fellows who'd take a drink would give it up for the duration of training. We'd all be in bed at eleven."

Did it ever get boring?

"It never would. Hail or shine we trained every day but we wouldn't walk in the rain."

Mick talked about the buildup to the Polo Grounds All-Ireland of 1947.

"John Joe was our captain then. Personally, I didn't realise at the time the significance of playing the final in New York. The subs and the officials went by boat and the teams travelled by plane. It was a twenty-seven hour journey by plane with a stop for refuelling at Gander travelling by the Azores. We got a breakdown and were stuck there for four hours. When we went to take off, it just wouldn't. Planes weren't what they are like now. We weren't too happy and when we arrived in New York we decided we were coming back by boat."

What was the whole scene like then?

"We travelled out five days beforehand. There was no big send-off for us from Cavan. There was a great reception for both teams when we arrived. For years no team had travelled to the States from Ireland because of the war. We stayed in the Commodore Hotel. We knew the Kerry fellows well - Paddy Kennedy, the two Lynes, Jackie and Dinny, Dan O'Keeffe, the goalkeeper, Teddy O'Connor. We met often in those days."

Was the atmosphere strange the night before the final?

"I stayed with my uncle. Phil Brady stayed with his aunt, but the rest stayed in the Hotel, a first class hotel. The Polo Grounds was packed for the game."

You remember clearly the game itself.

"Kerry started in a whirlwind fashion and led us eight points to two after fifteen minutes - Batt Garvey getting two goals - they were all over us at that stage and you'd nearly think we had stage fright. The funny thing about it though, the two points we got from the balls that came up to us, we got them fairly easy I thought. I remember saying to Tighe if we get enough of this ball we could beat these fellows. A switch made around that particular time was important. Duke was brought back to halfback from left three quarters and from that point on, we seemed to get a grip on the game. That and an injury sustained by Kerry's Eddie Dowling. Dowling was fielding everything and he was playing terribly well. He went up for this high ball and whatever way he over-reached, he came down on his back. The ground was tremendously hard and he fell more or less on his shoulder and had to be carried off and that didn't help Kerry's cause. We were leading by a point at half time and we finished up winning by four. Peter Donoghoe was deadly on the frees."

Did you enjoy the game?

"I really enjoyed the match. You get a great thrill pulling down a lead - a better thrill than if you are in front."

Coming home to Ireland with the Sam Maguire Cup must have been unique?

"It was only when we arrived in Southampton that we realised the importance of it all. We travelled home on the Queen Mary, then up by train to London and there was a big number of Cavan people there - from London, Birmingham and other places. After that it was home on the boat to Dun Laoghaire. Even then to us it was just an All-Ireland and I'd sooner have won it in Croke Park. You'd get a better thrill coming from behind in front of your own supporters."

What were the receptions on Irish soil like?

"There was a big reception in Dun Laoghaire given by the Town Council. They met us at the boat and brought us to the Royal Marine Hotel. Then into Dublin to the Mansion House and the Lord Mayor at one o'clock. Next day we were invited to Arus an Uachtaráin by the President, Mr Sean T. O' Kelly, and O'Connell Street was packed as we drove through it in a bus. Back to Cavan the second evening after arriving home. We were met outside of Virginia on the Cavan-Meath border by a large number of cars and people and after that we stopped everywhere en route to Cavan to be introduced to throngs everywhere. We were four hours late for the reception in Cavan."

Was what it all meant beginning to dawn on you?

"It was only then I realised what it meant to our people at home. We went back to play Kerry in Croke Park about four Sundays afterwards and they beat us well. We didn't like it either."

At this stage we discussed the tragedy and sadness of the untimely deaths of P.J. Duke and the 1947 captain John Joe O'Reilly.

"We didn't even know P.J. was sick. He was a student in U.C.D. at the time and he got pleurisy. He was very strong and probably thought he'd fight it and wear it off. It was a terrible shock."

Was P.J. the great footballer that lives on in legend?

"He was very good. And we hadn't seen the best of him. He was about twenty-three or twenty-four when he died."

It must have been a very sad funeral?

"Hard to believe. A person in his prime to be just taken away. It struck me very forcibly and all the fellows were visibly shaken by it. We all carried his coffin into his native village of Stradone. It was hard to believe that you won two All-Irelands with him in 1947 and 1948 and you were burying him in 1950."

John Joe died in 1952. That must have been a terrible shock too?

"He was our captain in 1947. I would safely say John Joe O'Reilly was the greatest Cavanman of them all. He was very easy to get on with and as captain he'd point out your mistakes and was a wonderful clean footballer. You played centre half yourself, you know, and you have to be fairly strong. I never saw him take an unfair advantage. Never in club football or in training. I usually played on him and there was always that rivalry between us, trying to outwit each other. I'd safely say we never had a heated exchange and we were great friends. I looked up to John Joe."

Wasn't John Joe a younger brother of Big Tom?

"Yes, he was. Big Tom was a good footballer too, but he was a different character. Tom never took football as seriously as John Joe. John Joe took everything seriously."

What happened to John Joe?

"He went in for an operation on a kidney. He got a knock playing football and kidney trouble was diagnosed. He died in the operation. It was hard to believe because in

1952 when we won the All-Ireland, he had retired and he was at the hotel and was with us training and at the match as well and then in November he was dead."

Was there any intimidation then?

"Ah no. No striking off the ball. You'd never hear tell of that. You could stand up looking at the ball at the other end of the field and no one would ever touch you or you'd never dream of touching anybody. You could block off then as the third man tackle was in vogue."

Are managers getting too much attention?

"Yes, surely. I took on team management myself in Cavan, Longford and Donegal. We didn't have that much attention paid to us then. In accounts of games now, the managers are mentioned often before the teams or before any particular member of the teams. Unless you have a team you can't have a trainer."

Should their role be de-emphasised?

"Very definitely. They are getting too much publicity altogether. They are interviewed at every nook and corner. They aren't doing it for nothing anyhow."

Your greatest opponents?

"One of the best I played on was Billy Goodison of Wexford. He was on a team that were struggling. They were good at the time but they weren't outstanding. He could field a ball. He never hit or touched you and played the ball the whole hour. But then you had Jackie Lyne of Kerry and Jim McCullagh of Armagh. Every county had one or two exceptional players. Mayo had Carney, Prendergast and Flanagan. Antrim were good too. Goodison was the best footballer but not the hardest to play on. That was Jackie Lyne. He was tough, strong but fair. He played the ball. He'd play you too. And mark you closely. You wouldn't get away too handy."

The game of your life?

"The one I got the greatest satisfaction out of was coming from behind to beat Cork in the 1952 All-Ireland Semi-final. Cork were hot favourites but granted they suffered a blow before the match when Eamon Young was forced to cry off with injury. They were the better team for about three-quarters of the game and were leading us by five points with about ten minutes to go and we beat them by two points. The crowd were leaving Croke Park when we got a penalty and John Joe Cassidy took it. It was a well taken penalty and was saved and the ball was cleared down the field and put in the back of the Cavan net to leave them five points in front. We came back up and took it down point by point."

You captained that team to All-Ireland success. Was that a very special honour?

"At the time it didn't strike me until afterwards how special it was. It was grand to do it and to have it to say that you captained an All-Ireland winning team."

Used you get excited before games?

"No I never got excited before games or lost any sleep over football."

Any other anecdotes?

"We met Meath in the 1952 final and it was the first year the G.A.A. decided to bring the two teams together for a meal after the game, just the players and officials of both counties. We were staying in Barry's Hotel and I remember distinctly two car loads of us set off for Mills beside the Shelbourne where the reception was being held - Paddy and Edwin Carolan, Tony Tighe, Peter Donoghoe and myself travelled together. We arrived in early and being captain I asked the barman for drinks for the five of us. They ordered four bottles of ale and I decided I'd take a mineral, minding myself for the official duties afterwards. I took out the money to pay the barman, when he said 'No money - this is all on the G.A.A'. When I queried again he assured us the drink was free. 'Oh my God!' said Donoghoe, 'take down those four bottles of ale quick and put up four brandies'. So when we came back for the replay there was no free brandy."

The sporting passions in your life now?

"I go to games all the time. I pass my time more with greyhounds, not that it's very profitable over the past few years. I have four dogs at present and keep them down outside the town, in kennels."

What's wrong with Cavan football today?

"It's galling to see that they are so poor and the standard is so low. And it's hard to understand it as there is a great interest in the game still in Cavan. Maybe too much interest in juvenile football - schoolboy football, competition too early and too keen. It's the same with every club here in Cavan. They have about five good schoolboys or juveniles and naturally when they win, this five get all the attention and at that age the others are overlooked and can be easily turned off football."

Is there any hope for Cavan football?

"Not for a while. We have got nothing out of St. Patrick's College, Cavan in latter years. They haven't won the Ulster title since 1972. They won the All-Ireland title that year. Now they are very far behind and getting very bad beatings all the time. And we haven't had an Ulster minor title for years. Attendances I'd say at club football in Cavan are higher than in any county in Ireland. And if we had any class of a team we'd have a huge following still. I never miss them in the championships. I never remember Donegal beating Cavan in my time and they beat us regularly now. Once playing Donegal in Ballybofey, they kicked the ball into the river Finn. It took them a long time to get the ball and we thought they didn't want to finish the game."

Were you delighted with Donegal's success in 1992?

"Delighted. I couldn't believe they could come so far in a few years. They seem to have an abundance of footballers. I love their style of football, loose open play. Tony Boyle is an outstanding full forward, intelligent, strong and not afraid to have a go."

Are there enough goals in football nowadays?

"There should be a lot more because play is a lot looser."

Has the standard declined from the 1940's and 1950's?

"That's debatable. Personally, I don't think it has improved but then you'll get fellows to tell you you're living in the past. The standard isn't nearly as good, but it is more hyped up. There is no high catching. No brilliant fielders nowadays. Not like the Victor Sherlocks, Padhraic Carneys, Sean Purcells or to go farther back Tommy Murphys or Paddy Kennedys."

Who was the greatest fielder of them all?

"Paddy Kennedy of Kerry. Mick O'Connell in later years. Tommy Murphy of Laois too. I'd love to have played with Kennedy, O'Connell, or Purcell. Sean took the shortest way to goals. I played with Kevin Armstrong of Antrim for Ulster, another bonny footballer."

How many county Senior Football Championship medals did you win?

"Three, two with Mountnugent and one with Bailieboro."

When did you retire?

"In 1953. Then I took up refereeing for a time."

Did you enjoy refereeing?

"I missed playing for a time. I was never happy refereeing. 'What if I made a mistake',was the thought I always had at the back of my mind. I hated to do an injustice to any team. I think if you're a back, you'll referee as a back played, and if you're a forward, you referee as a forward. I'd always let forwards away and if they were half taken down, I'd let them go on. I refereed an All-Ireland semi-final, a few Connacht and Ulster finals in my time."

What about your training of teams? Which of the teams trained by you gave you most satisfaction?

"I'd say Longford. I thought they had nothing. I always remember it was Fr. McGee and Jimmy Flynn that asked me over. I was training Cavan and I went over on the understanding that it would only be for a few evenings!"

And it tended to grow from there?

"I always remember the first evening. I had two dogs running in Longford at the track and I left the two dogs there and went to the ground and only eight turned up for training. So I said to Jimmy Flynn, 'I'll be back next Friday night and if there isn't a whole team here I'm not coming back again'. I went down and collected my two dogs and both had won. So I said to the manager there, 'You'd better put them on next Friday night again'. I brought the two dogs again the following Friday, left them there again and there was a full house at training. When I collected the two dogs, they had won again. They were a team that came on in leaps and bounds."

Who were the good ones on that team?

"There were a few lads who had been there for a few years and then there was a crowd of young fellows, who were coming on. It was a case of a blend of too young and too old. If they were all coming at the same age more or less you could have stayed longer with them."

Name some of them for me?

"Brendan Barden and Larry Gillen of the senior lads were outstanding. John Donlon and Sean Murray, too. Of the younger lads you had Jimmy Hanniffy and Sean Donnelly. Jimmy Flynn very good too, at midfield. Pat Barden, brother of Sean, Jackie Devine a beautiful player, Mick Hopkins, Bobby Burns. They beat Galway in the National League final and won a Leinster Senior Football Championship too, their first and only one. They gave me great satisfaction in the Autumn of my life."

Above: The Bank of Ireland Hall of Fame Winners of 1985, Christy Moylan, Waterford (Hurling) and Mick Higgins, Cavan (Football)
Below: Mick Higgins leading out his Cavan team before the 1952 Final followed by 'Gunner' Brady, Victor Sherlock, Paddy Carolan and Tony Tighe......

Chapter 10

Ollie Honeyman

Of Leitrim

Over the past number of years, mainly since the team-managership of P.J. Carroll, now in charge of his native Cavan, and the advent of Mayoman John O'Mahony, there has been a great buzz to Leitrim football. Over the years in this least populated of all Irish counties there has been a huge interest in Gaelic football. Leitrim won its only Connacht Senior Football Championship title in 1927. In the late 1950's they were unfortunate to produce a fine team when Galway won five Connacht titles in a row defeating Leitrim in four successive finals 1957-1960 inclusive. That was the era of the great Packy McGarty, Cathal Flynn, Josie Murray, Tony Hayden, Paddy Dolan, Columba Cryan...After that you had Mickey Martin. But the man who best represented the Leitrim spirit over the last decade and particularly in the recent upsurge in the game in his county, is Ballinamore's Ollie Honeyman. Stocky, even portly, the balding smiling back from Leitrim belies his years. In recent years Roscommon were Leitrim's bug bears. But in that time when Leitrim had one fantastic League run, bringing dozens of bus loads of loyal fans as far away as Casement Park and Droichead Nua, no man came closer to the Leitrim fans' hearts than the likeable Ollie. When Ollie grabbed the leather and came thundering out of defence, this was Leitrim's clarion call and often inspired success.

Who first introduced you to Gaelic football?

"It was at National School in Ballinamore under teacher Gerry Mahon that I first became interested. He organised leagues inside the school and involved all the young lads. He actually became County Chairman afterwards and played for the county during his office. We were very lucky to have him as teacher. He was a great organiser, he often came out and played football with us and sometimes we'd try to keep him out playing with us rather than going back into class. Yes, we were lucky. We took those leagues very seriously."

Did any of your schoolmates follow you onto Ballinamore and Leitrim teams?

"There was a bunch of us together - Gerry Logan, Gerry Reynolds and Patrick McKiernan. There used to be a Festival in Ballinamore every Summer and Gerry Mahon used to co-ordinate sets of teams for the Festival, two semi-finals and a final. That was the first big issue. That was the first time I ever played football on grass. Before that it was on the concrete schoolyard. It was a massive thrill that. I'm talking of under-age now. I got an awful gunk in the first game to find myself picked in goal because I thought I was playing well outfield in the schoolyard. That needled me."

The football heroes of your young life?

"In my younger days it was Mick O'Connell, Jack Quinn, Sean O'Neill, and Dan McCartan. I heard of Sean Purcell and Frank Stockwell. I never saw Packy McGarty play. In my early days I wasn't into going or wasn't brought to inter-county games. So a lot of that passed me by. Especially the Packy McGarty thing. But he is still big - real big in Leitrim."

Your first days in a Ballinamore jersey?

"We played U-12 first for a few years. So I was only nine or ten when I first wore the club jersey. We had a great tradition of winning under-age championships in Ballinamore. There was a terrific thrill in winning my first Leitrim U-12 title. I was very small at the time. We went on to win a few U-12's, two or three U-14's, three U-16's, four minor titles in a row and we carried that onto senior as well. I've won five County Senior medals. I'm not a great man for medals or memorabilia kind of stuff and couldn't tell you how many medals I have. They are all over the place. I suppose I should attach more importance to them and I know there will come a time when I may be sorry."

The club is called Ballinamore Sean O'Heslins.

"Sean was a teacher and highly respected in the area."

When did you wear the Leitrim jersey first?

"I played competitive football at senior level (Senior Football Championship) against Sligo in 1979, a game we won too. I played three or four years minor as well, of course. And I was selected for Connacht a number of years as well. That was a big honour. A good scene to be involved in."

Is Leitrim, as a county, football mad?

"There was always a great club interest in football. When P.J. Carroll came along he injected winning into it. He deserves the greatest credit. It hurts me to hear people condemn him. We were at a pretty low ebb when he took over. He put a bit of magic into the thing. I'm eternally grateful to him."

How did he change the scene?

"First of all he started to train people and there was regular training of teams and he isolated players on the team. Not that we never trained before but he brought a professional approach. He was tactically aware too. He knew the limitations of people and he picked his teams correctly. When he took over, the team took on a certain shape. He put players in positions they never played in before. That takes radical thinking."

Had he any faults at all?

"It used to be said that he could lose the head at times. He used to get so involved in the thing. For a Cavanman like, he used to have a fierce grádh for Leitrim and for winning. He cared for it so much. I nearly choke people that start knocking him. Where do they think they are coming from?"

Who else deserves credit?

"Tommy Moran, Tony McGowan, George O'Toole and all the men over the years who put in the great amount of work which is needed to keep the organisation going. All the other managers and players over the years too. They tried hard too."

Is football very important to you?

"Yes, it is. It is up high. When I was in U.C.C., it was high too. Nearly too high."

Has it helped you in life?

"It has, yes. I work as a Contract Salesman. It helps in a certain way but ultimately you have to rely on your own ability. But it is a meeting-point and a talking-point."

Is your day or week wrapped around football? (The week I interviewed Ollie was mid-April 1993. He had just seen the Leitrim U-21 Football team, which he co-managed, lose out to Roscommon in the Championship at Carrick-on-Shannon).

"At this time of year, yes. When I'm not playing I go to see a game on a Sunday. Last Sunday I had no game so I went to Breffni Park to see Donegal against Derry. Next Sunday we have a club league game against Melvin Gaels. This evening I'm in Carrick, to-morrow evening I'm in Cloone. For the last two months and the next three, every evening will be spent training."

Your greatest opponent? (It took some time for him to answer this one.)

"Probably McManus, you know, Tony. He was dangerous. He had a — eye for goal. An eye for a score, and a great man to pick up a position. He'd always be within a score with right or left foot. Always within striking distance. He'd catch it, kill it and you'd know if you didn't get a block in, there was a — score on."

Sweet praise indeed for the dapper Clan na Gael man. The greatest Leitrim player in your own time or before?

"The guy I thought was the best on the big day was Frank Holohan. A great footballer. I know he slowed down towards the end of his career. When he was U-21 and on from then he was a massive fielder of the ball. Strong as a bull. Frank was my kind of player. He was the business. He was from Drumreilly and I often had great battles with him. What I liked about him was that for the championship he got totally tuned in. He was physically intimidating too. Of the present team, Pádhraic Kenny has great spirit - right spirit. Like Holohan he has it here too in the heart. I like his attitude. I rate Declan Darcy too. Some people find flaws in his game, but I think he is a fine athlete and footballer. He didn't impress me early on. He was a bit loose for a while but he is much more commanding now. He looks the business. Mickey Martin was a lovely footballer too."

Is the G.A.A. getting stronger?

"The G.A.A. is marketing itself in a stronger way now than it has been. More people are talking about it. It is people like yourself writing books, and television and there is more hype in it. 'The Sunday Game' is a good programme and latterly we have had more live games on television. Ten years ago you wouldn't dream about having a game live on B.B.C.1 at four o'clock on a Sunday afternoon. The four game Meath/Dublin saga a few years ago set the G.A.A. on a new plane."

Have team-managers become necessary or too important?

"They are necessary now. You've got to have a focus, someone to manage the scene. It's a training scene, a working scene. You have to set out your preparation or you don't do it. Any teams that are doing it now have a serious professional style back-up. The make-up of the players of today requires management and a figure to look up to. The manager is as important as the team itself. I don't know whether that is unfortunate. Certainly some of the traditionalists don't like to admit that. If you don't jump on the bandwagon you're going to get left you know."

How does your present man John O'Mahony of Mayo compare with P.J. Carroll?

"He is a different style of manager. Quite quiet and serious and a very tough trainer. A very psychologically sound person. Two different men and good in their own ways. John is a very fine manager. Given the right material he would go far."

Is too much demanded of players today?

"I wouldn't be for players being paid really. I think players trained very hard years ago too. Fellows in my club keep telling us about their own time. Players should be remunerated if they were out of pocket because of training etc. Direct payment of players is not on really. I don't play football to get money out of it. Eventually it will turn towards professionalism but not at the moment. I don't want that day to come too fast."

Do you read a lot about the game?

"I read quite a bit. Papers a lot. My favourites are Donal Keenan, Peadar O'Brien and Con Houlihan. The latter I find very good. He is so abstract, off the wall, taking a different perspective on things, not a totally serious one. He has a good poetic way of interpreting things. He sees things others don't. I read him always unless he is on about horses in which I have no interest."

Do the media generally treat Gaelic games fairly?

"The media are getting more tuned into them as they get so popular. Even English people watching them on Channel 4 liked them too, even if some of them didn't understand the waving of sticks (hurling). Television and radio are very strong as media, local radio too. That is a big scene here now. Shannonside and North West. I have been interviewed by Shannonside quite a lot. I like Hogan Stand magazine too."

Refereeing? Will you become one eventually?

"I don't think so. There is a disparity of standards. I like Paddy Collins. Our own Seamus Prior is good. A bit pernickety and off-putting to players with his signals and his stance and the way he goes on but he tries hard. He is courageous too. Tommy McDermott of Cavan can be very good too. Paddy Collins is very sensible. The qualities I like in a referee are consistency, allowing the play to flow without pulling up for everything. Some referees can grab the tempo of a game. Consistency in interpretation throughout a game is very important."

The greatest players in the game today?

"Matt Gallagher from Donegal is a good defender. Very close. At midfield I wouldn't mind having Shay Fahy from Cork. Big and strong. Wins a lot of ball. Lets it off. Can score too. The forwards I like are Tony Boyle, Mickey Linden and James McCartan. The latter two have fierce pace on the break onto something. Very hard to have an answer to that pair. Especially Linden when he was at his peak coming onto a ball - fierce pace."

Will Leitrim ever win an All-Ireland?

"We won the B title a few years ago and that was big for us. It was a win. I think we will if we keep progressing as we are doing. Despite everything. I don't mind that stuff of everything being against you. If you have your panel of players and a bit of talent in it and work them hard and manage them correctly, I don't see that much of a difference between counties. Take for instance the hurling population in Offaly and Galway. Down hurlers latterly. It's intangible. It's about attitude. I wouldn't want help or a transfer system. The latter would kill it."

Is what Dermot Earley wrote in 'The Earley Years' about the growing intimidation in the game true?

"There was always a certain amount of intimidation in the game. Just remember some of the full backs of the 1960's and 1970's, Paddy McCormack, Jack Quinn. The off the ball thing is marshalled so much better than it used to be. Everybody, the two linesmen, the four umpires as well as the referee are all watching out for this now. Don't tell me it never happened before. There were far harder men around in former times. Some of them would break your neck then!"

The game of your life, Ollie?

"There are a lot of games I remember. The Connacht Senior Football club final against Salthill in December 1990 is one. The one that gives me the biggest satisfaction was against Galway in the Connacht Senior Football Championship in Tuam in 1981. We were beaten well in the end and I was playing centre half back. Dan Meehan was full-back. I was on Val Daly. Galway had just won the National Football League. Every where I went that day the ball followed me. A league playoff game against Offaly a few years ago when we qualified for the first time is another great memory. We played Offaly in Roscommon and Wicklow in Mullingar. They were massive games. The Senior Football Championship game against Roscommon in 1990 is another one. In

Roscommon I was on Tony Mac that day. But of them all that one in Tuam in 1981 is the most vivid. The ball chased me around that dreadfully wet December day in Athenry too. The B Final win over Sligo wasn't memorable as we won it too easily. In the end that game in Tuam, though we lost well, remains as the game of my life."

Above: Packy Mc Garty - 'real big in Leitrim'.

Above, left: Ollie Honeyman.
right: P. J. Carroll - 'put magic into it'.

Chapter 11

Peter McGinnitty

Of Fermanagh

Another Cinderella football county like Leitrim, Fermanagh has come to the fore in the 1992-1993 National Football League hot on the heels of St. Michael's College, Enniskillen winning their first ever McRory Cup. I worked in Fermanagh for a year 1954-1955 and found the county mad on Gaelic football. Honours won by the county were few. This was years before P.T. Treacy, Mickey Brewster, after whom the G.A.A. Park in Enniskillen is called, and whose son Paul captained Queen's University Belfast to 1993 Sigerson Cup glory. Peter McGinnitty, the St. Michael's College teacher and coach, retired from the game after a lifetime of service to Roslea, Fermanagh, Ulster and the game itself just a few short years ago. An absolute ornament of the game, let's take up his story.

When did you first play for Fermanagh, Peter?

"I started playing at the age of seventeen."

How many successive Championship campaigns did you play in for Fermanagh?

"1988 would be the last Senior Football Championship game and that was my nineteenth year at it."

Did you ever feel like giving it up?

"What frustrated me more than losing regularly was the year when we could have done better but because of lack of motivation or commitment from certain players we didn't put in the required effort."

Are Fermanagh up against it really?

"There is a dichotomy of opinion about this. I know Donal Fee who would have played on the 1982 team, doesn't like to hear Fermanagh people making excuses. But I heard it said once that half of Fermanagh is water and half of the remaining half are Protestants. Which means we have a very small pick in a very small county."

Would you want it changed?

"No. I think the achievement which will be Fermanagh's when we win an Ulster title - and they will win one - will be savoured by all the people who played in all the years that have gone before."

Are you sorry to be gone just when the wheel seems to be turning?

"I'd know most of this team through College. But I played on a good Fermanagh team before which reached an Ulster final and I feel this business of staying on too long, is a mistake."

Do you see yourself taking charge of the Fermanagh team in the future?

"No. I'm definite about that. I had a time as manager - as player-manager - for two Championships in 1986 and 1987 and it was a mistake."

Perhaps you were too close to the players?

"My most valuable contribution to Fermanagh I feel is to coach players at St. Michael's when they are receptive."

Do you feel there is a conflict between club and county within the G.A.A. scheme of things, Peter?

"The ladder as it is where you can start as a club player and raise your sights and become a county player and raise your sights again and become an inter provincial player and raise yourself again and become an All Star is quite sound. That's why I'd hate to see the Railway Cup going because it would remove a step up the ladder of achievement for all county players."

What are your thoughts on the experiment at International level with the Australian Compromise Rules game-series?

"I have very mixed feelings on it having been involved with Ulster and the Irish team. I think the two games didn't marry that well. The physical aspects of the Australian game and the poor definition of the tackle in the Irish game led to serious problems."

Is the G.A.A. getting stronger?

"We need professional people throughout the organisation and at the top, we need marketing. When you spend half a million pounds say on coaching, the amount is diluted down so that each individual club gets a fiver, let's say. And it might buy a football of sorts. What would have a much greater impact on the U-14 team you're trying to talk to would be if you gave a portfolio to the people who do the Guinness ads or Saatchi and Saatchi and said, 'Here is half a million pounds to promote us for six months', and you'd have billboards, television adverts, Tina Turner - you'd hit them all the time where they're at. Glossy magazines, glossy posters - your half a million would have a much greater impact than the fiver to each club."

Details of your own club?

"Roslea Shamrocks - twenty-six miles from Enniskillen. In larger towns people don't realise just how much part of a parish is the G.A.A. club. For me, growing up in Roslea, the parish and the G.A.A. club were sort of interchangeable. The people who ran the bingo were the same people who did the gates at Sunday matches - the people who helped out the parish. You knew everybody and in all I won three Senior Football Championship and six Senior Football League medals with the club."

The people who helped you along the way?

"I played absolutely no football until I went to St. Michael's College - never even togged out. But two men, Séamus Slowey, a next door neighbour of mine and Tommy Callaghan encouraged us no end. I went to study in Belfast 1972-1976 and transferred to St. John's in Belfast and won three Antrim Senior Football Championship and League medals. I won an Ulster Club medal and lost in the final to Thomond College.

The greatest learning experience of my career was with the St. John's lads in Antrim. Fermanagh won a McKenna Cup at the time beating Donegal - the year 1977."

Was that McKenna Cup the biggest honour won with Fermanagh?

"It was, I suppose. We won promotion in various divisions of the League at different times but for something substantial to look back on, it was an Ulster title."

Coming back to the club?

"I moved back to teach in St. Michael's in 1979. I feel the time I spent in St. John's away from Roslea was a time well spent. From 1980 to 1986 we won six Leagues, three Championships and reached an Ulster Club final. We lost the Senior Football Championship finals in 1987 and 1989 - that's the one I missed the penalty in. We were beaten by a point and the penalty was the last kick of the game. Not the game of my life, could be one of the worst moments in it. You mentioned club and county. I think there has to be a balance struck."

You are tall, Peter. Was that an advantage when playing?

"I'm six foot three and a half inches. It was an advantage surely. Sure isn't a big bad one better than a good wee one any day!!"

Did you ever play on Liam Austin of Down?

"I did surely. Played with him too many a time. Myself and himself played midfield for both Ulster and St. Joseph's (The Ranch in Belfast)."

Your Railway Cup record?

"My first game was in 1973 and the last was in 1987. I missed one year. Interestingly enough that first year I won't say who the manager was! We were playing the Combined Universities in Breffni Park, Cavan - 'twas the year they won it out. It was a burning ambition of mine to play for Ulster and at as young an age as possible. I got it in 1973 and went into the changing rooms - myself and Kieran Campbell and Phil Sheridan - the biggest representation Fermanagh ever had and Finn Sherry was on the

Combined Universities team, four Fermanagh lads playing Inter provincial on the same day. In we went anyway nervous and full of self-importance and the manager says to me, 'Here you are Kieran, here's the number three jersey', and then turned to Kieran and says, 'Here Peter, is your number ten jersey'. That pulled us down a peg not to be known and recognised by the great Mick Higgins of Cavan!"

Did you get an All Star?

"Yes, in 1982. Everything came together in 1982."

Did that Mick Higgins incident diminish your respect for the Cavan star?

"No, it didn't. There are certain things I remember as if they were told to me yesterday and James Lynch, God rest him, got Mick Higgins to come along to an U-16 training session in Roslea and he walked about and watched us and he talked and he saw that I was the freetaker. He came up and showed me how to set the ball with the laces as it was at that time, facing the goals, the idea being that the weight of the ball would draw it towards the goals. From that day on I always did as he advised and when the laces went I even set the ball with the little nipple facing the goals."

Your thoughts on the All Star Award?

"I'm not a great man for individual awards but there is nobody could come into this house and try to take that All Star Award away from me."

Your greatest opponents?

"Playing on Jack O'Shea in Railway Cup games was always a fierce delight. Brian Mullins was a great player to play against, because he would play his own game, but then if the notion took him, he could stop you playing. But the man I found most difficulty in playing, was a local club player here in Fermanagh from Peter Quinn's club, Teemore Shamrocks - Paddy Reilly. For about seven or eight years in the late 1970's early 1980's no matter what game I played against him, I had serious problems."

Other great club characters?

"One of the best characters that I was involved with playing county football, was Barney Reilly, again from Teemore. He won Championship medals in four decades. He won one in 1969, he won a 'slidder' in the 1970's, he won one against Roslea in 1983 and he won one with Navan O'Mahonys in 1990."

The great football men of Fermanagh?

"P.T. Treacy, Eamonn McPartland, Jimmy Cleary, Mick Brewster, John Donnelly, Phil Sheridan, Kieran Campbell. P.T. was playing corner back in the first Fermanagh team I played on. He had moved from full-forward back to corner back and he was a great corner back. In the 1960's when I was going to school he was the man in Fermanagh along with Mick Brewster. Mick taught in St. Michael's and he would have taught me most of what I would have known about football. Always when asked who contributed most to my career I would name Mickey Brewster. John Donnelly was a great servant of Fermanagh in a variety of positions. Irrepressible Barney Reilly. We'd have fought the bit out at club level and had the crack then at county level."

Has the game of Gaelic football improved?

"There are so many aspects of it that have improved, you get the feeling the game must have improved. I'm wary of looking back too much to the days that were always fine and never wet syndrome."

Is it faster now?

"Speed is a much more important facet of the game now."

Are the skills diminishing? Is the Peter McGinnitty style catch being taken out of the game?

"You look at it from the point of view of a team manager trying to counteract another team. One of the things you hear shouted at players by team managers from the sideline is 'No free catches'. You can't watch the other team continue to catch the ball cleanly. From that point of view, that skill is being diminished. But having said that, when a fellow does make a catch now, he is usually under pressure from somebody who is not trying to catch it with him but is trying to break it and it then becomes a great catch. It isn't a clean contest for the fetch anymore. The approach to games has become a little negative (perhaps that is too strong a word) in that tactics are much more used."

Are managers getting too much exposure?

"I think there is too much emphasis and talk about the expenses being paid to managers. There are some aspects of professionalism which we badly need. There are others which we certainly do not want. From a player's point of view we need a professional approach to the game in terms of commitment, preparation for game, general organisation of lifestyle. The players shouldn't be out of pocket for playing Gaelic games, nor should managers. Most of them aren't, I agree."

You have been doing analysis for the B.B.C.'s very impressive Ulster Championship coverage on telly in recent years. Is it interesting, Peter?

"It is very interesting. But I don't take myself too seriously on it."

Does the commentator give you a nod when he wants you to interject some comment?

"It probably has developed between Jimmy Smyth and myself to the extent that we nearly know now when I should come on. Early on he used to give me a nudge and he'd catch me off guard. There would be other times when I'd want to say something and you couldn't get him stopped talking. So over a couple of seasons we got to know each other."

What is the most enjoyable aspect of it?

"The thing I get the greatest hype from is the fact that I get to see all the matches in Ulster. Every single Ulster Championship game senior and minor and being involved at college level seeing the minor games is a great bonus."

How do you enjoy coaching St. Michael's?

"I like coaching. At St. Michael's we have been working very hard to get up with the big league - St. Patrick's Maghera and St. Colman's Newry."

Some great strongholds of the past, like St. Patrick's College, Cavan, have vanished from the scene?

"It will change now that the Southern Educational System is into a six year cycle. But Cavan are at a slight disadvantage now in that they would nearly be relying on repeats. Their educational system goes to eighteen. Ours goes to eighteen and a half. Six months at that age is significant."

Should the McRory Cup age limit come into line with the age limit in the other three provinces?

"There is only one team goes out of Ulster and even if the Ulster champions have to shed three or four players afterwards as St. Colman's Newry did this year, if we lowered our age limit we would be denying final year students in our schools the opportunity to play G.A.A. games."

The great players of today?

"I watched Fermanagh play Kerry here in Enniskillen and watched Maurice Fitzgerald and I saw the most complete footballer, maybe with one exception, that I have ever seen. He scored points with left and right from play. Caught some magnificent balls in the middle of the field. He defended well which is something I hadn't seen him do before. He hit passes with either foot. He got at the end of moves, scored 1-5 and I was very disappointed that he didn't take any frees with his left foot."

Who is the exception?

"Matt Connor, of Offaly. When I'm asked who is the player I respected most, there was something about Matt Connor and honestly this is not a sympathy ticket, as I thought this when he was playing. When it had to be done, he did it. Other players, myself included, could do it when you're winning by twenty points but I saw him in a

Railway Cup final in Breffni Park in 1983 and it was gone. Ulster had won it and they needed a goal. He engineered a goal from his own twenty-five yard line and ended up scoring it at the other end. Again his free taking ability, both feet. His point taking. A most effective player."

Why has Ulster football taken over?

"With the great Kerry and Dublin teams of the 1970's and early 1980's went that ultra-dominance. I don't think that will ever happen again."

Is Gaelic football getting dirtier?

"I don't think so. Maybe there is some cynicism in it but we are still a long way from Italian football."

Is refereeing improving?

"They come in for too much criticism. Most of it levelled at them, the source of it is interpretation of the rules. The tackle is still causing us serious problems. You watch referees from Sunday to Sunday and there are times you think it is a different game. They are attacking the problems now with grading etc."

Has Peter Quinn's elevation to Uachtaráin Cumann Lúthcleas Gael meant a lot to Fermanagh?

"It has in a couple of ways. To have somebody as President of a national organisation be it Macra na Feirme, or Young Farmers Association is good. To have a man as President of an organisation which has a great allegiance within the county and to have a man who cares about his local area is better. He didn't go away off to Dublin and forget about us. Teemore Shamrocks, his club, is very important to him. His roots are in Fermanagh."

The game of your life?

"The one I like most to remember is the Ulster Senior Football Championship semi-final of 1982 in Breffni Park, against Tyrone. We went into that game as underdogs having beaten Derry by a point in the first round. I was vice-captain and just before the game, Arthur McCaffrey, the captain, cried off with 'flu so I was captain for the day and led the Fermanagh team around in pouring rain. During that game it was one of those days when you felt you could do whatever you wanted to do. I can remember defending, pointing frees, one in the second half against the breeze from forty yards out when I had absolutely no business to be shooting. I couldn't believe I had scored. It was a wet dirty old day and yet my handling was good and probably most of all it was a very significant day for Fermanagh. It brought us into an Ulster final and more is the pity and the longer it goes away it still sticks in my throat that we lost by two points to Armagh."

Action from a club game between Roslea Shamrocks and Enniskillen Gaels taken in 1989. Peter McGinnitty watches his goalkeeper, Seamus Callaghan clearing the ball with John Reihill, Gerry Love and Kevin McWilliams in attendance.

Chapter 12

John Moloney of Bansha

Referee Par Excellence

When I visited the tall, long-striding Bansha farmer in early May on a gloriously sunny day, he was busy on one of his farming chores. The trees lining the avenue to his house were bursting into leaf and at least four dogs saluted my arrival in the shadow almost of the Galtee mountains. The Vee, Slievenamon, Knockmealdown and the Glen of Aherlow nearby. It was a beautiful pastoral scene. Helped by his six young sons, the eldest of whom is beginning to lessen the load on his father as he takes up full-time farming, John, almost fifty-nine years old, hasn't given up refereeing quite yet. He looks after the U-12's now, where it all began for him over thirty-five years ago. That night at Lisverane in the Glen he was refereeing an U-12 game of football between Aherlow and Lattin (Nicky English's home club) just underneath the Galtees. Always a man for the occasion, he asked me to speak to the two teams for a brief moment before throwing in the ball as he set off to referee his umpteenth game. The long stride is still there, the very direct signs, the loud blow of the whistle, the authoritative gait. There is a limp there now after a serious accident on his farm some years back. As I made my way back to Galway, I couldn't but admire once again one of my favourite G.A.A. people and a referee par excellence.

How did you first take up refereeing?

"I started by accident. A referee failed to turn up. I was Secretary of the club, lining the field and the two teams agreed to me. I actually enjoyed it so much that I felt I'd like to do more of it."

Did it just go on from there?

"I always loved the G.A.A. and its games. Being a referee meant I was totally involved in it. I was only a very average player. My age then would be twenty-three."

Was the club more involved with football than hurling?

"More than hurling, yes. Ours is a very famous football club."

Your favourite game of the two?

"When I'd be refereeing a lot of football games, I'd say football is great. Then I'd go on to hurling and think that was the greater. But I suppose being a Tipperary man, I'd have to say hurling."

Your refereeing career?

"It annoys me, when I see referees who are refereeing club games two or three years and they get annoyed when they are not refereeing inter-county games. I refereed from 1956 until 1965 before I made the breakthrough to the Munster Championship."

Did you get a Tipperary County Senior final assignment before the inter-county break-through?

"I did everything in my own county, my Division (the West of four Divisions in the county). I started there and progressed to refereeing finals in the other Divisions and eventually got my first senior final in the early 1960's between Carrick Davins and Roscrea in the era of Mick Roche."

Who helped you along the way?

"I was so interested in it that I studied all referees, even the rugby and soccer men, the whole philosophy of refereeing really. Gerry O'Keeffe probably, of the South Board in Clonmel, was the first man who really gave me encouragement. Another man Paddy Ryan, of Galbally in Limerick, Chairman of the South Limerick Board also gave me great chances with highly competitive junior hurling games there."

The books you've read on refereeing?

"One by Scottish referee, Tiny Wharton, and one by Clive Thomas of England, soccer referees and then from rugby I learnt a lot from Kevin Kelliher, a top Irish referee."

Your list of All-Irelands, provincial finals etc.?

"I refereed the All-Ireland Senior Football final five times - 1967, 1969, 1973, 1975 and 1977, and the Senior Hurling final in 1974. In Munster I think about nine Munster Senior Football and six Senior Hurling finals. The football finals were all Cork against Kerry. Regarding County senior finals I refereed them in Tipperary, Clare, Cork, Limerick, Offaly and Carlow. There was a Connacht Senior Football final too - a Galway against Mayo one in the 1970's. I did practically everything, College Finals, Railway Cup and National League finals."

The most precious of all compliments paid to you as a referee?

"One from the Colleges. In my last year refereeing for the Colleges they did a special plaque for me with all the finals I refereed for them listed and I really appreciated it."

Other compliments?

"Micheál O'Hehir on a few occasions. I got a famous compliment from yourself for an incident in an U-21 Football final in Duggan Park, Ballinasloe between Mayo and Kerry. The day Willie McGee scored all the goals to beat Kerry, back in 1967. Just before the throw in the legendary Paddy Bluett from Ballina who always marched with the Mayo teams in parades, came up to me to ask could he throw in the ball and I did that and you complimented me in various articles on that."

Pat Crerand, the well-known soccer star, when observing an All-Ireland once, paid John great compliments for his authoritative gait and command of the game. Did you work on developing that appearance?

"I feel there is more to refereeing than just blowing the whistle and giving frees. It is a communication with the players, spectators, officials. I made mistakes but I suppose I got on so well with people that they understood it and took it that it was a genuine mistake if I did something wrong."

Are you really aware of how well-known you are far and wide?

"Not really. A friend of mine who never goes to games was in the U.S.A. and he left the Airport by taxi for New York. The cabdriver who was Irish asked him where he was from. When he said Bansha the taxi man said, 'You aren't John Moloney are you?'"

The bugbears, if any, of being a referee?

"The easiest cop-out in the world is to blame the referee when you lose. Criticism is fine and I always welcome constructive criticism but some people for no apparent reason, pick on you and hold on to such beliefs. The media never really upset me. I always thought I got very fair comment from them. You can have an off-day like players."

Is it important to have the same four umpires with you always?

"The first All-Ireland I refereed in 1967 I hadn't my four usual umpires. My own trusted men were all from my own Bansha or close by. Originally, I had Jim O'Connor, local postman Eddie McCarthy, Larry Quinn who was away ahead of his time, Billy O'Donoghoe, and my brother Michael. Then in later years, I had Jim Byron, Maurice Keogh, Matt Nugent, Tommy Fanning. In fact six of my original trusted umpires are now dead. Yet another of the team was Paddy Ryan from Tipperary Town."

They were all local men from the Bansha Community?

"They were all dyed in the wool G.A.A. men, who had a great feel for the games. We were all Pioneers. That wasn't a deliberate thing. We never discussed things in public places like pubs. One thing I demanded from them was loyalty to me and to the game. We had such an understanding that their body movement conveyed something to me. Even by their lack of movement betimes. I'd always know when something was wrong."

Any particular lasting memory?

"To get things right going to a match one man always insisted we say the rosary. I remember one day we were going to Castlebar to referee a National Football League game between Galway and Mayo in February. We started the rosary after going through Milltown and before we reached Ballindine we were turned upside down in the snow. I often believe the rosary helped save our lives really."

Are you still heavily involved with the club, John?

"I'm still President of the club and attend all their games. I love to go to matches now and see my sons playing."

Is it very hard to give up refereeing?

"We are now in 1993 and I'm gone back to where I started, to the U-12's. I've got arthritis in my knees now and I cannot run too well. I had a very bad accident at one stage on the farm and that nearly finished me. I'm finding it very hard to break away from it."

Has the hype now associated with big games made the referee's task almost too responsible?

"Too much is expected of them now. I think they are being very unfair to referees presently. The video, television, they are picking up on every little thing. In our day it happened and it was over and that was it. Nowadays they are subject to trial by television really."

Is refereeing being treated fairly by all strata of the G.A.A?

"Gaelic football is difficult at the best of times. Of all the codes, soccer refereeing is simple, in rugby it is very complex probably the most complex but refereeing Gaelic football is pretty complex too and the rules are so hard to interpret with the speed of the game, that I think people aren't being fair to the referees presently."

What were your worst moments as a referee?

"I enjoyed it so much that I was able to switch off when I finished refereeing the game. I never brought my troubles in refereeing home with me. One of the negative aspects of it would be people who would come up to you after a big game and say thank you and then a few days afterwards I'd pick up a paper and find the same gentlemen nit-picking with me and picking out things which I did wrong. I liked it straight up."

Did anyone ever say 'You did us today' or something like that and how did you handle it?

"Oh they did. I'd say nothing. I always have the attitude that immediately after a game people are hyped up. I'd be hyped up myself after all the running for about twenty minutes afterwards."

Were you ever assaulted after a game?

"Oh God I was. When I was young I had a mighty head of hair and I was refereeing an U-21 Connacht Football final between Galway and Roscommon in Roscommon. It was a very high-scoring game and they were all confused about the score as the scoreboard was not working. Immediately after the game a big crowd gathered around me to find out the score. After a quick look at my notebook - too quick actually - I said Galway won by a point and this little man who was quite near just jumped at me and grabbed me by the hair and gave it a fair chuck. I gave it as the wrong score, saying I had to check it. When I got my umpires together, Larry Quinn said, 'John that's wrong!' There was a lot of points 0-17 to 3-8 or something and I checked it out carefully and the game was a draw and I gave it out then correctly. There was extra time and he came up to me afterwards and said he was very sorry. I got a belt of an umbrella from a woman in Ennis another day."

What happenings on a field annoyed you most?

"Sly people really. People trying to referee for me."

Are you forgiven in Cork for your refereeing of the 1976 Munster Final, Kerry against Cork?

"It started at one end with a free Sean Walsh took for Kerry. It was a powerful booming kick and Brian Murphy took the ball over the line. Now I didn't give the decision. The umpires called it. They immediately put up the flag. Unfortunately, the ball soon after went to the other end of the field and Declan Barron came in and fisted it into the net. We disallowed that not because of Declan Barron, a fact which often wasn't known. It was because a player who stood outside the field of play at the end line, stepped into the square as the ball was coming in and that was why it was disallowed. Cork felt very strongly about it."

Did the player interfere with the play?

"The rule states clearly that a player cannot stand outside the field of play. I got a lot of correspondence at the time after the game, all from Cork."

The qualities a good referee must have?

"The number one quality is integrity, fair play for both teams. Try to be fair and be seen to be fair. Common sense is very important too. The rules are there O.K. They must be observed. You can't break them but you can bend them. If you haven't a man of common sense refereeing Gaelic football or hurling then you'll have no game, especially in Gaelic football. Fitness is very important too. You must be fit to be up with the play. Work on the farm kept me very active but I trained always for games. And when the eighty minutes and seventy minutes games came in I had my own eighty minute jog marked out for myself through the mountains here."

The things a referee should not do?

"A referee should never, when booking people, pull them out to make a show of them. I would always feel a referee should go to meet the player or go half-way and not make a little schoolboy of him with a dressing down of wagging fingers. I wouldn't go for that. It is an amateur game played by fellows who get nothing but bruises and belts out of it. If you have to discipline a player do it quickly and fairly without a big show. This tendency is common to soccer referees and in latter times has come into G.A.A. refereeing."

Anecdotes?

"That crash in Ballindine I mentioned earlier. Who were the first to come upon us only John Dunne and some of the Galway team and they were so kind. They picked us up and brought us to Claremorris where I had a very good friend Fr. Martin Newell of St. Colman's College. He wasn't there when we called. They took me on to the game. I refereed it and the first man into me after the game was Fr. Newell. He had heard what happened. He took me back to Claremorris, gave me his car to take all of us home and that impressed me greatly."

Should the performance of a referee be subject to the criticism of players and officials as well as the media?

"I like fair constructive comment. I never minded it because players and managers are open to criticism. We should be answerable to somebody. We should be open to criticism, probably not in the public media."

Is trial by telly fair?

"No it is not. The analysts on telly have a great advantage. The game is played in the afternoon. They have until eight o'clock to play and replay it. They come up with something that nobody at the match may have seen. Maybe the cameras picked it up but the camera can also lie as regards lines and positions in the field of play. Nobody has a better angle on it than the referee."

Are some fairer than others over the years?

"I liked Enda Colleran's comments when he was there. He knew the game inside out. Colm O'Rourke I feel also knows the game. Micheál O'Hehir was brilliant. Micheál Ó Muircheartaigh, too."

Is the new scheme of assessment and grading of referees a step in the right direction?

"I think it is very necessary and they are going for great fit lively young fellows."

In your time as a referee who were the best footballers and hurlers you saw?

"'Babs' Keating was a super footballer. In football and hurling I thought he had no equal. Mick O'Connell and Jack O'Shea were famous footballers. I had a great time for a lot of the Cork team of 1973. Ray Cummins, Denis Coughlan and Billy Morgan.

I also admired Kilkenny hurling - Chunky O'Brien, Fan Larkin, a terrific little man, and Ollie Walsh in goal."

Were they easy to deal with?

"They were. Maybe that is why I remember them so well. They were so nice to me and understood what I was trying to do."

The game of your life?

"The All-Ireland football semi-final of 1969 between Cavan and Offaly. The draw and replay ran marvellously well for me. The draw was one of those games when everything slotted. It teemed rain. It was a great tough game of Gaelic football. That was the game of my life. The best game I refereed. One amusing story from it. Paddy McCormack came soloing out from his own goal and landed the ball in the Cavan square and when I should have been watching the ball, I had one eye on Paddy who kept coming and gave his man a great thump in the middle of the field. I blew the whistle on the spot and landed the ball straight back to Paddy for a Cavan free. After the game in very nice language, Paddy asked me how did I ever see his late tackle. I thought it was a great compliment. He was admitting he did it but was amazed he was caught."

Has refereeing made life better for John Moloney?

"I'll tell you, Jack Mahon, when I was a young fellow, I was very shy and inhibited. I would walk into a room of people and I would hardly lift my head. But when I started refereeing it helped me enormously. Even in my life as a farmer. Refereeing brought me all over the world, to all the thirty-two counties, Scotland, England, the U.S.A. I have trophies for everything I did but it wasn't that. It was the friends I made."

Do you look forward to refereeing that U-12 game later this evening?

"In the shadow of the Galtees. I always said that when the big games would get too fast for me, I would go back to where I started. Some friends have said to me that I should have gotten out long ago. I go where I enjoy the games now with the U-12's. That's where I like to be - I can just get around. That's their All-Ireland."

Later, as I said, I travelled with John to Lisverane, where I saw you greet the officials of both teams, and apologise for being slightly late. On the way you picked up two of your trusted umpires of old, introduced me to Tom O'Shea, 'A man who does great work for juvenile football here'.
Always the nice word. A highly respected gentleman. Lovely setting on a lovely evening for a lovely man. Yes, it was their All-Ireland.

Below: The handshake before the 1977 Final. From left: Jimmy Smyth (Armagh captain), referee John Moloney and Tony Hanahce (Dublin captain).

Chapter 13

Tom Cheasty

Of Waterford

He was not the most stylish of hurlers. But his swash buckling style and his never-say-die spirit made him special. The Ballyduff farmer was as tough as nails and in Waterford's sweep to the top in the 'fifties he was the play maker, making and taking scores from the centre half forward position. He is still a keen hurling fan and when I visited him on his farm just outside Waterford City on the Airport Road, he was full of the great Wexford/Cork hurling rivalry of 1993 having seen the second act of that saga in the rain of Thurles the day beforehand. The man is a folk-hero in Waterford. After he retired from the inter-county scene he won five County Waterford Senior Hurling Championship medals, one with Ballyduff - Portlaw and four with Portlaw. And to crown it all in 1983 at the princely age of fifty, he captained his junior club team of Ballyduff to county title success.

How did you first become interested in hurling, Tom?

"The first was during the summer holidays at my grandmother's place in Grange near Mooncoin. My aunt was married to a Mooncoin and Kilkenny hurler Martin Murphy and he was always bringing us to matches including All-Irelands. It was he who brought me to the 1948 All-Ireland when Waterford played Dublin. I was fourteen then. My mother was a Kilkenny woman from Mooncoin. During my National school days, I also played a lot of hurling in Grange, while on summer holidays."

Your National schooldays?

"There was very little hurling done in Ballyduff Lower N.S. I remember well we used to organise our games coming home from school. We used to have an old game coming home from school. We used to go into Harney's field about a quarter of a mile from the school and we often got into trouble with Mr. Harney, although the old field was good for nothing but perhaps that's a bit unfair. We probably went into the same field again after a short time. I was mad about hurling at that time. The first official game I played, was with the Ballyduff juniors and I was just fifteen. Then I played minor for Waterford at the age of sixteen. In all I played three years for the Waterford minors, wing half forward the first year."

Do you remember the first time you wore the Waterford jersey?

"That was against Tipperary in Mitchelstown in a minor and I was taken off. I was thrilled to wear the jersey and very disheartened to be taken off. I never get over things too fast."

Was there a good Waterford team coming up then?

"I was a sub when we played Limerick in 1955. Limerick weren't bad then. They beat us by one point. I remember going on for Mick Healy. He hit his head off the roller on the side of the field. While they were bandaging him up, they put me on for about five minutes and then took me off again. Mick was a Mount Sion man and they had huge influence. I remember coming back on again in the second half and we were barely beaten by just one point. That Limerick team were christened 'Mick Mackey's Greyhounds'. Mick trained then - they had Vivian Cobbe, the Quaids, uncles of the present goalkeeper Tommy, the Ryan brothers, Liam and Séamus."

Who was in charge of Waterford then?

"John Keane took over in 1956. We were beaten by a couple of points by Cork in Fermoy. That was the first time I made any real impression. I was playing on a young fellow. I was only twenty-two and he was younger than myself. Christy Ring was playing. He kind of beat us that day. Scored a couple of goals. We should have beaten them. Mick McCarthy was the fellow I was playing on. They brought Willie John Daly out on me. I got on almost as well on him."

Your early club days?

"We played in the County junior final about 1955 and lost. We had only a very middling team. Mount Sion were big then."

How did people take notice of you if you only played at junior level?

"The first chance I got really was in 1955. I remember going into the Sportsfield (Walsh Park in Waterford) and I was on the bank and somebody didn't turn up. They were stuck in a League game and they came out and asked me to play. It was against Kilkenny and I was put in at centre forward playing on Mick Brophy."

There must have been someone backing you from then on?

"That's a tricky one now. John Keane took over and he probably saw something. I was a tough aggressive player and had a bit of speed as well. I admired John as a trainer but I could have done with a lot more coaching. I didn't develop my right hand until just about All-Ireland time in 1957. After 1957 I trained and developed it myself."

The medals you won?

"Five County Waterford Senior Hurling Championship medals after my county days were over, the first with Ballyduff-Portlaw in 1970 and the last with Portlaw in 1977. I was forty-three when I won the last of them. I was sorry at times to have retired so early. You might remember I was suspended for attending an old soccer dance during the Ban days in controversial circumstances. The year was 1963. I played on until about 1967 but that suspension soured me. It makes me sad now to see a professional soccer player like Kevin Moran coming back from Manchester to play in an All-Ireland Final and I was suspended for going to a dance in the Olympia in Waterford. We always went there on a Friday night and someone spotted me and reported me. After we had been beaten in the 1963 All-Ireland. The suspension was for six months."

Getting back to the medals?

"Three Munster Senior Hurling Championships, one All-Ireland and I never got the National Hurling League medal on account of being suspended. We beat Tipperary in the home final. New York came over and played Waterford in the final and I was suspended at that time. (It isn't too late for Waterford to honour Tom, belatedly though it is, with a National Hurling League medal!). In the home final I had one of my best games ever. John D. Hickey wrote that it was one of the greatest games of hurling ever played. I won the Irish Independent Sports Star of the week award the next week. Played in four All-Ireland finals (1957, 1959 draw and replay and 1963). About twelve of the team played in all finals. As far as I know, I never got the medal, I don't have it anyway. The medal is not so important. It's winning the game that matters. They had to shift Tony Wall off me in the second half and he was a great centre half."

What is the greatest thrill you got out of hurling?

"Hurling is a thrill in itself. But my particular thrill was the solo-run. Beating a tackle maybe or putting the ball over the bar maybe passing the ball on to a better placed team-mate. You'd either score yourself or make the play. I liked the physical contact. You know the way a fellow would go for you, try and sink you altogether, that's when you could really make a cod of them. It's the cute fellow that shadows you is the hardest man to beat. It's the man with his dander up is the easiest man to beat. I'd like to make a fool of a fellow and then score if possible."

Did that taking on the man ever get you into trouble?

"It makes the game more physical. I was the kind of a fellow who didn't care if I side-stepped an opponent or if he hit off me. I took some punishment but I punished the fellows tackling me as well."

Were you ever injured?

"No, not much. I went off once against Cork about 1962. Broke my collar-bone. I waited 'till half time to leave the field. I never went off or was sent off the field of play in inter-county competition. Never even attended to during play in inter-county. Never down for any longer than it normally takes to get up again. I broke my fingers alright. I played on with one of those broken fingers. It was very bad and it never recovered. It was against Cork down at the Sportsfield (Walsh Park) in 1967. I remember getting fellows to put a bit of stuff on it. It was broken at the joint. It was a handicap after that."
(At this stage Tom showed me the shortened finger and regretted not having had it attended to properly at the right time).

Were you stubborn?

"I didn't want to go off. It was a tough battle. I wouldn't give them the satisfaction of going off."

Did you as a farmer find it easy to train?

"I used to train hard anyway. I'd get up in the morning and I might run about three miles. That is even when I'd be training normally in the Sportsfield for big matches. That three miles would be before I would milk the cows. I used to run cross-country and won the junior cross-country championship about 1958. Played Gaelic football as well and to be honest about it if I were in a football county I'd prefer football, as it was easier to retain possession and suited the kind of game I played. I played for Waterford seniors and liked the physical contact element of the sport. I remember playing on Paudie Sheehy above in Tralee at midfield."

Do they overdo the physical stuff in training nowadays? Do they hurl enough?

"It's more organised now and has been reduced to say Tuesdays and Thursdays only for training. They don't go down every evening to the field like we used to do. That is every evening that we could go. Every evening of the week Monday to Friday I did it. That was when I was in my prime. When playing senior with Portlaw, the two days a week came in then. I was married then - I didn't marry until I was thirty-seven. I thought all along that it wasn't a game for married people."

The great Waterford hurlers?

"I'd like to pay a tribute to the whole team I played with in 1957 and afterwards. The outstanding ones, I suppose, would be Phil Grimes, John Kiely at full forward, a great bit of stuff altogether. John was from Dungarvan and was very nearly over the top. He was brought back at the veteran stage and he took terrific punishment in at full forward."

What was great about Kiely?

"He had a great drive on a ball. A wristy drive and could double on it. Small too, five foot five inches about. He was hardy."

The others?

"Frankie Walsh and Mick Flannelly each side of me in the half forward line. Both very fast. We played well together. Martin Óg was a stylish centre half back. John Barron stylish in the corner. We were beaten by a goal and by a point and when we won, we won by seven points. There was nothing between ourselves and Kilkenny."

If you had to choose one from them all who would it be?

"Did I mention John Keane? I saw John playing, of course. John was a great hurler and a neighbour of mine at home, Mick Hickey was good too. John was a centre half back and they shifted him up to centre half forward and he operated well there at the end of his days. Vin Bastion was a great centre back too. Other stars from 1948 were Mick Hayes, Kevin O'Connor, Andy Fleming and Jackie Goode. I suppose Phil Grimes was best of all. It'd sway me a little that he is dead now. I was really cut up when he died and he fought a hard fight against cancer before dying."

Your greatest opponents.

"The two that stand out were Tony Wall and Willie Rackard and I wouldn't like to distinguish between the two. In club fare Pat McGrath from Mount Sion was a very stylish centre back."

Do you regret anything from your playing days,Tom?

"In a sense, I do. At times I played a very negative type of game. I tried to play negative, if I had one of my off-days. I tried to snuff out my opponent more than play myself."

Is Waterford hurling on the way back?

"It was marvellous last year to win the U-21. I saw all those games. The ones who impressed me were young Johnny Brenner, the outstanding hurler on the team, Tony Browne whose grandfather Fad was from my parish, (Fad was a former Mayor of Waterford and Fianna Fail T.D. and a great supporter of mine always. Fad played with

Erin's Own when he went to work in Waterford. One of my best friends. His son Tom Browne is now Mayor of Waterford), young Paul Flynn, a minor and a very promising player."

Why did it go down so much?

"To be realistic about it, Waterford hurling has always been in the shadow of Cork and Tipperary, as distinct from Kilkenny across the river. To get to the All-Ireland Waterford have to beat the two of them and that's a lot of it."

Who are behind the present push?

"Tony Mansfield is a good man but Georgie Leahy the Kilkenny man is the trainer at the moment. Ned Power, our goalkeeper, put an awful lot into it."

Are you still very friendly with your old team mates?

"Oh yes. We meet now and again, at games. We were all at Philly Grimes's funeral. Very sad then. We all met too, for the Centenary final in Thurles. That was our twenty-fifth anniversary and a special occasion. Micheál O'Hehir described me then as the ironman of hurling."

You told me of being Co-Sports star with Ollie Walsh in 1959. Did you respect Ollie?

"I think Ollie is one of the real characters of the game. He has a great old sense of humour. Everybody likes him. A brilliant goalkeeper too. He was so athletic. He'd come out like a shot out of a gun. Something special about him. A bit of a showman too but that's what it's all about isn't it?"

The great players of today?

"Liam Dunne, the Wexford centre half back, is a great player. Nicholas English is gone off a lot now but he was a real artist a few years ago. Joe Cooney too. The Connollys - Joe was my favourite."

The greatest hurler you saw, Tom?

"Ring, I suppose. I played with him in the Railway Cup. Have five medals from that competition, some as a substitute. Ring was a fanatic. He absolutely lived for the game. But then he had the power of a great county behind him. He was special though. Had very few weaknesses. Pat Delaney of Kilkenny a bit like myself. A better man to get a goal. A harder striker. Best man to hop the ball against the ground racing for goal. I used to do a bit of that myself earlier."

Best footballer you ever saw?

"Mick O'Connell the best fielder; Mikey Sheehy the best forward."

You're still cracked about sport, Tom?

"Sport is the only thing. It's the most important thing in my life. It's about youth and you tend to hang on to youth. I tried to prolong my youth by playing."

Do you mind getting old?

"I don't like it at all."

The game of your life?

"I suppose when you win an All-Ireland that's the important thing. I played a fair part in that scoring 2-2 off play. All off the right. In the drawn game I scored four points off the left. And some people still say I could only hit off one side. I always took frees though off the right. Under pressure I'd hit with the left. There was great satisfaction at winning but in the back of all of our minds at that time, we felt that we'd win another one. Most of us were only in our middle twenties, some less."

Any further comments?

"One man I'd like to mention is Michael White of Dunhill. I used to run cross-country with him. He was a good hurler and footballer too and I owe a lot to him. Monty Guiry was a great footballer too. Small hardy fellows like myself. With Portlaw the four

Phelans (pronounced Whelan in Waterford) played great hurling - Jackie, Frankie, Mossie and Peter. They were the mainstay of the team that won six titles. Mossie was a good inter-county hurler. John Galvin too, who won a couple of All Stars was another mainstay. Other great Portlaw men were, Paul Kelly, John Kirwan, Martin Hickey, son of Mick, Michael O'Regan and Paddy Hennebry. Players who played with me when Ballyduff won the Intermediate title in 1962 included, John O'Donnell R.I.P., Mick Power and Gerry McCarthy of the Irish Press, who was our full forward. Finally, the thing I miss most of all, is hurling in the long summer evenings in the field at Kildarmody. Yes, I miss that most of all."

Above, left : Tom Cheasty in his prime with Waterford
right: Nicholas English - 'a real artist'.

Chapter 14

Pat Hartigan

Of Limerick

Pat arranged to meet me in the Sacre Coeur Hotel at 2.45p.m. on Thursday, May 13th 1993. It was an unusually cold May day, after a scorcher the previous day. As I walked the short distance from my home to the "Sac" as it is known, at about 2.40p.m., I couldn't help recognise the tall frame and erect stance of the shirt sleeved man just ahead of me. Pat Hartigan could still conceivably be clearing balls from the Limerick goalmouth.

Is hurling bred into one?

"I suppose there is a common denominator between where you're born and hurling being bred into you. You could say that if you were born in any of the traditional hurling counties like Limerick, Cork, Galway or Tipperary for instance, the chances of your becoming a hurler are far greater than if you were born in counties like Cavan, Donegal, Wicklow or Fermanagh."

Is hurling a dying sport?

"I would expect it to continue, on more or less the same plateau it is on today. I'd be surprised and disappointed if I thought that hurling deteriorated to the extent that it became extinct entirely. We will always have good inter-county hurling but unfortunately, the club base is becoming more eroded."

Organisation is necessary all the time now?

"That comes from two factors. You have a society nowadays which is very affluent where young lads of twenty have their own cars, money, television sets. Today these young lads, instead of going to the cross roads to meet the lads to have a few pucks, are going into the city, to the lounge bars, socialising in what they regard as a easier way of life. Hurling in certain areas is not as glamorous as perhaps it should be."

Is it too expensive a game?

"First of all, it is too late in my opinion to try and develop a hurler at the age of sixteen. A hurler has to be taken care of from the age of six or seven. He has to have that awareness in him. In order to facilitate that, hurleys have to be available - ash hurleys not plastic, through subsidies, Government subsidies. Hurling is expensive for young lads at that particular age but when you come to eighteen, money is not so much a problem then. Young lads at that age have no problems buying sets of golf clubs, Raleigh bicycles, other things like Ski Boards, Surfboards, you name it. Far more expensive than buying a hurley."

Is it a dangerous game?

"No matter what contact sport you participate in, there are dangers and I'd be wrong to say hurling is not dangerous. There are dangers in it. It is a contact sport where players in opposition to one another have sticks and there is a ball and a lot of hard man-to-man pulling. Of course, accidents happen, but it is certainly not a dangerous game. I am a total supporter of headgear becoming compulsory."

Did you receive many stitches playing the game, Pat?

"I would hate to count them but certainly more than one hundred in my time. All my injuries were superficial, nothing serious, other than a totally accidental eye injury which I received in latter years. I started to wear a helmet back in 1968-1969 and it got to the stage that if I forgot my helmet, I felt as bad as if I had no togs."

Will the game remain an amateur game?

"I don't believe we will ever see hurling in the next fifty years becoming a professional sport. The backbone of an inter-county team are your club teams and to draw the line between the professional and the amateur within a club would ruin the whole scene."

Is hurling an addiction almost?

"The uniqueness of the sport and the skills involved in it, you've almost to be an addict to perfect it. I would call it commitment, not addiction. It's the will to conquer so many aspects of what is truly a magnificent game."

What in hurling gave you your greatest thrill?

"In my position at full back being the size I am, anybody that was foolish enough to send in a high ball to me was playing into my barrow. And the amount of high ball sent into my square still baffles me when I look back on it all. My strength and my identity was coming out to catch a ball in a ruck of hurleys and clear it. That gave me my greatest thrill. Catching the ball, facing an opponent, bursting out and not conceding ground."

How did you get hooked on the game?

"The first influence would be my elder brother Bernie (seven years older than me). He hurled with Limerick C.B.S. He had quite a good profile because Limerick C.B.S. started to come good in Colleges hurling at that stage. They were beaten in the Harty Cup final of 1960. I was ten then and he was hurling with South Liberties. I used to go to those club games, juveniles and minors. I followed him in all his games. The atmosphere soaked in and I wanted to hurl. And I wanted at all times to be as good as Bernie, who turned out to be a fine county hurler and a great athlete too. Interestingly, I followed him down the same road as a hurler and as an athlete too."

Your own schooldays?

"Sexton Street (Limerick C.B.S.) had their best innings ever from 1964 to 1968. During that period they won four Harty Cups. I played on the 1966 and 1967 teams. Eamonn Grimes captained the 1966 team and we won the All-Ireland title that year. A Harty Cup next year and we were going for a record five Harty Cups in a row only to be beaten by Coláiste Críost Rí of Cork who at that time were backboned by lads like Martin Doherty, Brian Murphy, Brendan and Ray Cummins and Séamus Looney. All these lads later hurled and played football for Cork. That great period in Sexton Street was the basis of the Limerick hurling revival in the 1970's."

Was winning the All-Ireland Colleges title a big thrill at the time?

"Bigger than we gave it credit for. Limerick C.B.S. had won it in 1964, beaten in the Final in 1965, won it again in 1966. We then felt it was our divine right almost. I was thrilled to see them win the Harty again this year."

The club - South Liberties?

"I'm indebted to South Liberties for hurling, for friends and for a whole philosophy of life. The club catered for people on the verge of Limerick City, a big parish consisting of Donaghmore, Knockea, Ballysheedy. Our club pitch and premises are outstanding. Fifteen years ago we had poor facilities and tremendous teams. Now it's the reverse but we have a very good under-age structure in the club with fine people like Ben O'Riordan and Fr. Tom Ryan, outstanding in their service to the youth. The club had a rural life style about it. We togged out in the back yard of a local hostelry. Often ended up getting a lift up to the field in the back of an old jeep belonging to somebody in the parish."

Some of the great club members?

"Willie O'Connell the local publican, was the hurley-mender, the bottle-carrier, the Treasurer and above all a tremendous character. Mikie Croker the Life President, who played for the club is another."

The number of county titles won with South Liberties?

"I won three: 1972, 1976 and 1978. In 1972 we won the Championship for the first time in eighty-two years. That was very special. Special in that Eamonn Grimes was captain and was automatically captain of the Limerick team for the following year, which won the All-Ireland for the first time in thirty-three years. Eamonn was a lucky captain. I was with him as captain in 1966 (Harty and All-Ireland) then in 1972 with the club and in 1973 for the All-Ireland."

Any other club members not mentioned?

"I haven't mentioned Joe McKenna but he was definitely Offaly's godsend to Limerick - a marvellous player. I knew Joe through the colleges - he went to St. Flannan's in Ennis and I had many a tussle with him. He joined South Liberties and became a vital cog in our wheel. J.P. McManus, the well-known horsey man. He ran his horses, whether in Cheltenham, Aintree or at home, always in the South Liberties colours of green and gold. To sit down and watch our club colours winning in Cheltenham was special to all of us. The All-Ireland club title has been a great success and is getting bigger. We never won it out but that All-Ireland club title has become a phenomenal success."

Club and county - do they complement each other?

"Inter-county players should always be available to clubs for their important games. They also help to raise the standard of the ordinary club players in both the training ground and in games. When the county players attend club training, the standard is always upped."

Is the G.A.A. over national? Pat, you won the Cooley Mountains Poc Fada Competition twice. Surely winning that rather unique event showed another side to the G.A.A.?

"To take up your first point about the Irish identity of the G.A.A. I think that as players we don't reflect too much on the Irishness of the G.A.A. We didn't look beyond the playing of it. There is a mystique about the Cooley mountains. It's a vast mountain terrain, four and half miles, and to conquer that twice in four years, and be second twice in the other two years was a huge thrill. I retired in 1979 and won the Puc Fada first in 1981. Lost it in 1982, won it again in 1983 and was runner up in 1984. There is one particular spot, a ravine you have to cross and it certainly reminds you of Cúchulainn. The ravine is eighty yards wide and if you miss getting over it, it is almost impossible to get out of it. You feel a wee bit like a Cúchulainn as you face the ravine. Man versus mountain, basically. You win if you get the ball across."

Did you like the buzz of being an All Star, Pat?

"In all I won five All Stars. I was on the first All Star team as full back in 1971 and held that position for five years in a row. One of those was an automatic selection - that of 1973."

How did you regard an All Star in the honours list?

"I remember asking Eddie Keher in 1971 how he compared winning an All Star Award against winning an All-Ireland medal. The All Star he held to be a very personalised award. You get it for your own contribution to the game, for your skill, your sportsmanship and ability. Winning Five All Stars in a row at full back with the exception of winning an All-Ireland with Limerick in 1973 gave me the greatest personal satisfaction. It's nice when you retire to look back and say I did it for my contribution to full back play. I'd be identified as being a hurling full back rather than a physical full back."

The All-Ireland of 1973?

"At the time we won it, it didn't stand out in my mind as the greatest thrill, then. Yes, it was tremendous. But I was the type of player that once the game was over, I wanted to put it behind me and set off after another one. The next game was the next All-Ireland."

Has hurling helped you in your career?

"People of my own age group tend to recognise me. The younger bunch in their teens and twenties don't recognise me but then I'm not in their circle."

Do you tend to have friends in every corner of the land?

"I tend to be known wherever I go. My work takes me throughout the West of Ireland. I work with Grassland Fertilisers and I travel from Sligo to Kerry. No matter where I stop, there is a G.A.A. man with whom I can identify."

Fame has spoilt the lives of many G.A.A. stars? Did this bother you, Pat?

"It never bothered me. If fame lures guys away into a different life that they might not have had otherwise, I think this would have happened with or without hurling. Many a non-hurler falls by the wayside too. Hurling kept me on the straight and narrow. I believe I didn't need hurling to do that. But there are people out there who needed hurling and football or indeed any sport to get through the critical period of life, say seventeen to twenty-five. Being a former G.A.A. player has opened doors for me but it has needed my own character to keep those doors open."

Why isn't Limerick a bigger force in hurling?

"No matter what you're doing, let it be a business or developing a team, you have to be where the people are. Where the people are in Limerick, the hurling is not and that is Limerick City. Cork's hurling is arguably strongest in Cork City. Hurling is relatively strong in Co. Limerick but the numbers playing the game aren't enough to give you the depth of players necessary. Just look at the rugby scene in Limerick City. The rugby clubs are stronger while some hurling clubs have gone out of existence practically."

Will Gaelic football oust hurling in Limerick eventually?

"Limerick has always been identified as a hurling county. Yet we have only managed to win one All-Ireland (Senior Hurling) title in fifty years. Subconsciously people are geared towards hurling. Football is a Cinderella sport and has never been really given the chance to develop. I played football with Limerick in my own day and never took it too seriously. There has been progress made in the attitude to Gaelic football. Bringing Kerry's John O'Keeffe in charge brought a certain seriousness to it. It has to go back further. The schools in Limerick haven't pushed Gaelic football as much as hurling. It will take time."

Your greatest opponents?

"The best were Ray Cummins, Babs Keating, Pat Delaney, Kieran Purcell, Tony Doran and Noel Casey. Ray Cummins was the best player I ever played on. Best from the point of view that if a ball was coming in to the square - say a line ball - he was always standing in the position where I wanted to be. His two feet were always where I needed mine to be and that's where the jostling would start. Negotiating for position. He was indeed a very sharp player. A quick thinker and a good reader of the game."

Anecdotes?

"We were playing Clare in the Munster Senior Hurling Championship around 1979. In fact it was my last Championship match and I was on Noel Casey, and Pat Herbert was on Enda O'Connor. I think the best way to describe their duel was that they reminded me of two guys inside a small room with two little sticks trying to kill the one fly. Noel Casey and myself were not exactly on speaking terms either the same day. It got so hot at one stage that Enda passed by and said to Noel 'Case, it's about time we let down the mowing bar in here'. On another occasion also against Clare I was coming out of Thurles and walking down with a friend who slightly resembled Eamonn Cregan. This elderly woman jumps out of a car and prods me with an umbrella saying 'Casey is the boy for you' and she turned to my friend - not a player at all - and prods him harder with the umbrella saying 'And Jackie gave it to you, too' referring to Jackie O'Gorman who had been playing on Eamonn Cregan."

The great players of today?

"I like Brian Corcoran as a player and I think the G.A.A. as an Association needs a personality like Brian coming forward. We have heard a lot about Nicholas English and justified may I add, but unfortunately backmen never get the recognition forwards get because there is less glamour to defending. Michael Houlihan of Limerick is a nice player. I like Joe Rabbitte. For a big guy he has a great turn of speed. His temperament might be questionable. Joe Cooney, of course, a marvellous player."

Is the game improving?

"Every generation has said the game wasn't as good as it used to be. I remember when I started with Limerick in 1968 it was so. Same again in every decade. Hurling is still turning out outstanding games. Maybe the overall skills aren't there because the physical contact isn't as much part of the game as it was. The game has changed. The over-head pull is gone almost. In the old days you tended to want to keep the ball moving. Then you had the third man tackle and it was a liability to take possession of the ball at times."

Any pet hates?

"Club teams and players that don't tog out properly."

Your achievements for the record?

"Two Munster titles in 1973 and 1974, the All-Ireland in 1973, a National Hurling League medal in 1971, Division two of National Hurling League twice, an Oireachtas medal in 1971, two Railway Cup medals in 1976 and 1978, the first as a full back, the second at centre back, a Wembley Tournament, a New York Senior Hurling Championship with Clare."

You never consumed alcohol, Pat?

"I never drank or smoked."

Do you still keep fit?

"Yes, very much so. I do a fair amount of weight-lifting, something I did a lot of during my hurling career also. You see I was involved in athletics and shot-putting at national and international level."

Your weight and height now?

"I'm sixteen and a half stone now and my height is six foot four inches."

Team-management or coaching?

"My involvement at that was at under-age level with South Liberties. I brought a group of lads through from age sixteen to twenty-one and we had quite a lot of success."

Do you read the papers about games?

"Not particularly. I read them about games I wasn't at."

The game of your life?

"We spoke about the 1973 All-Ireland. The win of my life was that game. I played a lot of matches for South Liberties in East Limerick - in Caherconlish - a small ground which invariably had four thousand people at the games. The atmosphere was electric and the winning with South Liberties in East Limerick took an awful lot of beating. The games that stand out in my mind though are two. The Munster final of 1974 against Clare is one. To me it was my best game and I got the Irish Independent Sports Star of the Week Award the following Friday. In 1975 we played Tipperary and we were nine points behind at half-time and we ended up drawing with them. Probably my second best game ever. Those two games were stepping stones to the ultimate. The 1974 one against Clare is number one."

Above, left: Pat Hartigan
right: Eamonn Grimes - 'always his captain'.

Chapter 15

Matt Connor

Of Offaly

He was one of the greatest ball players the game of Gaelic football has seen. The whole of Ireland was shocked on Christmas Day 1983 when Matt was driving to Walsh Island and home for the Christmas turkey and had a car skid. The resultant injuries confined him to a wheelchair for life. The whole nation was stunned. We would never again see the boyish Matt, a real gentleman footballer, solo, as he only could do, and score goals and points at will. Statistics tell us Matt played one hundred and sixty-one senior inter-county and representative games starting in March 1978 and ending in December 1983. In those games he scored eighty-two goals and six hundred and sixty points for a career aggregate of nine hundred and six points. What a man! Elsewhere in this book other players have paid him due tribute, stressing it had nothing to do with sympathy. Matt would not want it otherwise.

When did you first get interested in Gaelic football?

"I was always interested in it as long as I can remember, from the age of four or five, I remember trying to kick the ball out of my hands at that age. My brothers were all very interested and involved. I was the second youngest with four lads older namely Murt, Willie, Rich and Séamus. Murt played for Offaly in 1971-1972, when Offaly won their first All-Ireland senior title and he was a big influence on me. Then Rich and Willie had played minor and U-21 before me also."

Matt hails from a great football stronghold Walsh Island, fifteen miles from Tullamore. Is it a typical rural village?

"A Church, a pub and a school. About one hundred and sixty or one hundred and seventy families. There would be fifty Bord na Mona houses there as well, and they certainly added to the area."

His national schooldays were in Walsh Island National School where your teacher was Donald Dunne. Four or five years ahead of Matt, Richie's class won absolutely everything at National School level. That particular bunch won everything at U-12 and U-14 in both hurling and football for three or four years. He never attended the National School with Murt who was about ten years older than him. It was a football school really. Did Matt captain his school team when his time came?

"I don't think I was ever a captain but we won out in my time as well. I was never a captain. Richie was captain of nearly every team I played on. He was a good captain. I was too quiet on the field. I never wanted it."

Secondary schooldays?

"Portarlington C.B.S., a good footballing school as well. We never really won anything while I was there but an awful lot of players from the school played with Offaly and Laois subsequently. Six of our 1982 Offaly panel, John Guinan, Mark Fitzpatrick, Richie and myself and my cousins Tomás and Liam Connor, were there. Ger Lalor, Stephie Allen from Laois too."

How many Connors played for the club Walsh Island?

"The six brothers in our family all played and two cousins Liam and Tomás. Generally on that team, there were eight Connors playing. Murt, Willie, Rich, Séamus, myself and Sean of our family. Cousins Liam and Tomás were double first cousins, our mothers being sisters as well as the fathers being brothers. In all we won six Offaly Senior Football Championship titles in a row, 1978-1983 and two Leinster Senior Football Championship titles."

Did the club mean a lot to you?

"Yes an awful lot. In Walsh Island when my father was growing up in the thirties, they had a great club team. The Mulhalls and the Connors were the middle of that team as well. As we grew up, we heard a lot about this great team. The pressure was on us to emulate them. For four or five years we did very well in challenges and in leagues but never got to winning it. The Bryans, Willie included, were first cousins also, so you had ten brothers or first cousins playing for the club. We lost the Club All-Ireland semi-finals to Scotstown and St. Grellan's, Ballinasloe."

Is the club All-Ireland a good competition?

"It's a great competition. The best football played, is played in it. More open and more enjoyable to play in than inter-county. Teams don't know one another that well and you're allowed to play more because of that. Portlaoise had a lovely team, a very good footballing side. Eire Og looked very good on telly."

Wearing the Offaly Jersey?

"Amazingly, I wore it first at thirteen in an U-14 competition and it meant a lot to me. It was always an ambition to wear the jersey. I was dreaming about that always as a young lad. Wearing the senior one was the real ambition. That came in 1977 against Meath in the National Football League and I had been an Offaly minor that year. In six months I made a big transformation. I was light enough as a minor and then got big and strong in about a year. The first Senior Football Championship game was against Longford in 1978. We won it. I scored a goal and was taken off. So those are my memories of the first big engagement."

Honours won?

"Six Offaly Senior Football Championship medals, two Leinster Senior Football Championship and Senior club, one All-Ireland, three All Stars, two Leinster U-21 medals."

The All Star Award?

"A great honour. The night itself is brilliant. Meeting all the players. Nice to be selected. But the All-Ireland is the prize. I wouldn't swop the All-Ireland medal for anything. But my first County Senior Football Championship success a very big thing too. Almost as big. The first one in 1978 was against Rhode."

Your greatest score?

"The most important score was the goal against Dublin in the 1980 Leinster Final. It was in the second half and we were under great pressure. It was the goal that won it really. It was my first Leinster title and a vital goal. But probably the best scores I got were at club level. One particularly against Ferbane in a County Senior Football Championship semi-final where the game was gone. I think we were two points down in a replay as well and I got a goal to win it, really out of nothing."

Scoring feats? (Matt was reluctant to talk of these. I could never imagine the man boasting).

"I got 2-9 in the All-Ireland semi-final against Kerry in 1980, my highest at inter-county level. At club level I got 5-4 one day against Dunlavin - my highest score ever."

Greatest opponent?

"John O'Keeffe, the hardest man I ever met. So good all round, fast and strong. Would always play the ball as well. He'd always find a man with it, which is a killer. A lot of backs under pressure cannot do that and as an opponent you get satisfaction that you might have stopped them. Within Offaly the most difficult opponent was Liam Currams. He had great speed."

The greatest Offaly footballer?

"I looked up to a lot of fellows and was very influenced by the 1971-1972 team. Especially by Willie Bryan and Tony McTague. They had the skills. Tony put up the big scores every day and he had an amazing sidestep. As a forward I would have modelled myself on Tony a bit."

Did you ever train on your own, Matt?

"Oh all the time. Always with the ball. I never trained that hard but played with the ball a lot. Loved playing with the ball. Your skills have to improve if you keep playing with the ball."

Back to great Offaly players?

"Willie Bryan's fielding and his ability to be in open space all the time and to get away from trouble were pretty unique. He always seemed to have loads of time on the ball - the sign of a great player. Another who had it was Jimmy Duggan of Galway."

Of today's players, anyone to turn Matt on?

"Maurice Fitzgerald of Kerry and Mickey Linden of Down are class players. If you had the two of them on any forward line of the moment, you'd be nearly there. (Here I interjected if they had Matt Connor in the full forward position and Maurice and Mickey either side the scores would come!)"

Staying on the greatest Offaly footballer?

"As a driving force it was hard to beat Martin Furlong. A big influence on me in 1982. Great goalkeeper. Anything Offaly won in football Martin was involved as goalkeeper. A minor in 1964 - our first ever title, a team which included Willie Bryan and Tony McTague and still highly regarded in Offaly - he was still playing in 1985 and still a driving force. He wasn't very stylish or skilful with the ball but full of heart and extremely brave. Terrific in the training scene. His encouragement was constant and he was never afraid to stretch a point and take somebody on in the dressing-room, if it needed to be done. He hit as hard in training as in games. I know that from experience. Willie Bryan was the classiest footballer of them all."

Influence from within your own family?

"Murt had a huge influence on all of us. We saw him being collected by all the team and that was so influential. Great to have the fellows calling and I was waiting for the day when I'd be called for."

The influence of Eugene McGee?

"His organisation and professionalism was very good. I never was under any other management really, but I was happy with him. He talked to every player a lot. Rang them a lot. A serious man to a lot of people but Eugene could be very witty."

Anecdotes?

"Eugene would often go strong on a point and betimes it went wrong in the game afterwards. Once in Birr against Cork in a very important challenge game in preparation for some big test for us, our full forward line was Johnny Mooney, Sean Lowry and myself and Eugene's speech was really about us taking points in deference to Billy Morgan's great expertise as a goalkeeper. The theme was 'take your points the goals will come'. Within five minutes the score was Offaly 3-0 Cork nil and each of the full forward line scored a goal. There was a bit of a laugh at half time that day."

Is the game improving?

"In ways, yes. The crowds and the hype are terrific now. The skill level with young lads is gone a bit. The young lads are not playing enough on their own now. Everything has to be done in groups and organised. Players are fitter. Easier to train physically in groups than on your own. There is much more variety in playing moves. I can't see a return of the great skills because there are so many other things to do now for the young lads of today."

Will it go professional?

"No, but players will get more out of it. Even today ten years since I played almost, players are being treated an awful lot better. Everybody wants good management now and they are prepared to pay for it."

The Open Draw? Railway Cups?

"I'd love to see the Open Draw across the board. Absolutely. Perfectly made for football 32-16-8-4-2-1. I think it would be terrific. Teams can meet one another too often. Say Cork and Kerry. If they went five years without meeting and then were drawn in an Open Draw that would be a real big event and would be great for the game. Playing every year, the event gets smaller. The Open Draw in the provinces recently has helped greatly. I'm really very keen on the Open Draw. The Railway Cups are nearly gone and it's a pity."

Do you feel bitter about your accident Matt, which has confined you to a wheelchair for life?

"I still feel bitter, of course. The business of football is elementary compared to the whole business of life. I don't think football worried me until a couple of years after the accident. You miss an awful lot of things before you miss football. After a while when you have settled in to everything else and you have managed everything then you start thinking that you'd like to be playing again. If you saw a new talent in the county you'd just think I'd like to play alongside him. That's the way it would hit you. It's the very same, I'm sure, as when someone retires."

Talking of the fateful Christmas Day accident.

"I was thrown from the car and was conscious but I didn't realise then, what was wrong. I went through the first twenty-four hours not knowing, and feeling that I'd be alright in a few days."

Did your G.A.A. past help to sustain you afterwards?

"A lot of times I'd prefer just to be out of the limelight a bit. It does, of course, because I have a great interest in it. I love going to games. I'd never miss a Championship game for Offaly, any grade. My whole life revolves around it. I've been a minor selector for over seven years. I wouldn't really be able to manage a team. Basically, I wouldn't be a good motivator. I got great help when I was in hospital for the first six months with loads of people visiting me. That helped me to take my mind off it. My family were great. The Garda Station here in Tullamore too and the G.A.A."

Was the benefit game the following April very emotional for you?

"Very. I didn't cry that day. I had got over that by then, in the hospital."

What bugs you most now?

"People in life are so critical of everything. In football it is the same. If teams aren't going well, the trainers and selectors are always blamed and they are all doing their jobs to the best of their ability. Here in Offaly in the last eight years we have had four or five trainers and every one of them has come under terrible pressure. When you haven't got the players you haven't got them and no county wants to admit it hasn't got the players at the moment. But that's life generally. Same thing in politics. You can't make a decision but there is somebody against it."

Anything in the game?

"I never favoured rough play but still feel teams need hard players. I don't like dirty play at all and never did. There is room for the good tough player. Off the ball stuff I detest but on the ball I like good hard play."

The best footballer you ever saw?

"They were many. Brian Mullins was brilliant, so important to Dublin and Eoin Liston the same to Kerry. Two very effective players. Talking of skilled players, Willie Bryan, Tony McTague and Mikey Sheehy were the tops. Mikey had terrific skills and quick thinking too. Always a few steps ahead."

Your greatest thrill in football?

"Scoring goals. I loved scoring goals. Soccer or Gaelic. I'd probably go for them, when I shouldn't go for them. Often got the works from Eugene about it."

The game of your life?

"The feeling when we had won the All-Ireland. When it was over. It's a week later that it really sank in. You had done what you always wanted to do. It passes you by a wee bit when it happens, but then it dawns on you that you had got what you wanted to achieve in football. From the time I was four or five years of age I wanted to win an All-Ireland medal in Croke Park. The boyhood dream. And I got it and that was it."

Matt Connor scoring his greatest score against Dublin in the 1980 Leinster final.

Chapter 16

Michael "Spike" Fagan

Of Westmeath

Gaelic football has always had a high status in Westmeath, though very few provincial honours came the county's way. In the International series between Ireland and Australia in the Compromise Rules experiment, Michael "Spike" Fagan first came to be known to Irish sports fans. He wouldn't tell me the origin of the name "Spike".

Michael, what gave you the interest in Gaelic football first?

"My father was a big help to me when I was growing up. He played hurling for Westmeath being more of a hurling man but in Mullingar at the time there was very little hurling. So he encouraged me to play football. I got involved at school level in the street leagues where I played with Millmount where we lived then. That would be U-12 and U-14. That was around 1970. We won it one year and lost in the semi-finals on other occasions."

Was there a big family involvement in the game?

"I have four other brothers, three of whom played the game. John, my oldest brother, played for Westmeath senior team at one stage. That was a slight influence but not a major one."

When did you feel that you wanted to play for Westmeath?

"I was playing minor and senior for Mullingar in 1979-1980. That's when I first had aspirations to play for the county. I got picked to play before I had my eyes firmly set on playing senior for the county. I had been playing minor for Westmeath, having missed out playing U-14 and U-16 county football."

Where did you go to school?

"In St. Mary's C.B.S. in Mullingar, where one of my teachers was Sean Cleary of Galway three-in-a-row fame. He was a big influence on all of us playing football. He was always slagging and joking that we in Westmeath were never any good and Galway were always the best and that we didn't deserve to wear the maroon and white, ours and Galway's colours. He joked, of course, but was very serious in his preparation for games and he encouraged a lot of fellows into Gaelic football."

Were you keen on soccer as a youngster?

"Yes, I played all sports - soccer, rugby and hurling as well as Gaelic football. The latter wasn't as well organised in 1970 as it is now. So when you had any free time you normally played soccer. At one stage my father banned me from playing soccer."

Your father, Jimmy, was a true blue G.A.A. man?

"I remember sneaking out to play soccer, returning and saying nothing and maybe later on the same evening playing a Gaelic match."

How do you now compare the games?

"To be honest I prefer Gaelic football a lot more. It's a better game. The more I got into it the more I liked it. There were better chances, too, of going places with it."

Why is Gaelic football superior?

"Soccer has too much playmanship in it. Too many players going down injured and nothing really wrong with them. To me it wasn't a man's game. Not a tough enough game. More skill level to Gaelic with the high fielding, tackling the whole lot."

Was your club, Mullingar Shamrocks, a big influence?

"Yes, Terry Dowd, the main man in charge of U-14 football in the town helped me in a big way to stay with the game. We won the U-14 Westmeath title under Terry in 1973. I'm thirty-two now and shoving on!"

The progression from there?

"We lost the U-16 title in a replay but went on to win at minor level. Our great opponents then were St. Malachy's (out Castletowngeoghan way) for whom Mick Lowry played. He was an opponent all the way up and we played county together afterwards. Stephen Hanratty was another Malachy's man who became a great friend and is now in the U.S.A. Joe Grennan was another, who shot to fame with Carmelite College, Moate, an opponent and friend and colleague later too."

Interest in Gaelic football in the county?

"Great interest in the county. Some people in charge have a short sighted policy in their attitude to all other sports. In Mullingar the interest is very high. We have Bernard Flynn of Meath with us now. We are Westmeath Senior Football Champions for 1992, his first year to play for us. He was very quick to mix in with us. It took us a while to get used to his style of playing and he had to adapt to our style, too. He seemed to be moving a bit too soon for us. Played very well in the County final. A really fine player."

Was Flynn's presence at training very beneficial?

"It was indeed because Bill Sex from Kildare also joined us and we now had three internationals as such on a club team - a huge influence really. We ended up with a bigger quota than usual at training sessions."

Do you ever give up hope after so many defeats for Westmeath year in year out?

"I still enjoy wearing the Westmeath jersey. I always will, although I've given up hope several times. Several times in the future too I'm sure. Sometimes it bothers me when so many of us are putting in a huge effort and one or two guys take it haphazardly. But I'm sure all counties have this problem. These won't make the sacrifices other lads make."

Has Matt Kerrigan of Meath brought hope?

"Matt encourages and praises players. Sometimes I feel he could be a bit harsher on people. But he has taught us to get out there, get into a game and not be afraid of the opposition."

Your career successes in brief?

"Four Westmeath Senior Football, two U-21, one-minor, one U-14 Championship medals, a Railway Cup medal in 1987 (on the panel) and the three Test series appearances for Ireland against Australia in 1986 under Kevin Heffernan in Australia, a series we won 2-1, 1987 under Eugene McGee at home, one we lost 2-1 and 1980 again under Eugene when I was called out to Australia to join the panel for the second and third Tests which we won again 2-1."

You shot to national fame in that first Series, Michael.

"In 1986 I had a great desire to get on the Irish panel for Australia and I knew if I got the chance I had the determination to make it. I got nominated to go forward for trial along with Tom Ormsby and Aidan Collins from Westmeath and I kept getting called back after that."

Not being a big man how did you feel you impressed Kevin Heffernan?

"We had played Dublin in the Centenary Cup of 1984 in Mullingar. We beat Dublin and I held Barney Rock scoreless that day. One of the better games of my life. Ever since that Gerry Hargan reckoned, when I chatted to him on the plane journey home from the first Series, that Heffo had me in his eye from there on. In the trials he tried me out in various positions and gave me difficult men to mark as a test."

Was he a good coach?

"Outstanding. Best tactical manager I've ever experienced. If he had fifteen fellows who'd do exactly as he told them, there is no way they could be beaten. He had a great hold on players who looked up to him so much. The atmosphere was electric when he was in charge. In the dressing-room giving a talk he had charisma. I remember talking to Jack O'Shea who used to compare him to Micko, whom I'd love to have trained under, too, but he too could look up to Heffo also despite the close rivalry of that time."

Is there a future for that Australian link?

"There is a great future for it, in that it gives a chance to lads from the weaker counties to taste the limelight but there isn't enough support for it here or in Australia. Some of the diehards here don't favour it."

Are the games too far apart for marriage?

"We still have a hybrid game, half of one, half the other. If it was all one, it would catch on better. I enjoyed the game as it was. Far faster, far more scores, far harder, better entertainment for spectators but an international outlet for the game would be a great spur for the whole scene."

The Open Draw?

"A good idea. Gives everybody a fair crack of the ship. This thing of seeding teams is hard on players and officials. If Westmeath drew Kerry in the Open Draw, just think of the hype generated in my county and if we drew Carlow or Kilkenny and if we got by there would be the chance of another exciting draw. Some day you'd bring off something special."

Suggestions for the G.A.A. in the future?

"Rules need to be tightened up. Referees' decisions are too varied."

Are referees improving with all this analysis on 'telly'?

"Looking at Joe Lennon on the Saturday Sports Stadium in recent times, I think his explanation of the rules is one way of improving referees. But the rules need clearer definition. Players don't know the rules in full. They know the basics and they often end up arguing with referees on an issue in which they are wrong themselves. So this Joe Lennon exercise is to be encouraged. For the ordinary fans too."

Your favourite referee?

"Paddy Collins, not because he is a Westmeath official - actually he is with the St. Loman's Club here in Mullingar - one of the best I've ever seen. He refereed in Australia in the two referee system, one referee covering one half of the field, the other the other half, and he was absolutely fair. We felt their referee was more lenient towards them. Not so Paddy to us. Paddy saw it for real. If he saw it he blew it."

Do you read much on the game?

"All the paper articles in preparation for games. I like autobiographies in general. Doesn't have to be a sports personality. My favourite is Bob Geldof's. Phil Neal's of Liverpool is good too."

The Irish sporting writers?

"Donal Keenan, Pat Spillane, Colm O'Rourke and Eugene McGee (*Evening Herald*). Con Houlihan for his wit would be my favourite. I relate very much to him when he writes on football."

Your pet hates?

"Administration and fixtures. Sometimes no fixtures at all for a while and then five or six games all thrown together. At a local level Westmeath don't go too far in the inter-county scene generally so I don't know what would happen if we did well for a change! Our League final of 1992 is not finished until well into 1993. A regular game every Tuesday night would be no problem, allowing space, of course, for preparation of the county team for major games."

Anything about the game itself?

"The tackle has to be sorted out."

The great people in Westmeath who have kept the G.A.A. flag flying over the years?

"Paddy Collins is County Secretary for many years. Some people like him, some don't. He is very good in some things. Other things I wouldn't agree with. But it's hard to please everybody. Paddy Flanagan is also very involved. He writes in the local paper too. He is Treasurer of Leinster Council now and a former Westmeath player. Great man to produce match programmes and, believe it or not, the Westmeath Senior Football Championship trophy is the Flanagan Cup called after Paddy. We honour our men in Westmeath while they are alive!"

The heart and soul of your own club team?

"Tom Hunt, our Treasurer, is a great Gael. Originally from Waterford he looks after every penny. Mick Greene from Clare is another and since Clare did well we cannot keep him down! Richie O'Donoghue, a Kildare man, one of that footballing family so well known for its footballers, has been in charge of the Shamrocks team since 1985 and is one of the main reasons why we have done so well."

Your greatest opponent?

"Dermot McNicholl of Derry. I only played on him in training but I found him very difficult to mark. Every player is difficult in his own way. I marked Pat Spillane in training and he was difficult too. Always felt I had the edge on Barney Rock after that 1984 game but they all present difficulties ."

Anecdote?

"An old man Mick Gaye used to live with us, a great friend of my Dad's and he lived with us for thirty-five years and he was famous for giving out to referees. Anytime I got a belt playing football he'd be out with the umbrella shaking and wanting to go for the referee. If I got knocked over it was always a free for me! If I knocked somebody else over it was fair enough. He was my greatest supporter. One day Tom Farrell, a man involved with the County was refereeing a game and he soon got fed up with Mick giving out, so that after about fifteen minutes he sauntered over to Mick and said

'Who is refereeing this game anyway?' and Mick replied 'Neither of us'. Tom shut up and went away laughing."

Any other amusing story from football?

"We have another chap involved with Westmeath and Mullingar at the moment named 'Killer' Byrne, who boxed for Ireland years ago. 'Killer' is our masseur and has been involved with Shamrocks for ten years. Sometimes in his frustration or anxiety to do something when somebody is injured he often grabs the wrong leg and you'd hear the injured one roar 'You're at the wrong one'."

The greatest player?

"Jack O'Shea, overall, my favourite player. I played with him. He is a superb sportsman. His fitness and athleticism were great. As a forward I had great time for Pat Spillane and Mikey Sheehy. Spillane was magic out in the half forward line and Sheehy when he got towards goals couldn't be marked."

People from Westmeath?

"Terry Dowd as I said was a big help to me in getting involved. Leo Dowling a former trainer of Mullingar and Mick Fennell of Laois, who now lives in Cavan. Mick took me away from soccer and encouraged me to play rugby as he felt it wouldn't hinder me. I took up rugby then and I found it a more physical contact sport and enjoyed it. My knowledge of rugby, its tackling and being used to getting hit helped me in getting on the Ireland team to play Australia."

The best Westmeath player?

"At the moment Larry Giles, when he is on form, is one of the best footballers around. He is a corner forward. Very cute, two good feet."

The greatest thrill he gets out of the game?

"The camaraderie there is in the scene. At County level at the moment, a club spirit exists. After a game everybody can sit down, have a few drinks or a chat and generally get on very well. If we lose we're all down together. Same with the club. Our club is going very well. We are pulling together like a happy family and the two newcomers, Bill Sex and Bernie Flynn have fitted in well."

You are a top business-man in Mullingar with Fagan's Office Supplies, Michael. Does football help the business?

"Definitely it does. In business it helps to be well-known."

The game of your life?

"It has to be the second Test against Australia in 1986. I got the Man of the Match Award for that game. I went out there hoping to get on the team. I was a substitute for the first Test and came in after ten minutes and was selected at midfield alongside Jack O'Shea for the second Test. We won the second Test having lost the first one. I played out of my skin that day. That definitely was it. The game was played in Melbourne."

Would you have loved to have played that game before your own in Mullingar?

"They were all, I believe, watching it back home in Mullingar and were quite proud. The local club lads tell me a good story about it. They were listening to the game on the radio or seeing it on telly and Shamrocks were playing a club game afterwards in which my brother Patsy was involved. He hadn't been playing too well that year. After that game he went out and played a blinder, I suppose to prove it was in all the family that day!"

The reception in Mullingar on returning home?

"Unbelievable. I was paraded into town and we had a special banquet in the Lake County Hotel with about five hundred present. Everybody in Mullingar it seemed shook my hand. People from all over Westmeath. I was representing them in Melbourne. That was the football night of my career."

Spike Fagan in possession from 1993 Leinster Senior Football Championship game, watched by Pat Gilroy (Dublin) and David Prendergast (Westmeath).

Chapter 17

Tom Prendergast

Of Laois

He was one of the most stylish forwards ever to wear the blue and white of his native Laois where interest in Gaelic games, football particularly, is paramount. Laois has won few titles but in the thirties they stormed on to the scene with Tommy Murphy, the Boy Wonder midfielder, and all the Delaneys making headlines. In fact the footballing Delaneys of Laois was the first big family to attract national headlines, a pattern setter for the Fennelly, Cuddy, Quigley, Rackard, Gribben, Connolly family inter-county involvements of later times. Tom Prendergast's style of play is what endeared him to friend and foe.

I asked the Portlaoise star, who works as a Garda in Abbeyleix, which was the most popular game in Laois, football or hurling?

"Football would be number one. More football clubs and bigger attendances at club football games."

Are you still playing?

"I finished up last year at thirty-six years of age. I was a wee bit sad hanging up the boots and at times wondered had I made the right decision to retire, but there comes a time to make such a decision and after being beaten in the 1992 Laois Senior Football Championship semi-final I felt the time was ripe to quit."

Are you still interested?

"I go to all the club games involving Portlaoise and as many county games as I can. I hope to coach some of the juvenile teams in time."

Did you play hurling, too?

"Yes, I played the game as a youngster from U-12 to about eighteen but after that I concentrated on football. The club wasn't very strong on hurling then but that developed in a big way later. Actually the club brought off the Laois double Senior Football and Senior Hurling Championship success three if not four times in the last decade."

Your first interest in the game?

"Going to National school the first man to encourage me was Br. Beausang in Portlaoise. He was in charge of both hurling and football in the school. We won two U-12 Laois Championships (schools) in hurling and football under his guidance. A lot of the lads of that time continued on with me to win other club awards together later, lads like Liam Scully, Colm Browne, Billy Bohane, who hurled for Laois, and Jimmy Bergin. My father was more of a hurling man, being from Freshford in Kilkenny. In his own day he won a minor All-Ireland hurling medal with Kilkenny in 1937. He was keen on football, too, and supported me in my interest."

Secondary Schooldays?

"I went to the C.B.S. in Portlaoise where we got to a few Leinster finals in the B Division in football, never winning one. But football was a big influence in the school. Br. Paddy Kelly, a Clareman, was the man in charge and he was a fine hurler."

Your club Portlaoise was special to you?

"I trained to be a Garda in Templemore and remember Mattie Coleman of Galway trained there with my old school mate Colm Browne and myself. The club was a huge influence on me from U-13 up, and the man I must give absolute credit to is Bill Phelan, who was Vice-Principal of the local Vocational School. He was in charge of us in juveniles and was in charge at senior level when I reached that stage."

The club successes under Bill?

"We won every competition in Laois up along, U-13, U-14, two minor and four U-21 titles. We actually won seven U-21 titles in a row (I was on four of those teams). Mostly I played either at left half or centre half forward."

Your favourite position?

"Centre half forward because you were right in the middle of all the action. Near midfield, you could go left or right whereas on the wing you were often left stranded with all the play on the other wing. At centre half forward you could dash into the full forward line, out to midfield, or to any side. The playmaker really."

Were you two footed?

"Not originally. After minor I used to spend hours and hours kicking the ball with my weaker left foot. Also in training. I'd have scored more with my better right foot but was always confident if I had to go on to the left foot."

Is the club as successful now?

"Not as much as it was. By the way, our club colours are green and white. We won so much at club level over the past fifteen years that not as much effort was put in at juvenile level."

Your club achievements?

"In all I won ten Laois senior from 1976-1991, four Leinster and one All-Ireland club medal (1983) in the green and white. We beat Clan na Gael (Roscommon) in the final."

Was that the game of your life?

"I suppose it would in the sense that you get great satisfaction out of winning with your own club. You are playing with fellows you grew up with and kicked with since you were nine or ten. To go from U-12, after nearly fifteen years playing, to when you are twenty-six or twenty-seven to win an All-Ireland Final with the same lads was a great thrill. That was played in Cloughjordan (Co. Tipperary) and I can remember the whole aftermath well. The excitement in the Pathe Hotel in Roscrea was huge. The parade into Portlaoise led by the Portlaoise Accordion Band up to our G.A.A. club centre followed by thousands is unforgettable."

The game itself?

"On that day things went well for me too. We won by 0-12 to 2-0. I scored 0-3 from play. We got on top from the word go even though the conditions were poor. The game had originally been fixed for Tullamore but it was unplayable there and had to be switched elsewhere."

Your opinion of the All-Ireland club title?

"A great competition, particularly for the weaker counties who don't win All-Irelands usually. Take the recent successes of Baltinglass and Éire Óg. Also our own. A lot of the weaker counties have strong club teams able to match the top clubs of strong counties. Club success can help county spirit subsequently too, because it gives confidence to the successful club players who are afterwards selected for the county."

The death of Bill Phelan?

"He died in 1993 at fifty years of age. He was the man who set it all up. The whole club was upset and the funeral was a tribute to a great man - the largest I have ever been at. And all the clubs he helped to beat were present too, even from the Austin Stacks club in Tralee who were represented by Tony O'Keeffe and Ger McKenna."

When did you first wear the Laois jersey?

"The first league game against Armagh in Lurgan in 1975. The first Championship was in 1976 against Kildare down in Carlow. We lost to Armagh, my debut wasn't great. The first thing I noticed was that a lot of them were so strong, I was only about nineteen at the time and not much more than eleven stone. We won the game against Kildare and then lost to Dublin in the next game in Tullamore. Kevin Moran and Tommy Drumm started that year. My own opponent was Paddy Reilly. They went on to win the All-Ireland."

Your career with Laois?

"From 1976 to 1987. My last Championship game was against Meath in Portlaoise, which we lost by five points to a team which went on to win the All-Ireland."

Should Laois have done better?

"We won the National Football League in 1986. I had left the scene in 1984 because I wasn't too happy with the set-up as regards management and training and had lost interest. The new manager, Kieran Brennan, had a good personality and a good way with players and he gave us a feeling we could win something and we did. I came back in 1986 to that new set-up."

Why did you leave it there after that?

"After winning the National Football League we met Wicklow down in Aughrim in the Championship six weeks later. Nothing went right for us that day. The venue didn't help. There was poor stewarding of the crowds who kept moving in on the pitch. We had two players sent off (one being myself). Wicklow played a very physical game. Three players, two Laois and one Wicklow, were sent off in the first ten minutes and after that we were backpedalling. It was frustration on my part and that defeat was a huge disappointment as we had high hopes of adding to the League success."

Things seemed to have improved for Laois in recent times?

"Richie Connor has established a good structure. He knows what it takes to win All-Irelands. I personally would love to be younger and to be able to play under him. I have great respect for him having played against him for many years at club and county level. I have great time for him and he has good talent here in Laois at his disposal."

Laois always had that talent?

"Laois always had but he is getting them together. A good set of forwards, good defence and midfield. A small bit of luck and Laois could go places."

Great Laois players now or before? Who did you look up to as you started off?

"The players I looked up to as I started were Bobby Millar of Éire Óg fame in 1993, John Conway, who played for Laois and Leinster, Eamonn Whelan, my own clubman, Colm Browne, who came up along with me. Johnny Lawlor of Emo impressed me a lot. I never saw Jack Kenna play but I heard enough about him. I actually met him once two years ago when visiting Tullamore Hospital to get a pin out of my leg which I had broken during a local League game against Timahoe. I got it out and my wife had gone down shopping. I was on crutches at the time and, it being a sunny day, I hopped out and sat on the wall to wait for her to return. While there, this car stopped and the driver hopped out and asked was I Tom Prendergast. And though I had never met him in my life, I spontaneously replied, 'Are you Jack Kenna?' and it was Jack. He sat up on the wall and we chatted away. We knew each other from photographs I suppose."

Breaking a leg must have been a shattering experience?

"I went for a ball with a couple of players and one of the Timahoe players fell across my leg and it snapped and the pain of it was something else."

The best Laois player of today?

"Martin Dempsey is a very solid full back, committed and safe. He'd never let you down. Of the younger fellows Michael Lawlor of Emo and Leo Turley are good and I have great hopes for Hugh Emerson. I think he'll be great. But of all the players I played with, Eamonn Whelan of my own club would be number one. I won about eight Laois titles with Eamonn. He was a stylist and a mighty fielder, great spring, lovely solo and a special way of kicking the ball."

Your own style always impressed. Did you work on perfecting it?

"I always liked looking at players who always looked well. One man I'd pick out here was Willie Bryan of Offaly. A lovely way about himself on the field. He always looked the part. I would have worked a lot with the ball on my own in the field. Hours and hours kicking and shooting. I'd have two or three footballs and I'd often try to get some young lad living nearby to kick the balls back out to me. I never took frees so it was always off the hands. Any style I had was natural but I worked hard at the game. I had good pace with the ball over a short distance and this was a great help. Players who have it are Martin McHugh, Joyce McMullen and David Beggy. The latter has not that much style but he has marvellous pace."

Is Tommy Murphy still talked about?

"As a young lad growing up he was the player most talked about in Laois. A legend."

Do they talk too much in the past in Laois and in other unsuccessful counties?

"I suppose if you don't have that much success you tend to do so. Counties winning All-Irelands or Provincial titles have plenty of fellows to talk about. Every decade would have players for the young lads of that county to look up to. You mentioned Tommy Murphy. The Delaneys are special in Laois still. Bill is alive still. Jack was involved in the Portlaoise club and his sons all played for the club. They hailed from Stradbally."

Your greatest opponents?

"The two best I suppose would have been Tommy Drumm of Dublin and Pat Fitzgerald of Offaly. They could read the game so well. Could anticipate your next move. See what was developing, even the way the ball was going to be played to you. You'd have to try and be one step ahead of them mentally as well."

Greatest players seen?

"Brian Mullins, John Egan, Pat Spillane, Jack O'Shea and Matt Connor. Another player I always liked was David Hickey."

Biggest thrill from playing the game?

"Getting a good score. Kicking a point from a very awkward angle or shooting a point after going forty or fifty yards and in the process sidestepping three or four players. Goals too. As a forward you'd always enjoy scoring."

Your greatest score?

"Against Austin Stacks of Kerry in the 1977 All-Ireland club semi-final in O'Moore Park, Portlaoise. It was my second goal against them that day, having already scored one first half. We were a point or two down with about ten minutes to go and I took a ball on the run from under the stand, carried it twenty or thirty yards and shot to the roof of the net from twenty yards or so. Unfortunately, they came back to win the game by two or three points. But they had great players like Ger Power, John, Ger and Tony O'Keeffe."

Can the game of Gaelic football be improved?

"The definition of the fouls is not too clear. So much dragging and pulling at the moment. Teams are so well organised now. Defences can foul so much. A defender could foul an opponent seven or eight times and not be sent off. The personal foul war is largely ignored now. If that could be cleared up it would help the game which is basically good, has plenty of scores and compared to a soccer match is far more exciting for spectators. A good Championship game is well worth seeing."

Any pet hates within the G.A.A?

"There is much talk of opening up G.A.A. grounds to other organisations. At times you'd feel they should do it but you could not expect that every club grounds would automatically open up its facilities to other sports. That wouldn't be fair at all. But on certain occasions particularly where a soccer club wouldn't have such facilities on a once off basis, I'd see no harm in it."

Your opinion on the moving managers, to coin a phrase!?

"I'm all for it. A great thing for the G.A.A. particularly for the weaker counties. First of all if you bring in people with proven abilities as players or coaches, the players will look up to them and listen."

Will one of these train an All-Ireland team now?

"In the next few years definitely."

The Open Draw?

"No, I wouldn't favour it across the board. There is something special about the Provincial set-up but I'd favour the Open Draw within the provinces. I wouldn't like to see the Provincial finals being lost to us."

The best footballer around now?

"Mickey Linden of Down. Great skills and pace. Can score left and right. Natural talent abounding."

Favourtie sports writer?

"David Walsh writes some fine stuff."

Are you a sports fan?

"Yes, I watch all sports. I like rugby. I prefer it to soccer. It's an amateur sport and they give it everything. Not that I mind players being paid. But then I look at soccer. You see players getting a tip and they are down roaring and screaming often being paid £5000 a week when in similar circumstances a G.A.A. player would be embarrassed to lie down like that."

Your one wish for the G.A.A. in 1993?

"Laois to win a senior All-Ireland, of course."

Refereeing ambitions?

"No, not refereeing. Coaching, yes, in the future."

Dirty players were anathema always?

"I never like players carrying on in a dirty manner. Players are so fit nowadays that a big strong back can get stuck in to a forward, stay with him, hassle him, intimidate him. The same back doesn't have to be particularly good but it's a lot easier for the back to dominate. It's harder for the forward. He has to turn, twist, work into positions for scores. A forward is a sitting duck for these guys who are favoured by the game and its rules. Unfortunately, this type of back is becoming more numerous. Most counties have these athletes as I'd call them. They wouldn't be good footballers. They are there to do one job and that is to intimidate certain players on certain teams. That needs to be tackled. It annoys me to see a forward getting a belt while the ball is at the other end of the field and the umpires observing it and doing nothing about it. Sometimes they just don't want to see it."

Tom's family trauma?

"We have two daughters, Sarah and Kate and my wife Antoinette, who is a teacher, has a great interest in the G.A.A. and goes to games regularly. Always did. We suffered much trauma some years back when my youngest daugher, Kate, had to have a liver transplant in Birmingham in 1989. We knew nobody over there and eventually met an Irish family, Con and Phil Cunningham, a great G.A.A. family (Con is from near Tuam and Phil is a Mayo woman) who were so kind to us when we needed it. We ended up staying five months with them in Birmingham and later on, after the transplant, for another operation which necessitated a three months stay. Kate is well now and is four and a half years old and the apple of our eye. But that was a traumatic time. It was through the G.A.A. we met Con and we are extremely grateful to the Portlaoise G.A.A. club and the Laois-Offaly Gárdaí for their help in that critical time. They really turned up trumps and you saw another side to the G.A.A. and your club and your working colleagues. Happily it all ended well."

Left:
Willie Bryan - 'a lovely way about him on the field'.

Right:
Tommy Drumm- 'great opponent'.

Below: Tom Prendergast with ball in action in a Laois Senior Football Championship game against Ballylinan in 1987.

Chapter 18

Eddie Keher

Of Kilkenny

Eddie Keher, great Kilkenny hurling stylist, has always been one of the most relaxed of men. When I visited him in his living quarters over the Callan Branch of the A.I.B., of which he is Manager, he was, as always, relaxed and chirpy. He was about to leave for his native Inistioge, where he coaches the home team. He still loves hurling hugely and likes nothing better after a day's work than to be involved out there on the field with hurling and with hurlers.

Is hurling a way of life in Kilkenny?

"It has to be. The calendar is drawn up by the matches. Fellows in the county organise their holidays around Leinster Championships, League Finals, All-Ireland Finals and indeed club games."

Is it a drug almost?

"It is. Kilkenny wouldn't be regarded at all, in any stretch of the imagination, as a footballing county. But we don't regard hurling as a superior game. We think it is a great game, the greatest game in the world, but we love football as well."

Could you imagine yourself playing football Eddie?

"I did play football at under-age level and with the colleges. But when you came to a stage where you were involved with hurling and had lots of games at all levels, you tended to drop the football."

Had you always a hurley in your hand in your native Inistioge?

"There wasn't any hurling tradition in my family. My father was from Roscommon and played football. My memory goes back as far as living beside the Ryan family in Inistioge (Mike Ryan was from Slieverue and was a great hurling man and they had three sons just around my age group) and as a youngster of three or four I remember hearing the hurling going on next door. They had a pub and we had a shop and there was a big garden on both sides and a yard at the back. Then the bigger lads would be playing on the square, which was in the village. The square was railed in and, if you looked at it now, you'd wonder how the hell you hurled in it. There was a monument and a fountain in the middle of the square and we used to hurl around it. That's where we started."

Can you remember your first puck of the ball?

"Not particularly. I do remember when we started off holding the hurl the wrong way, left on top, like golfers hold their clubs, and I remember myself and the elder of the Ryans, Miko, out on the square and Jimmy Phelan and Fr. Michael Noonan coming along and telling us we were holding the hurl the wrong way."

National School days?

"One of the things that has been very good to Kilkenny hurling over the years is the contribution of the teachers in the schools. These teachers did and are doing a marvellous job to promote hurling in the county. We had one such teacher, Martin Walsh, and there were a few around the South locality bordering on Wexford, notably Mick Moore in Graiguenamanagh and Peadar Laffan in Thomastown. There was a school's League but apart from that we used to play a lot of inter-school games."

On to St. Kieran's College and the influence of Fr. Tommy Maher?

"Fr. Maher arrived in my second year in the college. I remember Miko Ryan, my next door hurling companion, telling me during the holidays that Fr. Maher was to be our new Dean and had done wonders for hurling in Crumlin, producing players like the Boothman brothers. So, Fr. Maher arrived amid great anticipation, following a period when St. Kieran's were down and immediately took on the teams and changed the whole scene. I made the senior team in my second year but we were beaten. We went on then to win the senior All-Ireland twice in 1957 and 1959. So I was on the senior team for four years."

Would Kieran's be the cathedral of hurling for you?

"Oh it would absolutely, and particularly under Fr. Tommy. He had a whole new scientific approach to the game. We worked on it and studied it. I remember going up to his room one day and found him weighing hurling balls - sliothars, looking at hurleys, trying to improve them. He studied other games at the time. One of his other qualities was that he could mould players and develop them into positions and get the best out of them."

Was he the greatest hurling influence on your career?

"In 1957, Paddy Grace approached Fr. Maher to coach the Kilkenny senior team. They won it that year and it was a team moulded by Fr. Maher. Most of them were from junior hurling clubs and they beat Waterford in the final."

Getting back to days in Kieran's and the first All-Ireland colleges success in 1957?

"Ted Carroll, the County Secretary now, and his twin brother, Mick, Miko Ryan from next door, Ollie Harrington, Martin Campion, now a Monsignor, Dick Walsh from Thomastown, Martin Walsh, a fellow third year, brother of Tom the forward for Kilkenny, were all team members."

Were you captain in your senior year of 1959?

"Yes. In the final we beat Tipperary C.B.S. and that was a big honour."

Returning to Fr. Maher's coaching days with the county?

"When he took over, his coaching methods raised many eyebrows. His theory was that if you do the simple things well, perfect them, there will be a few players who will do the extraordinary things. He had them out handpassing in 1957 and I remember hearing of the remarks of some of the diehards 'What is he at?' They couldn't believe this was training. I'll give one instance of his method. I remember in 1957, the Kieran's against Flannan's final, the training he did, he had me on the wing where I had plenty of speed. We trained a couple of evenings a week and he kept me several evenings after training with our full forward, Dick Dowling, later to become a Fine Gael T.D. He had me for about half an hour soloing down the left wing in towards the middle and handpassing it in to Dick. Just the two of us on the field again, again, again, and again. Then when playing Flannan's, we had only scored two points in the first half and about fifteen minutes into the second half we hadn't done any better and they led by eight points. We were out of it. Beaten. Then I got a ball, soloed down the left wing, programmed to do so! Handpassed it to Dick, and into the net. Did it a second time, was fouled on the way in - twenty-one yards free. A goal. Third time, did it again. Was fouled again. Another goal. We got three goals from the ploy and won the day."

Your minor days?

"I played minor then for three years 1957-1959, having been a substitute in 1956."

The hurlers you admired as a youngster, Eddie?

"My first hero would have been Jim Langton. When I was out hurling on the Inistioge square, I was always Jim Langton. Later on Sean Clohessey was the hurler I admired and wanted so much to be like. My dream was that when Sean would retire I might get his place. As it turned out I played with him from 1959-1963 when he retired. Christy Ring was a national hero and was the hurler of hurlers for everyone. I wouldn't have seen Christy in Munster finals or his last All-Ireland win in 1954. We heard of him from Micheál O'Hehir and from the papers. I played against him in the League final of 1962, when he had a great game at full-forward, though we won. He retired then in 1963. We were bordering Wexford and they were the team of the 1950's. The Rackards, Nicky, Bobby and Willie - fine big men - Ned Wheeler, the late Mick Morrissey, his namesake Jim, Tim Flood, Nick O'Donnell. That was some team."

Your freetaking skills. The deliberate pick-up. Did you hone that yourself?

"Fr. Maher never imposed anything on you. He just gave you guidelines. I was the freetaker in Kieran's. I hadn't any particular style, as such. I did my own thing. Just went out, lifted the ball and tried to score and so on. He was always aiming for a higher success rate. He emphasised the importance of lifting the ball properly for any success to be achieved with consistency. So he made me practise this and it worked fairly well for me. Over the years, I changed my style but I always realised that the most important thing was to lift the ball properly. And that got my full concentration."

Your senior debut?

"The 1959 replay was my Championship debut. I had been brought on for two games between the draw and the replay."

Your last game for Kilkenny?

"Against Wexford in 1977, in the National Hurling League."

Did you play a tougher game as you grew older?

"I never advocated any sort of dirty play, but I felt that being big, strong and fast, I had no fears of using my body. I tended to take on the backs with the ball. Earlier on I would probably have avoided tackles. As the years went on, I went into them. Particularly in the late 1960's, Kilkenny were short of a bit of toughness in the forwards and I'd say we did change our style into a tougher type of forward play."

Was it successful?

"It was. We overcame Tipperary in an All-Ireland in 1967 which would have been a milestone as far as Kilkenny were concerned. It was forty years since we beat them in a Championship game. Now if you went back on the records, they didn't meet that often but at the same time the thing was there: 'Ye'll never beat Tipperary in a hard game', and it was getting bigger."

The great Kilkenny players of your time?

"Sean Clohessey I've mentioned. Ollie Walsh was a guy who really made the position of goalkeeping a sought after position. I remember when we used to be arranging matches as youngsters the last fellow always was saddled with, 'Will you stand in goal

Johnny?' It used to be the pits to be asked to stand in goal. But Ollie made a whole new glamour position of goalkeeping. As a result, Kilkenny produced a whole series of good goalkeepers. 'Chunky' O'Brien, Frank Cummins, Kieran Purcell, Pat Delaney, Mick Crotty, Mick Brennan and Billy Fitzpatrick were just coming on the scene in 1975."

If you had to choose one from them all who would it be?

"If I needed a man on the team to have a complete influence, Frank Cummins would be the one."

The man behind the scenes?

"Paddy Grace was a unique character. There will never be another Paddy Grace and that's a pity. He was a player's man. Always took care of them. He was the man who always let in youngsters to play at half-time in Nowlan Park. All for hurling and the player."

The great thrills of the game of hurling?

"The game itself, of course. I loved scoring. As a forward I regarded it as my job to score or make scores. I loved to see the ball hitting the net or sailing over the bar. Just loved that feeling whether it was in a tournament or All-Ireland Final. I enjoyed the thrill of hitting the ball and, as a forward, angling myself for a score."

Personal thrills?

"The first All-Ireland in 1963 was tremendous. Winning the first in Croke Park is special. I was captain in 1969. I was on the team from 1959, let's say, and our club the Rower-Inistioge wouldn't have been regarded as a hurling stronghold. And we won the junior Championship and then went senior and we won the Kilkenny Senior Hurling Championship in 1968 which meant I was captain for 1969. You know when you are just one fellow on the county team for years and you're playing with all these lads and getting nothing and suddenly they come up to senior and win it and then there are four of them on the panel for the All-Ireland Final. The whole honour is being brought into the little village."

Are you still as keen as ever on hurling?

"Probably more so. I'm training the home team, The Rower-Inistioge this year, going back to the home place. They are gone back to Intermediate level for the past five or six years and I'm trying to get them back up to senior status again."

Resumé of career?

"Six All-Ireland medals, ten Leinster, five All Star Awards, one Kilkenny Senior Hurling, two All-Ireland Colleges, four Leinster Colleges, ten Railway Cup medals and a Texaco Award Winner. The first All-Ireland medal of 1963 would be my most precious award."

Scoring achievements?

"I used to have the record score for an All-Ireland Final 2-11 against Tipperary in 1971, a day we were beaten, but Nicky English has it now since the final against Antrim in 1989. His was 2-12, I think."

There was a famous photograph of yourself and Nicky Rackard taken at a National Hurling League game. What was that about?

"I had passed him on the number of scores for a year, a record he held, in an actual National Hurling League game against Wexford in 1971 in Nowlan Park. I was two or three points behind his record coming into the game and passed his record during the game. He came in to congratulate me after the game. So big of him, and a photographer was there to capture the moment. I phoned Nicky English myself to congratulate him on beating my All-Ireland record, about a week after his All-Ireland win. Scoring was important, the amount didn't matter."

Did the euphoria ever invade your privacy?

"Not really. In Kilkenny people don't fall over you because you're an All-Ireland man. They take you for granted. There are so many around with All-Ireland medals that they don't go overboard at all. It isn't a major thing."

Greatest opponent?

"Could I name a few people? I always had the most difficulty with good ball playing backs. Lads like Mick Burns of Tipperary, who hurled the ears off me in 1964, John Nolan and Vinny Staples of Wexford, Eamonn Russell of Clare - all hurlers and very hard to beat. I had great tussles with Willie Murphy of Wexford, with whom I'm great friends since, even though people, who remembered us playing, might think we were deadly enemies. Len Gaynor of Tipperary and 'Fan' Larkin from here in Kilkenny, whom I met in club games, all great players."

Greatest players today?

"Nicholas English, two or three years ago, was great, but has had injury problems since. Jimmy Barry Murphy was superb too. Today, D.J. Carey is one I admire tremendously. He is a lovely chap for a start. Tremendous skill and he practises all the time. He did this growing up too. He has great speed, great off the mark. Dedication to the game. He has all the skills. And he is still only a boy. A great ambassador for the game. Brian Corcoran is a lovely fellow too. And a lovely hurler. And a great ambassador."

Any fears for the game. Will it die?

"I don't think so. I know people are inclined to say that the hurling is not as good as it used to be. I think the game is great. Some great games. And it has all the skills. The game is evolving all the time. People say there is no overhead hurling now. There is plenty of overhead hurling now but it is done with a purpose. I remember the Wexford team bringing in the catch rather than the overhead hurling. I saw that catch coming into the game. No one ever put up their hand for the ball before Wexford developed the skill of being able to protect their hand with the hurl and catch it even though the opponents were pulling. Other teams had to develop an antidote to that."

Did any other skill come in since the catch?

"All the skills are still used. We perfected the handpass under Fr. Maher."

Would you ban the kicking of goals?

"No. Nor would I take a handpassed goal out of the game and it was taken out. What I was afraid of and I have spoken at Congress on this. Hurling as a game, that has been made great, gave room for the individual and for the heroics. If you keep closing off the options, you weaken the game."

Your days in management?

"I took over Kilkenny in 1979 and was lucky to be in charge when we beat Galway in the final of that year. I was manager in 1980 when Offaly made the breakthrough and beat us in the Leinster final of that year. I was back again later. At the time I enjoyed it mostly because it was nice to maintain the contact at that close level, but I don't think I'd enjoy it now. The pressure is too much."

Is there a definite Kilkenny style of hurling?

"There is. The priority with Kilkenny is to try and develop all the skills that can be used at any one time. These are developed at juvenile level. Mostly right hand on top and being able to hit left and right equally. Use the ball and let the ball do the work. I love to see the game spreading. Take the rise of Down and I hope that Kilkenny have played their part in developing other teams."

Your greatest score?

"The one I most enjoyed getting was in a game against Dublin in Nowlan Park where Martin Coogan took a sideline ball and as it sailed across the goal about twenty-one yards out, I came in from the back, jumped up very high, trapped the ball on to my hand and shot it to the net."

The game of your life?

"The 1972 final against Cork. We were down nine points in that game with twenty minutes to go and sort of out of it, I suppose, and came back again and won by eight or nine points. It was a marvellous comeback in a great game to play in. Cork were brilliant first half. We had no answer to them. Full of great scores which is what the game is all about. Pat Delaney nearly made the ball talk that day."

Nano Brennan?

"She is dead now poor Nano. Our greatest ever supporter. She was from Callan but lived in Kilkenny and I remember her from my own minor days. Always at training. Knew us all, once we wore the black and amber. We all loved her and we were all at her funeral. She got the tributes she deserved. At the funeral Mass the McCarthy Cup was brought up among other hurling memorabilia in tribute."

Above: Eddie talking hurling to Muhammed Ali

Below: Three Kilkenny greats - Paddy Grace, Jimmy Langton and Fr. Tommy Maher

Chapter 19

Tony Doran

The Man from Boolavogue

That is what Pádhraic Puirséal, that most lovable, racy, *Irish Press* writer, dubbed the red-haired Tony Doran, when he first hit the headlines as a youngster in 1968, donning the mantle of Nicky Rackard, another Pádhraic Puirséal favourite. Since his one and only All-Ireland senior medal of 1968, it is correct to say that Tony Doran became one of the most loved hurlers, making his club, Buffer's Alley, famous throughout the land in much the same way as the Mackeys did for Ahane, or the Quigleys and Rackards did for Rathnure. There is something special about Wexford hurling. Like Galway in the past, they have had many hard luck stories, beaten by a point in dubious circumstances. Always the underdog. Big sporting men. The 'yellow bellies' are the most popular of men. Tony Doran for years and years was their hero, their inspiration. When I visited him at his farm in Monagreine, Monamolin, I found a G.A.A. mad family. The sideboard is laden with trophies. Tony won the G.A.A. One Hundred Questions quiz in the 1992 Christmas issue of *Hogan Stand* magazine. That wouldn't surprise you after a chat with this cheerful ever-smiling Wexford star, who at forty-six years of age will still rally to the club colours if needed and enjoys playing in the masters' competition masterminded by former President Dr. Mickey Loftus some years back.
It was difficult finding Tony. Earlier in the day he suggested a route through "The Harrow" but I drove through Oulart - enemy country - and got final directions at the impressive Buffer's Alley G.A.A. field.

I put it to him that it was difficult to find him.

"A hard place to find alright. It's only a very small place on the map."

Your way of life is wrapped around hurling?

"Everything is worked around the hurling and vice versa. I live here about three miles from the field and Boolavogue is another three miles away. This area is actually Buffer's Alley as such, an area taking in a few townlands."

Your first interest in hurling?

"I can't remember when I wasn't interested. Growing up in Wexford in the 1950's it couldn't be otherwise. My father was involved with the local club when we were growing up and he played the game himself for the club. In fact he played junior for Wexford in the late twenties, early thirties. There were five of us in the family and I was the second youngest. Four played hurling. Colm, who also played for Wexford was the youngest of us. Bill was the oldest and played with the club for years before we started. Joe, two years older than me, also played."

Was hurling very much part of the Doran household?

"Very much so. The local club trained in a field of ours just across the road from our house. It used to switch around from one field to another. Maybe one field would be tilled one year and we'd switch to the one beside it."

When were you noticed first?

"Back in 1956, there was a competition started by Nicky Rackard, called the Rackard Rural School's League and it was in that I first started to play."

Did wearing the Wexford jersey for the first time mean a lot?

"Oh God, it surely did. The first time I played for Wexford in the Championship was minor in 1963. We played Laois in Croke Park. Started at centre half forward and we won the minor All-Ireland that year, Wexford's first ever minor title. I played at centre half forward mostly and full forward then. That was a big breakthrough. Ned Power was the trainer and he was the one we all looked up to."

Others from that 1963 minor team?

"Vinny Staples, Mick Kinsella, the current County Secretary and Pat Quigley."

The people who really influenced you as you grew up?

"Nicky Rackard was the one we all looked up to at that time. When you'd be out at the back of the house playing, you'd be Nicky Rackard one evening, someone else the next. Nicky was the king. None of them were from this area and we wouldn't have been hitting up against any of them."

Do Wexford people realise how popular they are nationally?

"A lot of that came from the team of the 1950's. Big strong men who came up from nowhere in a football county and became immensely popular. We are worn out talking about hard luck defeats."

Your first Senior Hurling Championship game with Wexford?

"Not until 1967 and Laois again. We won that and Kilkenny beat us in the Leinster final. It was close enough, but in the end they won by about four points."

The 1968 story?

"We beat Kilkenny in the Leinster final that year. To beat Kilkenny was always a thrill but at that time in the 1960's, we ended up about fifty-fifty in games with them. So it wasn't a nine-day wonder. We always met often over the years but it wasn't as big a deal to beat them then as it would be now."

Would the 1968 final be the game of your life?

"I suppose it would, being the only All-Ireland we won but at the time I was only in my second year playing Championship hurling with Wexford and it was a bit too early in my career to appreciate it."

Do you regret that nothing like that ever happened since for Wexford?

"I honestly would have loved to win an All-Ireland at a later stage."

Your career with Wexford?

"From 1967 to 1984. Eighteen Championships in all. I had played in the League and other things for Wexford before the 1967 Championship."

Does the club Buffer's Alley mean a lot to you?

"It meant an awful lot to me because it had come from nothing. I remember when I started with Buffer's Alley in 1962, we were just a very poor junior club. We won our first Wexford Senior title in 1968 (a great year that), having lost the 1967 final to Rathnure. So it was Rathnure man, Dan Quigley, who captained Wexford in 1968. That rivalry with Rathnure developed over the years since. We have won eleven Wexford Senior titles in all. We only beat Rathnure in one final, in 1988, so it took us over twenty years to do it. We went on to win an All-Ireland club title in 1989, the 1988-1989 title. I was just a few weeks short of being forty-three years old. Definitely that was the greatest kick I ever got out of playing hurling."

Take us through what a county final means to a club, Tony.

"The build-up around the area, especially in the early days when it was new to us, was huge. We'd have a reasonably big following but we are working from a small base. The population in the area would be about fifteen hundred. We'd have reasonable support from neighbouring junior clubs as well."

The great men of the club?

"When I started, the first ones were Tom Donoghoe, who is still active, the late Tom O'Leary, Tom Butler who actually died at a county final, Ger Dempsey, father of Tom the county star. It all seems to run in families. My own brother Bill was involved too. My father, Willie was beginning to take a back seat at that stage. He died watching his four sons playing in the 1970 County Senior final. He never used to show his excitement. Kept it all bottled up. We won easily that day but I remember seeing a spectator being stretchered away and a very worried looking cousin of mine, Pat Nolan, walking alongside and knowing it must be my Dad. They told us at half-time he had a turn but I feared the worst. I don't remember much of the aftermath of that final."

Do you miss it after giving it up?

"It's a big difference looking at, rather than playing in a game. You always think that if you were there yourself, you'd do this and that but out in the stand watching, you can't do a lot, can you?!"

Do you still hurl a bit with them?

"I played junior last year and we were beaten in the County final. I was forty-five at the time. I had been playing for the Wexford O-40's and that's how I came to be involved again."

The great thrill of the game of hurling for you?

"Playing as a forward, the greatest thrill was to see the net shake. Every forward thinks he should score a goal every time."

Your greatest score?

"The one that put us in front in the 1968 All-Ireland. That was something special because the game was after being level from about half way through the second half from the time Paul Lynch scored the goal from the '21' to even it up. It see-sawed then for about eight or nine minutes without a score. Then I got the goal with about seven or eight minutes to go to put us in front. Another one was in the 1976 Leinster final against Kilkenny. They had beaten us for five years in a row. It was early in the second half and we had led at half time by six points and, of course, everyone expected the usual Kilkenny comeback was going to come and I remember getting a goal five or ten minutes into the half which killed it off as a contest. The only other one sticking out would be the 1984 Leinster semi-final, against Kilkenny too. We were complete underdogs and I had just made a comeback in time for that Championship. Again it was level and with a minute or two to go I got a goal that won the game."

Did you overdo the palming of the ball for scores?

"I palmed a good few goals but the greater majority of them were scored with the hurley."

Was it wrong to ban the palming of scores?

"I'd think so. Every change that has been made seems to have been made to cut down on the amount of scores. Making it more difficult for forwards to score. When I started you would charge the goalie. That has gone and maybe quite rightly so, leaving that area to him. Then they banned the dropping of the hurley to pass the ball. Now that was acceptable too. Next one was the banning of the palmed goal. Now you see so many kicked goals. I hope they don't ban that too. The banning of the palmed scores has led to controversy over penalties a forward should or should not have got. A back can easily tie up the hurley of an opponent at close quarters and it leaves him with no alternative. Kicking the ball is both more dangerous and untidy than palming it."

Still a Pioneer and non-smoker?

"Never drank or smoked and hope I don't at this stage."

Greatest opponent?

"I think your most difficult opponent is always your next one. In club games in Wexford Dan Quigley was a very effective back. Two other great club stalwarts were Jimmy Pender and Georgie O'Connor of Faythe Harriers. At county level, you had an awful lot of very effective full-backs like Pa Dillon, Brian Cody and Nicky Orr of Kilkenny. Nicky wasn't a great hurler but was a very effective back. Pat Hartigan, Martin Doherty and before him Pat McDonnell. Eugene Coughlan of Offaly was very deceptive. Much faster than he appeared to be and a good ball player as well. He was one of the best to tap the ball out of the way."

Rough play?

"I never favoured it. Hit hard but I hope I never made bad friends. You'd have tough clashes with everyone but at the end of the day, it is all over when the match is over. I never took a grievance with me. I'd like to think that I could talk today to anyone I ever played on about a lot of what happened between us."

Injuries?

"Very lucky. Very few injuries. Never wore a helmet. Not a lot of stitches, just a few here and there. Broke a thumb and a finger, strange to say, not on the hand I was catching the ball with and both happened against Galway in different games."

The best Wexford hurler to play with him?

"If you needed a score, it's a forward you'd look to. If you needed to hold on, it's a back you'd need. Back in the first half of my career, one of the men to rally us was Phil Wilson, out around the middle of the field. Very inspirational in that way. On the club scene, I'd have to include our own Bill Murphy. In the 1968 County final, our first ever win, we were down eight points with seven minutes to go and he scored 2-3 for a one point win for Buffer's Alley. He pulled us out of the hole that day."

Greatest hurler seen?

"Mick Roche of Tipperary. I started at centre half forward on him for the first twenty minutes of the 1968 final. He was as good a hurler as I have ever seen ."

The best today?

"The ones pulling games out of the fire for the past few years are Pat Fox of Tipperary and D.J. Carey of Kilkenny. I'm not going to say Pat Fox is the greatest hurler in the game but he has done an awful lot to win games for Tipperary."

Are Wexford on the way back?

"We had a few great chances in the 1993 National Hurling League final of winning something. We are there or thereabouts. We lack a bit of the killer punch when we have a team on the ropes."

Is the game of hurling improving?

"Yes and no. There is a much greater emphasis on physical fitness than when I started. That time a few laps around the field and a few sprints sufficed. There is less emphasis on skill now. I always preferred training with the ball. You had to do a certain amount of the other thing as well but an awful lot was done with the ball. Now they put too much into the physical end of it."

Did you hurl beside your home?

"You'd always have hurled against the wall of the house. You'd break the window now and again but you'd get over that. I remember one evening when the goal was between the two windows and I hit the post that day! A costly job that one! Clean through it."

Is there a Wexford style of hurling?

"The Wexford style of hurling always seemed to be - pick and lift the whole time. We have been criticised for it fairly often down through the years. The team of the 1950's - all big men - could play that type of game. Later on with a smaller team we tended to play the same type of game. Sending high balls into the forwards. They seem to be changing a certain amount away from that now. Personally, I never minded high balls coming in. I won't ask you what way would you like the ball. My answer to that always was 'often'! The passing game is coming in and that can be overdone as well. Passing to a purpose is good. I always liked to see a team moving forward in a passing game not across the field."

Anecdote?

"One year on an All Star trip to America with Fan Larkin we were out pucking a ball around. Light hearted exercise killing time and that. Someone challenged Fan to a race to the other end of the field. 'Oh be God you won't,' says Fan, 'but I'll tell you what, I'll race you to the twenty one yards line. That's as far as I ever do have to go'."

Railway Cup and All Star?

"I have seven Railway Cup medals and one All Star award in 1976. The Railway Cup looks to be dead, which is a pity. I always loved playing in it. But the interest in it is dying. The club All-Irelands have taken over from it but it's a pity there can't be a place somewhere for it."

Micheál O'Hehir?

"O'Hehir was an institution. I can remember the days of being tuned in to a bad radio. The dry and wet battery type and O'Hehir's voice keeping you in touch with everything that was going on. He was part of the hot days of our summer youth. Of the present media-men, I'd be very fond of Micheál Ó Muircheartaigh and love his commentaries."

Little annoyances at the moment?

"All-ticket games are very awkward for people. No need for it at all in some cases. I go around to games every evening of the week and usually have four youngsters with me. To bring them to an all-ticket game you'd have to fork out for five tickets before you left home. That's not on. I hate to see the traditional things that were part of the scene being discarded. Like keeping the crowd out of Croke Park after finals and big games. They are part and parcel of the G.A.A. and we are dressing ourselves up too much in that way."

Refereeing?

"A very difficult job. We are all good at the job when we sit in the stands or out on the sideline. The annoying thing about it, when I played was, you'd get away with a thing today but wouldn't the next day."

The game of your life?

"Winning the club All-Ireland was the one for me. Possibly at the time it came because it was something that I thought had passed me by. Here we were doing it for a small community and to see the joy it brought to all the people in this one little area was a great feeling. We were a club which came out of the ashes and here we were the best in the land. That was the crowning of everything. We have our own club-house now and lovely field just up the road from me. My sons are playing the game, though they're young yet. I hope they go on to get the same enjoyment from the game as I did."

> *Gaelic games have a high profile in the Doran household. One of the younger lads, who has G.A.A. heroes in every county, after a row with his older brother, set off upstairs to pack his bags and leave. When his mother enquired as he raced upstairs where he was off to he said, "I'm going off to live with Larry Tompkins!"*

Above, left: An action shot from the 1976 semi-final against Galway. Joe McDonagh of Galway on the ball.
right: Tony with a B&I monthly award.

Chapter 20

Robbie O'Malley

Of Meath

He is taller than he looks on the field of play. He follows in the great tradition of Meath cornerbacks, like Mick O'Brien and Kevin McConnell. Firm handshake, forthright in his opinions, we met in his plushly appointed bar in the centre of Navan town. The place abounds with photographs of Meath's recent glory years. Not all of Robbie. All the heroes of Sean Boylan's great successes and a place of honour for the late Noel Keating's photograph beside a version of the "West Clare Railway".

How did it start for you, Robbie?

"I suppose it was primarily at school along with school friends. There was never a really strong tradition in the immediate family at home. My father played a bit of club football or school football in Castlebar, where he was from and my mother's brothers in Castlecoote, Fuerty, Co. Roscommon were all accomplished footballers. I went to Donacarney National School, not far outside Drogheda."

Club days?

"The local club was St. Colmcille's, a club very much into youth policy, which was fortunate for me. That area just outside Drogheda was a growing area twenty years ago with improved road facilities etc. Dublin was becoming ever nearer."

The people behind that club?

"In particular we had Pat O'Neill, a former Chairman of the Meath County Board, who was one of the prime movers behind the club's youth policy. The club won its first Meath juvenile title at U-14 level in 1973. In 1979 we won our next U-14 title. I was on that team. We went on then to win U-16 in 1980 and 1981, minor in 1982 and 1983 and I was with them in that great run."

Secondary schooldays?

"I went to St. Mary's C.B.S., in Drogheda. The big influences there were a couple of Christian Brothers namely Br. Gerry Carberry who later went to Tuam, Br. Daithi Kennedy, a Galway man, and in particular a lay teacher named Pat Colgan, an Offaly man, who had a great interest in young lads and football."

Young team mates at the time?

"The most obvious one was Bernard Flynn. We were born and reared together. Other lads included the Carr brothers, Kieran and Joseph, Mark O'Neill, Joe Stafford."

Had you a desire then to wear the Meath jersey?

"I suppose down the road we had this fairy tale dream Bernard Flynn and myself. We used to sit at class together and we dreamt about playing for Meath together someday."

What was your debut in the Meath jersey?

"I'll never forget the first county representation with the Meath U-14 team. A clubman of ours and a good under-age mentor Paddy Brannigan brought me to a game one day and he said to me in the car coming home 'You know, generally, if you stick at it, they'll stick with the same players right up through the ranks.' I suppose he planted the seed that day."

Minor days?

"I was fortunate to play minor for Meath for three years 1981-1983. Left corner back, midfield and right corner back were the positions respectively."

Were Meath emerging as a football force then?

"I think they were. At senior level there were a few shattering defeats in 1981 and 1982 at first round level. This was a low, as Meath had run Dublin very closely in the Dublin glory years. Then along came Sean Boylan to take over in late 1982 and things began to take shape. He brought in a whole new training regime, new disciplines and all of a sudden Meath qualified for Division one of the National Football League. We went on to draw with Dublin in the first round of the Leinster Championship and were beaten in extra time in the replay after two great games which had the whole country talking."

Your breakthrough onto the senior team?

"After minor, I played U-21 for a few years. I finished playing minor in July 1983 and was called on to the panel in September 1983. Things were starting to move."

Family background?

"My father works as a technician with Telecom Éireann. A very keen golfer, that is probably where I got my competitive spirit."

County Senior Debut?

"My first competitive game was in the National Football League against Down in Newry in February, 1984. I played at right half forward."

Who was it saw a future in you?

"The biggest influence, motivator and my idol really, in the years before that was Matt Kerrigan. I certainly saw an awful lot in him and I'd like to think it cut both ways. He was involved very much with coaching minor teams at the time and it was more so his manner than what he did specifically at coaching which made the impact. He was very laid back, yet was great to get the message across to young people."

Back to the debut?

"That day against Down was cold and wet. My opponent was Brendan McGovern of Burren. A great day for me, even though we lost by two points and my first big step on the road. I remember speaking to Sean Boylan beforehand about positions and I told him I'd play anywhere. That's how keen I was."

When did you make the right corner back position your own?

"That took some time. First right half forward, then centre half forward. Then later that year we went on to win the Centenary Cup and in the semi-final I came back to right full back because Phil Smyth got injured. That's how it started. I played in that position on my Championship debut against Westmeath in Mullingar."

Achievements?

"Five Leinster Senior Football Championship medals, two All-Irelands, two Leagues, three All Stars Awards (1987,1988 and 1990) all for right corner back."

Did Bernard Flynn's career take the same course?

"Almost identical. He got on during the same National Football League campaign and we then started the process of travelling to games together. There was a great character from Stamullen named Jim 'Scupps' White, who has been carrying Meath players in his car since 1958. It's his life and he does it out of the goodness of his heart. The Meath team is his family. He carried us everywhere along with players from that area, such as goalkeeper Mickey McQuillan and Philip Smyth before that. He still takes me. There is mighty crack in that car."

When did Meath realise there was an All-Ireland in them?

"We hit a big low after the initial high of 1983 and 1984 (in the latter we lost to Dublin in the Leinster final by four points in a typical Meath-Dublin game of the time, we had 60% of possession yet they scored enough to win). In 1985 we hit a low being beaten by Laois in Tullamore by ten points. That was a watershed in so many ways. So we sat back and asked ourselves have we got it? There was a hell of a push made in 1986, when we made the big breakthrough of beating Dublin in the Leinster final which we hadn't done since 1970. Our first Leinster in sixteen years. Kerry beat us by four points in the semi-final. We should have beaten Kerry that day. I remember the series of clashes between our backs which led to Ger Power's goal. Inexperience beat us, but things were on the up. We won out in 1987. But a big day for us was the Leinster final of 1987 because it was important for us to beat Dublin again to maintain our superiority."

Sean Boylan? What kind of a man is he?

"He is very diplomatic, a gentleman, very friendly and helpful in any way he can. His biggest plus points are two. First, though he'd not be the greatest tactician in the world, he is excellent at physical fitness. He has the knack of bringing a team to the boil on the big day. He times his run very well even though some of his training methods would be considered off the wall. He is into different things and his whole system is full of variety. One year it could be the Hill of Tara. Next year the sand-dunes in Laytown or Bettystown. Or the swimming pool in Gormanstown College. Or an all weather horse-racing track around Summerhill. And you get no intimation of this beforehand. You just arrive at the usual training area such as Dalgan Park and then off together to somewhere offbeat."

Are county players still informed by post of being selected for their county?

"Still happens in Meath. Our Secretary is Liam Creaven who has been in that position for years. He stays true to the old tradition. It's a nice touch and it is foolproof. You get the written details. Nowadays, I take these for granted, but the first few were precious."

The second Boylan plus?

"The second more important one is that he is an expert in man-management. He will help you in every facet of your life. Whether it be your work situation, love life, the situation at home. If he can help any of your family, he will. He is an outstanding Herbalist. A man you'd confide in. No matter how crazy some of his training sessions may appear, there would be a great sense of loyalty to him. He brought us to train in Dalgan Park for important games, again something different, taking us into a Columban Fathers' College and afterwards we used to dine with the Sisters of Sion at Ballinteer."

Noel Keating of Kepak?

"Noel, our greatest fan and sponsor, who died recently, is a huge loss to Meath. I met Jack Boothman recently at a race meeting largely organised by Noel before his death, as a fund-raiser for his beloved Meath and he put it well to me with a real country saying: 'You'd feel a fair breeze when he's gone'. Noel Keating was one of the greatest people I ever met, a very special man and we are not over his death yet. He could tolerate second best but lack of 100% commitment bothered him."

The great men of that Meath team?

"The big four that Sean picked as his generals from the late 1970's and the early 1980's were Mick Lyons at full back, Gerry McEntee at midfield, Joe Cassells who floated round the team in different positions and Colm O'Rourke."

Was Mick Lyons a tough player?

"A friend of mine, Jim McGovern, who owns the Goblet Pub on the Malahide Road always says this of Mick. Jim, a Leitrim man, says that Mick always did things openly. That you always saw what he did and was never underhand or hit you from behind. If he hit you, everyone saw it. He might have been rugged and rough but he was straight."

Are Meath Dublin's bogey team now?

"I have to be cautious here, because we play each other so often and fortunes tend to sway. It has to be remembered how close Dublin were to us on so many occasions. Nothing between us but the rub of the green. A kick of the ball."

Do you like playing Dublin?

"There are two sides to it. On the one hand anybody with a bit of experience has to look forward to the big day with the sun shining, if you're lucky, Croke Park, fifty thousand people or more, media hype. There'd want to be something wrong with you not to want to be involved in that. That's it. The big one. On the other side, the big fear of playing Dublin in the Championship, is if we are beaten, what do we do with ourselves next week. That's a big motivator too. The fear of losing."

The top Meath stalwart?

"If you press me, I'd go for McEntee before all. McEntee was as intense a man as I've ever met. He has lived about four lives in one already. A top class inter-county footballer for fifteen years. Married with three kids. He has gone to the top in his field in medicine. You couldn't use words to describe what Meath football means to him. All you'd have to do in a dressing-room is look at him. Ferociously intense. Runs in his veins. He wasn't the most gifted footballer in the world but he was the most motivating footballer I saw."

Colm O'Rourke gets better with age?

"Very hard to appreciate the great influence he had on all the younger players around him. When you're talking of these players, it's their leadership qualities and the example they give not their footballing talents, which really mean so much and O'Rourke would be up there with the best of them. His greatest score to my mind was one scored with the right foot at a crucial stage of the replayed All-Ireland against Cork in 1988 with about ten minutes to go. Twelve or fourteen years or so kicking them with the left and if ever we needed a score we needed it then. Joe Cassells was the role model for us all, the perfect sportsman, the father figure."

Are you now with a new wave of young Meath players, Robbie?

"The under-age structure in Meath for the past ten or fifteen years has been very solid, going back to the Pat O'Neills and the Matt Kerrigans. Given the amount of time put into it, good players had to come along. In particular this year Enda McManus, Graham Geraghty, Jody Devine, Cormac Murphy are coming through. I'm almost twenty-eight now and for fellows like me, they are a breath of fresh air and they have necessitated a new thinking for us. That minor team of 1990 was a great one and their coach Paul Kenny, who went on to be in charge of the 1992 minor All-Ireland team as well, is very special too."

Your favourite player?

"Growing up Jack O'Shea is the one I looked up to. Purely as a footballer, his fitness level and workrate were superb. Also as a scoring midfielder. One day against Galway in 1984 he must have scored six points from play. Others would include Mike Sheehy, Matt Connor and John Egan."

Greatest opponent?

"The one I hated marking most was Barney Rock. At the end of his career he ended up in the corner. You could, and I did, mark him out of the game for sixty five minutes but yet you couldn't relax with him for the last five."

Refereeing?

"Bothers me a lot at times. Inconsistency. Even lack of knowledge of the rules. What bothers me is referees not calling the rule where forwards use far too many steps before scoring goals. Like Martin Lynch against Wicklow or D. J. Carey once or twice in hurling. It happened me personally in 1989 when Kieran Duff took eight or nine steps. That annoys me. If a player makes a bad decision or plays a bad game or does a thing wrong he pays the penalty. But if a referee makes a bad decision, there are very few recriminations."

Rules? Should they be changed?

"I sometimes wonder about the mark as applies in Australian Rules, whereby you are rewarded if you make a good catch, the loss of which, people are lamenting. We don't see enough Teddy McCarthys, if you like. The breaking ball now is the prime source of possession for a team. There was something like forty kickouts in the replayed National Football League final between Dublin and Donegal. I was at it and if I remember three or four of those being caught cleanly, that was the height of it. In other words 90% of the ball was won on the break. We should experiment at least with the mark."

Does the G.A.A. ever embarrass you?

"At times it does. There is an awful lot right with it, let me say firstly. For one hundred years plus it has been the biggest amateur sporting organisation in the country and given the volume of people that play it and support it, I think it is a testimony to them, that they have kept it so well, for so long."

Sunday. Your day?

"It's what we all work for all week. What you train for. I get up early. Get the big fry as Matt Kerrigan used to say and the bit of porridge. Polish the boots. Off in the car and you all meet in the hotel. The biggest drag about Sunday is the couple of hours leading up to the game. They go so bloody slow. All you want to do is get out there."

Your greatest thrill from playing the game?

"I suppose it has to be when you do something good, whether it be catching a high ball or blocking one and you get appreciation from the crowd. You're only human at the end of the day."

Game of your life?

"Two games if I'm allowed. One was the 1988 replayed All-Ireland Final against Cork. We lost Gerry McEntee early on and were down to fourteen men. Everybody had to up their work-rate by at least 5% to win. And everybody answered the call. That was the most satisfying of victories. The other one, perhaps a bit off-beat, but will stay with me forever. I'll never forget playing the first Test of the Compromise Rules Series in Australia in 1990. I was captain of the team that year. It was a great experience overall because we were all part of a group of players from different counties who were knocking hell out of each other, Sunday in, Sunday out, for the rest of the year who came together to play for their country in an international against professionals, who really didn't have that much respect for us and thought they would win easily at home and to go and beat them that night and the camaraderie and fun and sense of achievement in faraway Australia gave everyone of us intense pride."

Does coming home to your plush bar in Navan after losing or winning bother you?

" Win or lose, I'll go back to Noel Keating's idiom, 'If you've done your best, you should be able to hold your head high in any company'."

Above, left: Robbie O'Malley, right: Sean Boylan - 'an expert in man-management.' Below, left: - 'you couldn't relax with Barney Rock....', right: Matt Kerrigan - 'my biggest influence, my idol, really...'

Chapter 21

"Nudie" Hughes

Of Monaghan

His full name is Eugene Hughes but in his native Monaghan, indeed anywhere in Ireland, he is known as "Nudie" Hughes and just plain "Nudie" in 'Blaney. It was the week after Monaghan lost to Derry in the 1993 Ulster title race that I met him in his bungalow, set in a lovely rural area about four miles from the Castleblaney he loves. I called to see their G.A.A. Park, so like an amphitheatre, which is a testament to their fine club history and the deep interest in Gaelic football in the area. Castleblaney, as well as being the Irish Nashville, is Monaghan football country and "Nudie" Hughes, its favourite football son.

Whence the name "Nudie"?

"Someone of my own family or a relation couldn't pronounce Eugene right and I have never known myself to be called anything but 'Nudie' from the age of five or six."

The early football days in 'Blaney?

"It began in street leagues when I was only about eight or nine. When we finished school, we used to play in the commons, which is about sixty yards long and forty yards wide, all gravel. We played there every single day. In summertime, up to half eleven at night."

Any young lads from those days in the commons who stayed the course?

"In fact my age group was one of the club's most successful to come through to senior ranks eventually. We may not have been the most successful at under-age level because Monaghan Town and Clones were very strong at the time. But we had in that gang 'Gunner' Brady (son of the legendary 'Gunner'), Noel Shields, Aidan McNally,

Anthony McArdle and others who went on to club success at senior level later. In fact when Monaghan won the Ulster Senior Football title in 1979 for the first time in forty one years, Anthony McArdle and myself were on the team."

The people who helped along the way?

"At that time all we ever knew was playing football - I played a bit of hurling too - but everything was coached into football. Liam McGrath, one of the most successful managers in the country, asked me to play for the club Castleblaney Faughs in the 1975 Senior Championship. I was only eighteen then."

Your career with 'Blaney?

"We won seven Monaghan Senior Football titles in all, winning two Ulster Senior Football club titles in 1986 against Burren and in 1991 against Killybegs."

Do you still play with the club?

"I still play a bit but I'll finish out the 1993 Senior Football Championship with them. I have an unbroken senior Championship sequence since 1975. Played in the minor final before the senior final of 1974 which we won."

Your weight today?

"I'll not disclose that but I'm working at it. At my fittest, I was twelve stone ten to thirteen stone weight. My height is five foot eight and a half inches."

It used to be said of Monaghan that there was more interest among the players in club than in county?

"'Blaney was one of the most successful clubs in the 1960's dominating the scene really and were hugely interested in the County title, showing little interest in the new provincial club title which had just emerged. There was a distinction there that some players wouldn't turn up for the county or if they did they wouldn't pass a ball to different players on the county team. When I started out, it was mostly five selectors in charge of teams in Monaghan. Then along came Sean McCague on to the scene in

1978 and we lost to Antrim in Casement Park but we stuck with his system of three selectors and himself in charge."

The breakthrough in 1979?

"I was right full back on that team. The first ever Senior Football Championship game for me was against Tyrone in Dungannon in 1976, when I played at right half back and was opposed by Brendan Donnelly and they won well that day. I was very lucky to hold on to right full back in 1979, having received an injury shortly before the Ulster final and being challenged strongly by Brian Daly from Donaghmoyne. Dessie Mulligan, one of the stars of that 1979 team and previous years too, used to train with myself four or five times a week. I used to spend a lot of time playing ball with left and right foot from close in range, out to thirty five yards and would never move until I had scored ten with each foot. I'd always start in the centre of the goals on the fourteen yards line and go either side of the post ten yards, because after reading the Christy Ring story and listening to Sean O'Neill, I concluded that if you master the close in things, the rest will follow naturally."

You won an All Star as a corner back and as a corner forward, Nudie. Did you do all this ball-practice while playing in defence?

"Yes. I used to train non stop. One of the things I mastered was picking up the ball while sprinting without breaking stride."

Why did you put such emphasis on the pick-up on the run?

"It's the simple things you have to master. And picking up a ball is one of the most basic skills. In major games, at all levels, you'll see many examples of players being pulled for picking the ball foul."

All Stars?

"I won an All Star in 1979 as a corner back. For my club I used to play at centre half back, midfield or sometimes on the '40'. So I progressed steadily out the field for the county too. I first moved to right half forward and later on to corner forward."

Career achievement?

"I won three Ulster Senior Football Championship medals in 1979, 1985 and 1988. In 1988 I won the man of the match award in the Ulster final against Tyrone. Everything went well for me that day. The ball broke right and I ended up scoring 1-3. It was a unique occasion for Monaghan in that we scored 1-13 in all from play."

The two positions. How do you compare them?

"I preferred centre half back to anything. You have to be a stopper and a creator. I was going for a record in the Railway Cup, which I think would not be beaten. I won medals as a right corner back, right half back and right corner forward and captained the team in 1986 against Leinster in Breffni Park which we lost by a point, this time at right half forward."

The Railway Cup?

"It's a pity that other provinces didn't have the same interest in the competition as Ulster."

Injuries?

"Since I started I haven't missed any Championship, club or county through injury."

Schooldays?

"I went to the Boys' National School in Castleblaney and left school at an early age, fifteen to be exact. There were fourteen of us in the family, seven boys and seven girls. We lived in Castleblaney and there were two bedrooms in our house. Things were tight. I'm thirty-six now and I remember the old money days well. When I was nine years of age I was earning four pounds a week for peeling potatoes after school at the back of a chip shop. I know the value of money and you get nothing easy. My father, God rest him, is dead over a year and he hadn't it easy."

The great football interest in Monaghan?

"It stems back from the 1979 breakthrough, when Sean McCague as a one unit person took over the team. We had good players in the 1970's too, but there wasn't the same motivation as in the 1980's. At most, there are only thirty-two clubs in the county, eight of them being senior. At the competitive level you'd nearly be picking from the senior ranks but in Monaghan, the players at junior level were just as good. After 1979 when some of the old guard retired, a good crop of players came through from the Scotstown area which was dominating Ulster club football. We got a good blend of players through that time like Gerry McCarville, Fergus Caulfield, Gene Sherry, Ray McCarron. We came from Division 3 to Division 1, just losing one game in each Division in each year and we contested the final of the Open Draw Centenary Cup with Meath in 1984. To get there we beat Limerick, Mayo, Offaly, Derry and lost to Meath by two points. That gave us hope and in 1985, we won the National Football League winning our first senior national title."

Was there great jubilation then?

"For a full week we were treated as kings and everybody enjoyed it very well. After that we got down to the hard graft of the Ulster Championship. The league was a bonus and we went on to win the Ulster title and lose to Kerry in a replay."

Did you really believe you could beat Kerry then?

"We were cruising very well at the start and were up to five points ahead of them. We had all the chances first half and didn't avail of them. Then just before half-time, John Kennedy hit a ball in from the wing very high and it hit the very tip-top of one of the posts and landed in Ger Power's hands ten yards from goal and he put it past Paddy Linden for a goal. If you were to hit one thousand balls up there, it would never come off the post the same way again. That was against the run of play and we went in at half-time just two points ahead."

The feelings at half-time?

"We could have and should have done better. At the end of the day I'd say that we were one of the unluckiest teams not to play in an All-Ireland Final."

The great Monaghan players of your two eras?

"Early on you had 'Bubbles' in goal, Gerry McGarry from Clones, Dessie Mulligan and Eamonn Tavey, one of the greatest players to wear any jersey. Tavey shone no matter where he played, long before 1979. He was a big influence on all of us in 'Blaney. Dessie Mulligan was another great clubman. You had Anthony McArdle, Gerry McCarville, Sean Hughes, Kevin Treanor, Tommy Moyna and Jack McCarville. That 1979 one was a very tough team. Gene Finnegan was another of the staunch ones."

The second wave team?

"Gerry McCarville continued as one of the staunchest and Fergus Caulfield. Gene Sherry came through then as a fine corner back. Another clubmate, Eamonn McEneaney became the main man up front along with Eamonn Murphy and Ray McCarron. Ray started off in 1983 and is still going strong. Declan Flanagan and Declan Loughman were others. McCarron was unfortunate this year in that his fellow forwards were not mature enough to really help him out."

How would you describe yourself as a player, Nudie?

"I have been described as another Christy Fisher or Billy Mason, former Monaghan footballers. Great to be remembered that way. I was very dedicated to the club and county. Training was no hassle, from the time I lived in Annalitton and when we moved out of Castleblaney town I would think nothing of training for an hour and a quarter at half six in the morning and going training with the county again that night. Christy Fisher was a postman here in 'Blaney and I knew him. We always had stars to inspire us in Castleblaney."

Other great Monaghan men?

"John Rice and big Ollie O'Rourke from Iniskeen. John Rice was an exceptional player, Vincent Duffy another."

How did you manage with referees?

"In County Monaghan, I've been known to take the whistle off the referee and take care of the game for him. Not literally, but next thing to it. John McAviney has some great snaps of me going through with a ball and being fouled and a pleading expression on my face more or less inviting a free."

Players from outside Monaghan whom you admired?

"Sean O'Neill of Down, very dedicated, methodical in his game and always advised well in his role as coach to Ulster. Another was Brian McEniff."

Other sports?

"I play a lot of golf. A lot of hurling as a juvenile. I was coached by Eddie Keher as a youngster, when six of us from Monaghan were selected to go to Gormanstown College at U-14 level for a Coaching week. I played soccer too and won awards here including the Evening Herald Cup."

Today's game. Is there too much hype?

"The hype in the present game is very good. Much better media coverage than in the 1970's or 1980's. Television cameras everywhere. Even getting into the dressing-room scene, unheard of before. It hasn't changed anything in toughness. Ulster was always a test of character. The game has speeded up."

The Dubs?

"The Dubs are again a formidable force. Their great problem is picking their team from such a big pool. They will always start out as favourites. They are good for the G.A.A."

Nudie is regarded as one of the characters of Gaelic football. Any interesting stories?

"One night we played Meath in the Susan McCann Cup in Castleblaney and I asked one of the boys would they come for a pint and the whole visiting busload stayed at a certain pub until half three in the morning. We had a draw that night. So we agreed to repeat the dose in the event of another draw. Meath beat us but we had the same venture again. You remember nights like that. I remember playing in England and our club game with Round Towers in New Eltham had been cancelled. These boys came up from Bristol and prevailed on a few of us to play against Gloucester in a league final, illegally, of course. I was the last brought on and about to hand my name 'Brian Murphy' to the referee. The official in charge called me back and said 'I'd better change that, as the other two I sent in were Brian Murphys and the referee would surely spot it.' So we changed it to Aidan something or other and went on to win the game."

Another story about John Egan?

"We were playing a Railway Cup game against Munster and Sean O'Neill was up and down the line and I was playing on John Egan, one of the greatest ever footballers and a character too. Egan was a creator and very hard to shake off a ball. We were standing talking - I always talked to opponents even though you would be told not to - and at one stage he said to me 'What's that man writing down on the piece of paper? Ah, sure he's an eejit like the rest of us. He's writing down...' and as I turned to reply the bould John had just stuck the ball in the back of the net. So I said, 'John that's the last time I'll ever talk to you during a game!'"

Players you admired besides Egan?

"Mike Sheehy too was very good. Mick Kennedy of Dublin was a very underrated player. Joey Donnelly of Armagh, another exceptional player. Padhraic Lyons from Meath, very good too. I'd put Eamonn Tavey as high as any of them, as a forward or a back."

The present Castleblaney team?

"I'm very lucky to be part of a Castleblaney club team at the moment which came up all the way together from U-10 and has never been beaten in any competition up along. Just another old fellow like myself left, Philip 'The Gunner' Brady, and there is twenty minutes of a game still left in me!"

What will you miss most when you hang up the boots?

"I'm very lucky, I can adapt to any sport. I'm a great competitor. Golf is number one at the moment after football. My handicap is ten and I have already won three captain's prizes. I have coached the club U-21 team to win two county titles and may get involved at county level later. At the moment I'd like to give a little time to my family and watch my children grow up."

Toughest opponent?

"Mick Kennedy of Dublin. We got on very well together too."

Game of your life?

"It has to be a club game as my top game even though I got more recognition for others. The County final of 1985 or the County semi-final of 1986. The latter one was a replica of 1985. Both were against our old rivals, Scotstown. We won the 1986 one. We were handicapped in 1985 without Eamonn McEneaney, allegedly sent off in a seven-a-side game in Dublin. Also without Declan Loughman, out with a broken leg. We lost that game by four points. I scored five points that day from centre half back, three with the right, two with the left. I could kick naturally with both feet especially after all the training with the ball. In 1986 I didn't score quite as much, but my mother, who is my greatest supporter, has all the clippings of those games and the Argus newspaper described that as my greatest hour. Hard to separate the two in my own mind."

Your work?

"I work as a Rep. for Tennents - Bass Ireland, and I get on very well with customers and people generally."

Is there something special about Clones on Ulster final day?

"I enjoyed the three I played there immensely. The following you get on the day. The congratulations. It's equivalent to a World Cup for me. Nice to win and be part of the team that wins. You'll not always be the star."

Anything else?

"I'm married now with two kids. Geraldine's father, Brendan Hammill won an All-Ireland junior football medal with Monaghan in 1956. The two lads names are Ciarán and Conor, and I hope they will wear the colours of 'Blaney and Monaghan. I'd better not forget me mother. A fanatical Monaghan woman. Maggie Waters before she became Hughes. You'd love meeting her. Her brother, Tommy, played for the county in the 1950's. Mammy would travel from here to Dingle. She has all the scrapbooks out at the house. All the trophies stay in Mammy's house. She is seventy-two years of age now and we all had a great party for her last weekend. And we hope to have more too. Here in Castleblaney we have many true blue supporters. You'd know two of them, Paddy Cole (Mr. Jazzman) and Big Tom McBride the singer."

Above: Eugene "Nudie" Hughes

Chapter 22

Benny Gaughran

Of Louth

Benny has reached the top of his profession as a leading solicitor in Dublin. Living in Malahide, he is still actively involved in sport. The bouncy effervescent character we knew as a Sigerson player with U.C.D. and in his county days with Louth, has been little affected by life in the metropolis. I do believe he will always make up fifteen, if he chances on a team that is short. I'm an all year round swimmer in my beloved Blackrock, Salthill, Galway. In March 1992 at a Combined Universities Re-union on the eve of the Sigerson Cup final, I invited a number of brave souls to join me for my daily swim at 10a.m. next morning. Never expecting any of them to be there, I didn't reckon on Benny. He was togged when I arrived.

What age are you Benny and have you finally retired?

"The answer to the first question is I'm forty-seven and I haven't retired."

You played Dublin Senior Football Championship football in four decades?

"It was with U.C.D. and with Civil Service. I started with U.C.D. in the middle 1960's and won my first Dublin Senior Football title with them in 1966. We won again in 1973. I joined Civil Service in 1974 and we won the Dublin senior title in 1980. That's three Dublin senior medals but I lost in finals too, the first the Louth Senior Football Championship final, when with Dundalk's Clan na Gael, we lost to the famous Newtown Blues in the 1960's."

The U.C.D. days?

"My first Sigerson was in 1964, when we were beaten in the final by Queen's University largely by full forward, Sean O'Neill, who scored about 2-3 and literally demolished us. He was marked by Paudie O'Donoghoe of Kerry and Paddy O'Hanlon the former M.P. was right full back. Sean ran into Paddy with a perfectly fair shoulder charge and knocked him out with the impact."

How many Sigersons did you play in?

"I played from 1964 up to 1972. There was a famous objection to me over in Galway when we beat U.C.C. in the semi-final. Then we heard that night that I was being objected to because it was claimed I was not properly registered, which I maintain was incorrect. However, the ruling body found I was illegal and threw U.C.D. out of the competition. It was the first time this ever happened in University competition. The following year I got back playing again as U.C.D. were adamant I'd return on a point of principle."

Did you win any Sigerson medal?

"I had the pleasure of winning only one Sigerson, in 1969 when I captained the side. We beat U.C.G. in the final. I remember Coleen McDonagh was captain of Galway and we marked each other. A right old tussle too. We played the final in Croke Park and I scored 1-7. Following that we were selected to travel to the Cardinal Cushing Games in New York."

Would you regard Sigerson as your greatest time?

"I always say that the proudest medal I have is the winning captain's medal for Sigerson 1969. It was a specially cut gold medal then. In those days, the captain trained the team and organised affairs. There were no team managers then. The captain had a large say. I was ably supported by an up and coming Eugene McGee who later took on the role of manager. We worked very much in tandem."

Did you win an All-Ireland Senior Football Club medal?

"Yes, we won the Dublin title in 1973 and went on to win the All-Ireland in 1974 and on the same weekend I won a Railway Cup medal with Leinster. That was a very exciting time and I joined Civil Service within weeks of that victory. So I left U.C.D. on a very high note."

Schooldays and your early life in Louth?

"I remember Louth winning the All-Ireland in 1957 and the Sam Maguire was taken to the Friary School in Dundalk. I knew Frank Lynch personally, even in those days as I think he was doing a line with my sister. My mother had a shop in Dundalk and I knew Stephen White well too. My idol was Kevin Beahan. I thought he was one of the complete footballers. He was a class apart. Everyone else seemed to be struggling and he'd be like a Rolls Royce."

The men who inspired you and set you going?

"There was a Br. Finbar in the De La Salle, Dundalk who introduced me to the local Clan na Gael club and in fact I didn't play club football until I was fifteen. I was very interested in soccer and the soccer mentors wanted me to stick at soccer because I seemed to be going places. My father, who was a former professional footballer with Dundalk, Bohemians, Sunderland and Southampton and whose old scrapbooks I still cherish, had taken a middle line on the issue. I don't think he encouraged me to play soccer. In fact various clues that I discovered as years went by, indicated that he very subtly directed me away from soccer towards Gaelic football and I think that is because he felt he wanted me to get a degree, a good education and he felt I might be enticed to play across channel."

The early motivators?

"The Dixons in the Clan na Gael club who are still associated like the late Tommy, Paddy and John. It was a great club for kids growing up."

Did Clan na Gael mean a lot to you?

"There is a saying in the club and a proud one 'Once a clan, always a clan' and I've never lost that. Everytime I go back to them there is a certain nostalgia."

In what way were the club days in Louth different from those in Dublin?

"The Clan na Gael club was a real family club and when you went out to play with Clans, you had a battery of support and if a row developed you had plenty of help. In Dublin, it was a bit different, dare I say more cold blooded and professional. With U.C.D. you were very much on your own. You had to fight your own corner. Whatever had to be done, we did it on the field. We were all students. With Civil Service it was much the same."

Your debut with Louth?

"I was playing minor at the time for Louth and one Sunday morning I was having breakfast and my father came up the stairs of the house very excitedly to say there was a taxi outside the house with one of the Louth selectors and several Louth players. What happened was Jimmy Mulroy and other Louth players had to go to a funeral suddenly and they were short and they had to play Meath in Navan in an O'Byrne Cup Senior Football game. It was 1963 and I had to fill in until the boys came back from the funeral. So I got on for the first half. I got two kicks, one on the head and I kicked the ball against the upright. I was taken off just before half-time when Mulroy and Co. arrived and there was one clap from the stand - my mother!"

The real debut?

"I was selected on the panel for the League campaign in 1964 and played my first full game for Louth. Let's say I had a clean run through until 1978. Then, rather mysteriously I thought, I suddenly wasn't picked for the new Championship campaign of 1979. I made a comeback years later."

The highs and the lows with Louth?

"We were an almost team. In the 1970's we had the doubtful honour of being beaten by three subsequent All-Ireland winners after hard close games, Offaly, Meath and Dublin. On that 'nearly' team Jimmy Mulroy was a classy footballer. He started his career with Louth at full forward and ended it at full back. There was 'Muckle McKeown' once described by Con Houlihan as 'A strange genius.' There was a lot of Newtown Blues players who had won six or seven Louth Senior Football

Championships - Liam and Mickey Leech, the Judge brothers. They were the backbone. And, of course, there was Frank Lynch and I also had the honour and privilege of playing with Kevin Beahan. My first Championship campaign was his last. Leslie Toal, another great. Pat Reynolds of Meath and I made our Championship debuts on each other."

Did your lack of inches come against you? What is your height?

"My sons and I have a debate about that. They measured me lately and I think we settled on 5'9" but they or I don't believe that! Nowadays, since Kevin Heffernan started the trend of picking good big tall players, you have to be exceptionally good if you're small but it has its own advantages. Generally speaking, it came against me. I played at midfield a lot for Louth. I had a great spring for the ball. At times, if you met a giant you had a problem."

Your greatest thrill from the game itself?

"When you're playing on a good team and everything is just purring like a good engine and you're part of a machine that is just setting up scores. The actual score itself is a big thrill but if I took part in that, not even the final pass, if I made the move that led to the final score, I just felt like ice-hockey that it was my score. For instance, I remember playing on a U.C.D. team that went something like forty plus competitive games without defeat and we got to the stage where we just felt we'd never be beaten. It was a great feeling."

That great U.C.D. team?

"John O'Keeffe and I played midfield for a long time together; Paddy Kerr, Frank Canavan and the famous John Purdy of Down who set up all sorts of records, John Kelly and Garrett O'Reilly."

Your earlier days at U.C.D.?

"Sean Murray of Longford was one of the greats of football. Sean Cleary of Galway, Georgie Kane (Westmeath), Bobby Burns (Longford) were others. Paudie O'Donoghoe and Barney Brady of Donegal. All of them interpros as well. I trained assiduously and even before I became a Louth minor I used to go out to the back garden in Dundalk and do so many pressups and situps a night, upping it night after night. I think it stood by me as I was small in stature. I didn't care who hit me. I was as tough as nails around the shoulders and body."

Honours won in the game?

"I played many times for Leinster starting in or about 1968. I was picked regularly up to about 1974. I played for the Combined Universities many times and captained them against one of the famous Australian teams captained by Ron Barassi, when they visited Ireland for the first time in 1967."

How did you enjoy that experience?

"It was phenomenal. I remember meeting Noel Curran of Meath (Paul's father) whom I thought was the best full forward in Ireland at that time. Meath had just won the All-Ireland. The Aussies were known then as the Galahs. I met Noel in O'Connell Street the Sunday night the Galahs destroyed Meath in Croke Park and I asked him 'What were they like?' He said they were a class apart. Ten times fitter than we ever were. Like flies, moving so fast, flitting here and flitting there. We played them in Croke Park. They had a giant at full back called Polly Farmer, an aborigine and a bit of a freak, about 6'6". And a fellow called Jesaulenko, the Australian player of the year. There were several players from the Carlton team. They beat us by five points. A great memory."

Any regrets now that you are semi-retired?

"We had Louth teams that almost did it. Just unlucky that we ran into great Offaly, Meath and Dublin teams. We certainly should have won a Leinster. Sorry too not to have won an All Star though nominated often."

Anecdotes?

"I remember playing against Down in Newcastle in one of the few games Louth picked me at half back. During the game Sean O'Neill came over and he was very annoyed and said something to me, abused me verbally, shouldered me and really seemed to want to fight me. As the game ended, he stormed off the pitch. The following St. Patrick's Day I was playing for Leinster against Ulster in the Railway Cup final at Croke Park. They beat us the same day and Sean came up to me in Barry's Hotel, shook my hand and apologised for something that happened in the Newcastle game before Christmas. 'Something was done to me during the match and I thought it was you and I found out later it wasn't you.' I thought it was very manful of him."

Your greatest opponent?

"I loved midfield and one of the greatest games I played there, I was up against a better man that day. My immediate opponent, Colm McAlarney. He had everything. Class, tough, great catch and a football brain. It was a National Football League game in Newry. I covered every inch of the ground and so did Colm that day. The crowd applauded both teams as they left the field. Down won by a point. I had played the shirt off my back but he was better. I could never get the better of Brian Mullins. I met him in my later days. I never really minded anyone in the half back time, as I felt I'd wear them down but at midfield Mullins and McAlarney gave me a lot of problems. So did Ken Rennicks of Meath. Hitting against him was like hitting a granite wall."

Greatest footballer you ever saw?

"Without a doubt Sean O'Neill. Kevin Beahan I've described as a Rolls Royce. Sean was even higher than that. Such a football brain. He was several generations before all other footballers."

What did playing the game do for you as a man? Did football prepare you well for life?

"If you take any sport seriously, I think it will prepare you well for life. Gaelic football did that for me. Firstly in U.C.D. one season we trained at seven o'clock in the morning. We did that for ten weeks, three times a week. You had to do it. Nobody was going to give you sympathy. It teaches you to take the good times and the bad times. You learn to be gracious in victory as well as defeat. You should never taunt your vanquished opponent."

Do the stars of today take everything too seriously?

"There is so much at stake now, I don't blame them really. I discovered that when I was brought back on to the Louth team in 1983. The difference between the media hype from 1978 was phenomenal. I was interviewed left right and centre and I was by no means the star of the team."

Are you sorry to have missed out on this?

"It has advantages and disadvantages. I just miss being young again playing football. A lot of the talent has evened out now. So that's why you get the likes of Donegal and Clare coming up. That is good for the game."

Why is Gaelic football as a game special?

"It has a manliness about it other sports haven't got. I often hear people say this or that fellow is windy or a coward. There are no cowards playing Gaelic football. I think there is quite a parallel with Australian Rules football. If somebody in that game gets a broken nose, he plays on. The injuries are just pushed aside. We hear stories of Gaelic footballers going over there like young Brian Stynes. His father sent him over a pair of gloves to wear in the Aussies Rules games and his coach told him on no account was he to wear those cissies' gloves."

The game today?

"The game today is tougher. Players today are fitter. Less margin for error and they analyse it a lot more."

Any changes you'd like to see?

"They will have to do something radical about refereeing . It's too much of a responsibility now on one man. Referees should be paid properly. They should send them to school. I know assessment has come in but they should have better assessments. More help from the umpires and the linesmen."

The game of your life?

"With Louth I remember Kerry winning the All-Ireland in the late 1960's and coming to Dundalk to play Louth in the National Football League. We beat them and the crowd went absolutely wild. Just to see the way the Louth supporters reacted to that was phenomenal. They carried us off the field in a tide of emotion. We did the same to Armagh after they lost to Dublin in 1976. We beat them in Dowdallshill in Dundalk and again the crowd carried us off the field. With U.C.D. captaining them to Sigerson victory in 1968-1969 was special. Also beating St. Vincent's in the Dublin County final of 1973 because they had beaten us the previous year and I had been unavailable. Going on to win the All-Ireland Club title and all those games in that series were memorable. A good few were very emotional including winning the Letterkenny All-Ireland 7's three times. But if there has to be one, the Dublin Senior Football Championship win of Civil Service in 1980, must be number one. We had got to the final the year before in 1979 and were beaten. People said we were too old to do it again. But we came back and walked the 1980 final."

Do you mind growing old?

"I think everyone minds growing old. You have to adapt your mind to it. For a sportsman you have to substitute, to find other things. I'm lucky where I'm living in Malahide because it's a real sporty town."

Benny Gaughran being chaired in triumph from Croke Park with the Sigerson Cup in 1969

Chapter 23

Frank McGuigan

Of Tyrone

It was the eve of the 1993 Ulster final when I met former Tyrone star Frank McGuigan in his native Ardboe, close to Lough Neagh. Frank was on crutches, recovering from a recent car accident, when he broke the same leg again that had already been smashed in 1984, bringing to an end a brilliant football career. Driven by his friend, local fisherman John Coney, Frank arranged to meet me in the Glenavon Hotel just outside Cookstown. Thence to Ardboe by the backroads and a most pleasant stay with the effervescent Frank, who could still be there fielding the high balls were it not for the tragedy which prematurely ended his career.

What age were you when you had the accident which finished your career?

"Thirty years. The year was 1984. The crash occurred in November."

That was the year of your eleven points from play, Ulster final win?

"There has been a lot talked about that final but to me on that day I didn't even realise how many points I had scored. I didn't know until Micheál Ó Muircheartaigh told me that I had scored eleven points. All were from play and seven were scored in the first half."

How were those eleven points constituted?

"I think maybe it was six with the right foot, four with the left and one fisted point."

You could kick with both feet?

"From a very early age, I didn't favour any foot. I was equally accurate with both."

Football was everything in Ardboe when you grew up?

"Where I come from, in Ardboe, it is farming or fishing stock only. Basically, at that time there was nothing else only football. During the summer holidays we'd get up early and go down to the shore and kick football until bedtime."

Can you remember your first medal?

"I do, well. It was an U-13 medal. We played in the final at Edendork and I was captain of the team. Austin Currie presented the cup to me and we beat Coalisland in the County final."

Your first time to wear the Tyrone jersey?

"As a minor in 1971. Arthur McRory was over the team. We played Derry in a Minor League game in Ballinascreen. There was a lad on the team from Ardboe called Sean Coyle. I was very shy at the time and he was instrumental in persuading Arthur to give me a run."

Who are the players from Tyrone you looked up to?

"You'd have heard of Jody O'Neill, Iggy Jones and all from that great 1956 Tyrone team. I even heard my mother talking about them."

Jones was special?

"I never saw him playing but from all reports he must have been. The 1956 team, Tyrone's first Ulster title team is very special still. You know the way they pick best ever Tyrone teams in pubs, you'll always find the bulk of the team comes from 1956."

The minor days?

"We got to the All-Ireland Final in 1972 and Cork, or rather Jimmy Barry Murphy beat us. I was captain that year. The previous year I was on the team which won out in Ulster but lost to Mayo in the semi-final."

Your first memory of Croke Park?

"Pretty shocked with the dreary old dressing-rooms in Croke Park in 1971. I had expected something like you saw on telly of soccer dressing-rooms like Wembley. The pitch was different."

Croke Park on Final Day 1972?

"Totally different altogether. Probably my proudest moment in football, to lead that team out in Croke Park in front of a packed stadium. I think we were leading just before half time and then Cork got a goal. Point for point from then on but they held on to win."

Was that the biggest disappointment in your football career, apart from the accident of course?

"Not really. I could always accept a defeat after that. I thought on the day it was a chance to get up on the Hogan Stand and get a cup presented to you. I had no speech prepared but I knew I'd have to say something. It's something I'll always remember."

What are your thoughts on dirty play and is Gaelic football getting dirtier?

"There isn't a doubt about the latter. I have no time whatsoever for dirty play. There are boys who would go out and maybe hit you a dirty kick or box but illegal tactics like pulling jerseys and dragging people can be very annoying too. Bigger physical men against smaller players often take advantages. Defenders get away with a lot of this all the time."

Are the rules protecting players now?

"The referee definitely cannot see everything that is going on behind his back on a big pitch and the ball at the other end. There is so much of this behind the ball stuff going on at the minute, that if the umpires or linesmen called the referee's attention to everything the game would never end."

Is it harder to win gracefully or lose with dignity?

"Harder to lose gracefully. I like to see the winners going over to console the losers. Cork were very gracious to us in that minor All-Ireland win."

Are team managers today given too much importance?

"I think football in general in the last ten years has gone too professional for an amateur sport."

What about the club Ardboe?

"This part of the country here is special. It means everything to me. It's where I was brought up and reared. My parents were reared here too. I have great affection for it and think it is a beautiful part of the country. Down around the lough shore. Fishermen and all that. Where I learnt my football. I had a lot of glory with the club and through my injuries they were very good to me."

Your successes with Ardboe

"Four Tyrone Senior Football Championship medals and a few Tyrone League medals. The Championship successes were 1971-1973. The fourth was in Centenary year 1984."

Ardboe's first ever title was in 1968. Was that big in the area?

"Ardboe through the years had great teams. People used to say that there was a curse on the team and that they'd never win. But that evening in 1968 in Dungannon when they won the cup for the first time was special."

Was that why you were captain of Tyrone at eighteen when they won the Ulster title?

"No. I remember the day in 1973 when we were in Ballybofey for the first round of the Championship and Jody O'Neill at a team meeting said 'By the way boys, Frank McGuigan is captain of the team for this year'."

Did it bother you to be captain of Tyrone at eighteen?

"I never took things like that too seriously. A lot of players today take it very seriously. To me it was only a sport, just a pastime."

Have you any regrets now? - That you didn't train hard enough? Would you have been better with less weight?

"There is no doubt about that. I suppose the weight only came on when I went to the States in 1977. I suppose I should have trained harder in those years and put more into my game but I never had to work hard at my game."

Of the two Ulster final wins of 1973 and 1984, which meant most to you?

"1984 meant most. I knew I was coming to the end of my career. In 1973, I thought these things might happen every year."

Tyrone were a bit of a disappointment against Dublin later in 1984?

"That Tyrone team could have put up a better show. We could have beaten that Dublin team if we had got it out of our heads that putting on a good show was good enough."

Is Dublin being up, good for the game of football?

"No doubt about it. Dublin being there you love them or hate them. They are good for the game and when they are down you miss them. The sight of the Hill is great."

At the end of 1984 an accident ended your football career. Tell us exactly what happened?

"I was building my house here and left about 2p.m. I'd have been working on the house all day only the Tyrone County Board came up with this idea of playing club league games on a Saturday. So I went and played for the club and then had a few beers after the match. On the way home with more than a few beers, to be honest, I crashed into a wall ten yards down the road from my home."

Were you knocked unconscious?

"I was surely. I was lucky I only got injuries to the leg (the right). When I hit the wall with the Hiace van the leg took the whole impact. The leg broke at the knee and hip."

When did you realise you were finished with football?

"Football never entered my mind when I was in the hospital. I was more worried was I going to survive and live. The doctors had told me I was a pretty sick man and no one was allowed in to see me for a couple of days."

But when did you miss it?

"I was over the worst when I missed it. I did miss it I suppose but I was thirty years of age and I hadn't that many more years to give to it. I had a wife and family. We had four kids at the time."

How long did it take you to walk properly again?

"I probably lay in the hospital for twenty weeks without getting out of bed. Then drawbacks and I had to go back into hospital again for another twelve weeks and it must have been a good year before I was out around again."

Did Tyrone hold a testimonial game for you?

"Not at all. They may have sent some small donation, whereas the club here in Ardboe did run a few things to raise funds for me. Basically my friends here including the G.A.A. friends, helped to complete the house. I am bitter towards the G.A.A. in general on that issue. As a body they didn't do a pile for me. Most of my money came from the States where I spent seven years. They ran a big fund for me over there. A few boys got together here and had a big benefit dance in a hotel outside Cookstown. The Kerry team was up here for a National Football League game and they came as guests."

Did you miss not being involved in 1986 when Tyrone reached the All-Ireland Final?

"Oh, I'd probably have been around in 1986 alright. Even if I had quit, I think Arthur would have coaxed me back."

The great Tyrone players of your time?

"You'd have to include Eugene McKenna, Kevin McCabe, Damian O'Hagan. McCabe was one of the best half backs I ever saw. He was more inclined to think 'I'll let the half forward mark me', which I think he did in that 1986 final. If he had marked Pat Spillane man to man, I don't think Spillane would have caused the damage he did."

Which of them all would best lift you if needed?

"It takes a special player to do that. I suppose McKenna would be the man. In my time the best players in Tyrone were McKenna and McCabe."

McCabe was a pure footballer?

"He had the speed of a sprinter. Great build and talent."

The most memorable social occasion in the G.A.A.?

"That night they ran that benefit dinner cum dance at the Prairie Restaurant, when the Kerry team as All-Ireland Champions of 1984 were there. Jimmy Keaveney, Tony Hanahoe, Nudie Hughes, Joe Kiernan, all our own lads and Matt Connor in his wheelchair all on his own. Matt drove all the way from Tullamore on a foggy night. He found the place with no help, parked his car and arrived at the door in his wheelchair. I'll never forget that especially."

Your years in New York?

"I was in New York for seven years. Football there was different. You only got a game about every three weeks because you only had one field. For the playoffs, they brought over fit players from Ireland and it was only three or four of the better players over there who made the teams for the playoffs."

Did you lose out on football back home during those years?

"1977 to 1983. I lost the best football years of my life in the States. We (Tyrone) won 3-in-a-row New York titles. I don't regret my time spent there at all. I had a great time and made some wonderful friends. I daren't say anything else because my wife is American."

Where did you meet your wife?

"Her name is Geraldine Donnelly and I met her at home, believe it or not, on a blind date. We have six in the family now and four of them were born in America. The first three were boys, the eldest now coming on to fifteen, then two girls and a boy. The older boys are crazy on Gaelic."

Your honours?

"Four Tyrone Senior Football, two Ulster Senior, two minor and two U-21 medals. In U-21 we were beaten again by Mayo in a replay in the All-Ireland semi-final and by Galway in Salthill in 1972."

That 1972 game was a tempestuous affair?

"My memory is the aftermath and the bit of a scrimmage with spectators. We were beaten by a good Galway team. Galway played the game hard and fair. They had a tough backline and one man stood out, Joe Waldron."

Did you ever win an All Star?

"Yes, in 1984, the year of my accident."

Is it a great honour?

"It was one thing I always looked forward to winning some day because I travelled five times in all to the States as a replacement All Star."

The All Star Award in 1984?

"People had pencilled me in for the All Star that year at full forward after Clones. I had scored five points in the first round from play against Donegal and two more in the semi-final against Derry before the famous eleven. I hadn't a great game against Dublin but I still got four points. I remember I came home from the accident and the All Stars were announced on a Friday night and I got a call with the news from Pat Shields, a great fan of mine who was recently shot dead here. I was still in pain that time and it certainly helped me no end. I'll never forget the next morning I turned on the T.V. in the house. I was bed-ridden that time. Michael Lyster was going through the team and he says when he came to full forward 'Frank McGuigan probably only got the position for sentimental reasons'. That took a lot of the glory away from my All Star Award. It still hurts to this day."

Is there too much hype in the game today? Too much telly?

"I don't think there is too much telly. I like to see the players getting all that prominence. When I was playing there was nothing nicer than to meet people who'd say they saw you on telly."

Should managers be back on a voluntary basis again?

"I think managers should be on a voluntary basis again. They should get expenses."

Your greatest opponent?

"The most awkward opponent and probably one of the best players I ever saw was Brian Mullins. He had it every way. He could play football, play it hard, had a footballing brain, everything."

Greatest footballer you've ever seen?

"A lot of players today work so hard at their game. I'm always one for the man born with the pure talent and skill. For ability and talent Matt Connor and Mikey Sheehy. There is one other and we'll never know how good he could be and that is Kevin

Moran. His best was still to come when he left the game. There have been other greats like Jacko and Spillane but they put a lot of work into it. Keaveney was a talented footballer. He never put a pile of work into it. His brain and his score-taking were great. Jimmy Barry-Murphy, a great opportunist."

Did you train hard?

"I never would have missed a training session and all my managers would verify that. I wouldn't have done extra training outside it which a lot of them are doing nowadays. The managers of juvenile teams have the kids running up and down the field now instead of giving them a ball. In our time we used to go to the Ardboe field about twenty players a side with one ball and play all evening."

Greatest player today?

"Natural talented players today are scarce. Colm O'Rourke may be one of the older players but he is the best around still."

Your biggest thrill from the game itself?

"Catching a ball. Without a doubt, going into the air and catching a ball. One which I took from Jack O'Shea in Gaelic Park is a special memory."

Game of your life?

"Against Bellaghy in the Ulster club Championship. They were All-Ireland Champions the previous year. The year was 1972. That was my greatest game. I was around eighteen then and played at midfield. Everything I did was just right. We beat them 0-8 to 0-6 and I think I scored seven of the points. They carried me off the field that day."

Were you often carried from the field in triumph?

"In 1973 and again in 1984 on Ulster final day. But I was very shy of it all. After a game I used to love having a few beers with friends and maybe not talking about football at all."

Is playing football in Tyrone a disadvantage because of the troubles in the North?

"No disadvantage at all. Life is very normal here as you saw today."

A final thought?

"In the best players of today, I'd have to include Martin McHugh of Donegal. Another oldtimer too. Tony Boyle is a decent player too and is very valuable to Donegal."

Frank McGuigan scoring a point against Dublin in 1984

Chapter 24

Ger Coughlan

Offaly and Kinnitty Hurler

He was a permanent fixture on all the great Offaly hurling teams from 1980 to 1990 inclusive. Though small in stature, his great skill and hurling heart carried him through against all foes in many a battle. He still plays club hurling for his club Kinnitty, always a stronghold of hurling in a county better known for Gaelic football. In fact, the recent rise of Offaly hurling has been the great modern G.A.A. story.

Age, weight and height?

"For a hurler, I was quite small, five foot five, my hurling weight was nine stone, five pounds, I'm thirty-seven now."

Are you retired from the game?

"No, I'm hurling stronger than ever before with my club Kinnitty and enjoying it as much and training as hard as ever."

Did your stature militate against you?

"When I started hurling with Offaly at the age of twenty-two, I suppose people were saying why wasn't he on earlier. A lot of people in Offaly believed I was too small and light prior to that. I got on the team first in 1979. Kinnitty won the County final in 1979 in a replay against Coolderry in Birr, and for that replay, Kinnitty moved Pat Delaney, who was a comrade of mine playing for Offaly at the time, back to centre half back and the two of us combined quite well, with me at left half back. That move really set me on my way."

How did you combat superior strength and physique in general over the years?

"You develop it yourself over time when you're playing the games and you realise you're caught in certain situations. You have to adjust with time. At wing back I learned to play more defensively in my game. I couldn't afford to sell myself completely in any situation. If I went for a fifty-fifty ball in the air full whack and I was beaten, then I had myself sold."

You didn't need to train much physically?

"Hurling is, I believe, basically around training with the ball. In hurling you're working your arms as well as your legs a lot. So if you spend one and a half hours hurling you're working a lot of your limbs and you will get fit just hurling."

Did you always dream of becoming an Offaly hurler?

"I dreamt first of becoming a Kinnitty hurler, my home club. I remember back to 1965, the start of the Kinnitty era. They were junior then and had not won a County title since 1930. In 1965 they were beaten in the junior final by a last minute score. In 1966 they won the junior title and in 1967 they won the Offaly Senior Hurling title. I was eleven years old then and the whole thing impressed me so much. The mentors were Paddy Joe Neill and Tim Egan, the latter, Secretary for forty years when the club had little or no success. With the passing years, I learnt to appreciate the importance of that victory because it brought a great change in hurling in Kinnitty. The captain, Pat Spain was carried shoulder high into the village. It was a small community and everybody had a sod of turf held aloft. The sods were soaked in oil and set ablaze, literally a torch lit acclamation. I was one of the young fellows carrying a blazing sod of turf alongside Pat Spain."

Any other memories?

"At that time, the Flahertys came on the scene, Johnny and Mick and the Moyles, Percy and Eddie, all young lads combining with the older fellows like Pat Spain. At that particular time hurling was very tough in Offaly. They had won through as hurlers in a very tough atmosphere. At that time Paddy Johnston of Kilkenny started to referee games in Offaly and he was the start of cleaning up Offaly's act a little bit and bringing Kilkenny discipline into it."

Your interest in hurling, Ger?

"From the time I was knee high every Sunday was spent going to a match with my father. Television was just starting then."

You grew up with the growth of Offaly as a hurling power. How did it all begin, as well as the Paddy Johnston clean up act?

"That was the start of it. Then Offaly made a small breakthrough in 1969 to get to the Leinster final before being beaten by Kilkenny. That gave great hope to Offaly. The team was a mixture of very young and very experienced players. The latter were Paddy Molloy and Barney Moylan. Both will always live in my mind as absolutely classy. The younger players then were P.J. Whelehan (father of Brian of today) and Johnny Flaherty."

Other factors in the rise?

"At the time I was going to the Presentation Brothers School in Birr and the Principal was Br. Denis from Cork. When I was a first year everything revolved around the training of the school senior team and we would have to spend our two breaks at 10 o'clock and for lunch doing a chorus in the yard, getting our vocal chords going for the games."

Would you give Br. Denis the credit for giving you the skill of hurling?

"I don't think anybody can give you the skill of hurling but he gave me the environment on which was built a deep love of the game. We trained so much and the atmosphere was right for development."

When did you realise you had the skills?

"I started to play teams outside the county with the school at U-14 level, teams like St. Peter's of Wexford and St. Kieran's, Kilkenny. Winning and beating those, I realised there was something there that maybe we should be able to carry through to senior hurling later."

Did you win a Leinster title with Presentation, Birr?

"We won at U-14 and U-16 level. The real turning point for me was when we played the senior final against Kieran's in 1975. The game was on about ten minutes when Aidan Fogarty who was playing centre back on Kieran Brennan was sent off and we lost the match by three or four points afterwards. We always felt that if we had him that we'd have won. He was our best player and they went on to win the All-Ireland afterwards defeating Faranferris easily and Kilkenny minors. With ten of the Kieran's lads aboard, they went on to win the minor All-Ireland. Presentation, Birr built on that result and went on to ultimate success later."

Who else was on that school team with you?

"Eugene Coughlan, Aidan Fogarty, Pat Carroll, Brendan Birmingham, Joachim Kelly..."

Did you realise how good you were?

"We realised how emotional it was. We returned to school on Monday and Br. Denis who was very disappointed brought us in to a room to talk to us. He was just about to speak to us and he ran out of the room. Same thing next day. On the third day he broke down. We realised how much it meant to him and that memory will always stay with me."

Any other people besides Br. Denis who deserve kudos for the Offaly resurgence?

"In my own club, Fr. Madden coached me from an early age. He gave me the right attitude to hurling. After that Br. Denis and Dermot Healy who came as team manager to Offaly in 1979."

What was Dermot Healy like?

"We knew he had success with Kilkenny at under age level and he came with a fair reputation. At that time Offaly hadn't won anything. What Dermot instilled in us was that we were good. As good as Kilkenny."

Had he something special as a manager?

"Because he was an outsider he built up a lot of respect. He changed the style of training in Offaly. Before that they believed a lot in physical fitness. Dermot changed that and 90% of all training was based around hurling."

Was it a tough struggle to get there?

"In 1980 we made our breakthrough in our first Leinster final against Kilkenny and we had to have our share of luck to get through that. Against that we were a shade unlucky against Galway in the semi-final. So we were hungry to get back at it in 1981. Winning the Leinster title again in 1981, there was a lot of pressure on us to win our first All-Ireland."

How did you feel when you had won the All-Ireland?

"I really understood it when we came back to Offaly with the McCarthy Cup and saw the emotion in the people. The expression on the people's faces is what I vividly remember."

The great Offaly hurlers of your own time?

"In the past it was Paddy Molloy, Barney Moylan and Johnny Flaherty. On the more current team we had Pat Delaney, Padhraic Horan, Mark Corrigan, Johnny Flaherty again, Joachim Kelly, Pat Carroll... At different stages different men pulled us out of the fire. In 1981 it was Delaney and Flaherty. In 1985 it was Horan. In most of the intervening years Mark Corrigan."

Pat Carroll's death must have been very severe on you all?

"That was sore on everybody. I had been in school with Pat. We sat together in our first year at Presentation, Birr. He lived for the game and sacrificed everything even his work at times. We were very close and in 1985 we were playing Kilkenny in the first Round of the Leinster Championship and Pat was playing centre half forward on

Ger Henderson. After the match, which we drew after being nine points down at half time, we met on the following Tuesday night for analysis. Pat took the total blame himself, giving the credit to his opponent, Ger Henderson for Kilkenny's supremacy and promising he'd do better on him if selected at centre half forward the next day. Following that meeting, Pat told me he was having headaches but he was afraid to tell anybody, especially at that time as it would have been taken as an excuse. We beat Kilkenny in the replay and Pat succeeded in halting Ger's domination."

What year did he die?

"He died in March 1986. All the players were at the funeral. The coffin was carried by players on the mile and a half route from Chapel to cemetery."

You had your own personal family tragedy, didn't you?

"In 1989 my younger brother, Seamus, who had hurled with Offaly in 1987, died in a tragic drowning accident in America the week before we played Antrim in the All-Ireland semi-final. It was a very traumatic time and I regretted afterwards that I played in that game."

Your greatest opponents?

"Billy Bohane (Laois), Ger Fennelly (Kilkenny), Joe Connolly (Galway) in the earlier days who was strong, forceful and determined and broke into Irish when he got really excited."

Greatest player you ever saw?

"Outside of Offaly (and I stress this), Ger Henderson was the greatest all round player I ever saw. He had everything. He was very strong physically. Tough and rugged but he never fouled. He had a tremendous will to win and he instilled that in the whole team."

Any changes you'd like to see in the game of hurling?

"More coaching. I know there is a lot of it taking place but we should look at the professional side of it on a more organised basis. There should be a full time hurling coach minimum in every county."

Any change in the game itself?

"In relation to time-keeping in the game, definitely we should have a stop-clock in place and everybody, crowd, players, officials can see this. That would bring a lot of excitement to the scene and take the onus of time-keeping from the referee especially the overtime given when spectators never know what to expect. The umpires for important games should all be top class referees themselves who should be brought into play in any matters that occur around the square. Most young players now have to wear a helmet and that is a good thing. I never wore one. Never had any need to. Got the first three stitches of my life two months ago."

Do G.A.A. players, especially Gaelic footballers take the whole thing too seriously now?

"Football in general has gone maybe more professional in its approach than hurling and maybe a little bit of the enjoyment will go out of it as a result. Hurling is still at a level which is less technical and less psychological. In relation to managers you'd have to question all the planning and sometimes the intimidating tactics devised for a game. A person my size wouldn't last at all in football because he would be taken out of it."

Is there too much hype in major games today?

"The more hype you have the better. Also this helps to attract young people into our games. Hurling has taken a back seat here as all the hype seems to be about football. I don't agree with the development of Croke Park. They should be looking at the positioning of a 'Croke Park', a stadium similar to Croke Park, down the country."

Is television giving fairplay to hurling?

"I don't think television does justice to hurling at all. You can't really follow hurling on television. People who don't understand the game wouldn't have a clue what's going on from television as they wouldn't see the ball."

Why is the G.A.A. becoming more successful in the modern era?

"I mightn't totally agree with the question. I'd be worried about hurling. It requires a lot of time and because of the competition from other sports, anyone playing hurling as well as two or three other sports is finding it difficult to develop the skills necessary for hurling. Football is developing O.K. because it is close enough to soccer and they can mix both games. We are getting bigger crowds at major games. But we aren't getting bigger crowds for ordinary club games and the club is the backbone of the G.A.A."

Your opinion of the All-Ireland club title?

"The biggest disappointment of my hurling life was that Kinnitty didn't win an All-Ireland club title. Offaly for me was a ten year period in the middle of my hurling life but my club, Kinnitty is my love and we failed to win the club title with a very good team. We won the County finals of 1978 and 1979 and then a 3-in-a-row 1983-1985. We never won a provincial club title and the team that beat us often went on to win out. But our club had Pat Delaney, the two Corrigans and Johnny Flaherty. It was a good skilful team but not the type of team required to win a club title. The club title is usually played during the winter in very mucky wet conditions. It's the most under-rated competition we have and needs to be projected more. It should be played in more favourable conditions for hurling. It was a huge disappointment to be beaten in a club final in Leinster by St. Martin's, Kilkenny in the middle of winter. That was 1985 and the venue was Athy."

Favourite sportswriter and commentator?

"Two favourite comentators, Micheál O'Hehir and Micheál Ó Muircheartaigh. O'Hehir did the G.A.A. a great service in earlier times and Ó Muircheartaigh in modern times. Paddy Downey (*Irish Times*) is my favourite sportswriter."

Achievements?

"Five Offaly Senior Hurling, seven Leinster Senior Hurling (actually played in eleven Leinster Senior finals in a row in the same position never missing a game), two All-

Irelands. I was never injured playing hurling until recently. I won two All Star Awards in 1981 and 1985."

Game of your life?

"Really when I look back on it in years to come I'll always think of the 1981 All-Ireland Final as being the special occasion. I'll always remember going out on Croke Park that day and feeling the hum of excitement in the air. The atmosphere Croke Park creates is not just the crowd shouting. It's a hum and players respond either positively or negatively. I'd like to think it made me respond positively. I can remember the tune the Artane Boys Band played. It gave me a dance in my step. The tune was Fáinne Geal an Lae. In the puck around before that game I don't think anything ever had such a settling effect on me as that tune."

The greatest thrill from the game of hurling itself?

"The greatest thrill for me as a defender has always been frustrating a forward and when he throws up a ball eventually blocking him."

U.C.D. days?

"Br. O'Grady trained us then and we won a Fitzgibbon under him. He had a similar type of hurling energy as Br. Denis. Hurling and the G.A.A. generally owes a great debt to the Irish Christian Brothers."

Family and final thoughts?

"My wife's name is Bernadette from Kilcormac. We have three kids, Colm who is five, Brian four, Roisín one and a half, the joy of my life. The boys come to the games with me and enjoy it. A lot of people spend much time criticising the G.A.A. and finding fault with it. If we look at it realistically a lot of the parents of this country could be very thankful to the G.A.A. for the contribution it has made to the well-being of their children. They know when they are out playing, being brought to games and out training that they are in good hands and a discipline is being built up in them for life. People who play games as youngsters are much stronger as a result and are better prepared for life. It promotes discipline and respect for people. The people coaching youngsters are all amateur doing the work voluntarily in their own time and in rural Ireland anyway, the people doing this work are very sound solid people."

Above, left : Ger Coughlan, in action in Croke Park in the 1981 final.
right: The late Pat Carroll, his schoolboy friend who shared many hurling triumphs with Ger.

Chapter 25

Noel Roche

Kilkee and Clare

When Clare footballers hit the limelight in 1992 by winning the Munster Senior Football title for the first time in 75 years, dethroning old rivals and hitherto unbeatable Kerry in the final, no one felt more pride than the longserving Kilkee man, Noel Roche, who had soldiered so long in vain for the Banner county.

What age are you Noel?

"Thirty-three at the moment, thirty-four in December 1993."

Your club?

"St. Senan's, Kilkee. 1976 was my first year playing with the senior team."

Who sowed the seeds of interest in you?

"Fr. Pat Culligan. He came to Kilkee when juvenile football was non-existent. He got together an U-14 team in 1969. Joe Hennessy was another great organiser. We were successful with a good bunch of players arriving together. I used to go to the field watching the U-14's train in 1969. Our colours were blue and we were well-known as the 'Blues of Kilkee'. We lost the U-14 in 1973 but won the U-16 in 1975."

The lads who were with you then?

"My brother Michael, now in America, was bigger and stronger than me even though we were born in the same year, he in January, me in December. I could never beat him. Martin O'Shea, also in the U.S., John Murray and Jimmy Murray."

Under age successes?

"My first major disappointment was losing the U-14 final as captain in 1973 to Kilmihill. We came good two years later in U-16, beating Kilmihill in the semi-final. There was great enthusiasm in Kilkee then for juvenile football which was just developing. We won the Clare minor title in 1975 and on to an U-21 in 1976 and 1979 and I was on both teams. We got to our first senior final in 1981 for about forty years and lost to Kilrush at Cusack Park in Ennis."

That must have been some local derby?

"There is always great rivalry between Kilrush and Kilkee. Kilrush were the kingpins in the seventies, winning five county Senior Football titles in a row. The Greens of Kilrush versus the Blues of Kilkee. We came along in 1984 (Centenary Year) to win our first Senior Football title in forty-two years. A big day for Kilkee. We weren't given a chance above in Carron, Michael Cusack's birthplace. We won by 0-10 to 0-5 on a dreadfully wet day against Kilmihill. The wind was howling across the Burren. Since then, we beat Doonbeg in a replay in 1989 and we beat Doonbeg in 1992, again by a point in the final. So I have three county Senior Football medals. The 1984 one would be number one."

Your first time playing for Clare seniors?

"I always had aspirations. I actually played minor, U-21 and senior in the same year for Clare - 1977. I didn't join the Army until 1984. Martin Maloney, a great footballer in his time, came into the factory in which I worked in Kilrush, Warner International and asked me would I join the Clare panel. I was dumbfounded as my dreams had come true. My first game was against Galway in Pearse Stadium in a Gael Linn Cup game. Tommy Curtin got the 'flu the night before and I was thrown in at the deep end marking Johnny Hughes of Galway. I had a baptism of fire. He knew I was young and he treated me like a baby. He played the game hard and fair and I'll never forget that game in September, 1977. And we beat Galway too."

Do you take the game seriously?

"Always did. Trained very hard. I don't drink or smoke. Whatever about drinking, I don't think I'll ever wish to smoke. I've tried many drinks but just don't like them. I have no problems about going to pubs after games or socially."

Your first Senior Football Championship game with Clare?

"In 1978 and I don't remember too much about the match. It was in the new Páirc Uí Chaoimh against Cork. My first impression was going through a tunnel area and looking out onto the pitch and thinking it looked so big. The first time out of Clare, playing an important game inside a kind of Colliseum. I was playing on Brian Murphy, the dual star at all levels, a big name at the time."

Did you ever think then that you'd play for Clare in a Championship before a packed arena?

"You would always hope to contest a Munster final some day. You'd often wonder would it ever happen and the years kept passing by so quickly, one after the other often getting beaten in the first round. There would always be enthusiasm for the Championship and we always trained hard."

Who were the ones who kept the flame alight in those days of hope?

"In all those dreary years one name always cropped up. That was Noel Walsh. He was a pure dreamer. His life and soul was Clare football. A Milltown man, he never gave up hope even when things were down in the dumps. He kept on pressing for the Open Draw in Munster and eventually got it in 1991. There was always the possibility that you might catch either Cork or Kerry in a semi-final but the chances of beating the two of them was remote."

Others who kept hopes alive?

"Down through the years we had different men looking after teams with little success. One such was Joe Taylor of Moyasta. He always said there was no difference between a Clare footballer and a Kerry one. If the attitude and dedication was right with the Clare players, success would come, he maintained. He prepared teams even as good as John Maughan. He probably lacked in the area of goals, putting the carrot out there in front of us. We had John McCarthy, a fantastic selector, David Weldrick in the 1986-

1987 era who brought us out of Div.3 into Div.2 of the National Football League. He introduced discipline and concentrated on tactics a lot. We may have lacked in fitness then. A great man for the chalkboard. Seanie Maloney was one of the greatest scoring forwards Clare ever produced. He took over the team at a low ebb and concentrated on ball work."

Once Kerry beat Clare in the Munster Championship by a phenomenal score?

"We will never forget or be allowed to forget that one. The year was 1979. The venue was Milltown Malbay. The score 9-29 to 1-9. We never gave up even that day. Very interestingly I was U-21 that year and the Wednesday night after that drubbing we had to play Cork in the Munster U-21 final in the Gaelic Grounds in Limerick. No one gave us a hope but we put our backs to the wall and they just beat us 0-14 to 1-9. We were disappointed when we saw Cork go on to win the U-21 title that year. On that night John McGrath had a magnificent game. One of the best fielders ever to come out of Clare."

Did you often feel like giving it all up?

"9-29 to 1-9 was a period in time when you said to yourself what is it all about? We had a lot of preparation done but we met a super Kerry team eager for more success. On days like that you sit down in the dressing-room and look down at your boots with your head between your legs. And you say to yourself 'God above tonight, it isn't worth this'. But then you have twelve months to think about it. Along comes the League and you win a few games and confidence returns. And you're raring to go again for the next Championship."

And then John Maughan?

"John was brought in, in 1991. He came in when Clare were at a very low ebb. I remember the first match we played was against Waterford in the League at Newmarket-on-Fergus and they beat us the same evening. We didn't do too well in that League. But then in the Championship against Kerry over in the Park (Ennis), they were extremely lucky to beat us."

Was he then beginning to have an effect?

"His commitment was total. He travelled down from Galway to Crusheen and never missed a session. Every training session was different. Before, they were all in the one gear. John has a way of getting the best out of players. One night he'd concentrate on one player. Next night someone else. His methods of training surpassed anyone I've ever trained under. Always let the players know exactly what he wanted. Told us always what was happening. Never contemplated defeat."

When did this confidence begin to rub off on Clare?

"It did take its time. First of all he knew our fitness level wasn't adequate. His first aim was to bring a panel of twenty up to the required level of fitness. Once he got the fitness right, he started work on the ball. That took a period of six months. His techniques didn't come to fruition until the Championship game against Kerry in 1991. Kerry got two late goals to put an untidy look on the score which was 5-16 to 2-12 in the finish. We had Kerry on the rack for a lot of that game."

When did Clare begin to capture the Clare public's fancy?

"When we won the All-Ireland B title that was a major stepping stone."

Is that B title worthwhile?

"It's a fantastic competition, because it gives you Championship type football. Tough fit teams and it's run in conjuncton with the League. In 1991 between October and December I think we had only three free Sundays because of our double involvement."

Clare's first successes?

"We won the B title and then went on to qualify for the Quarter final of the National Football League against Meath beating Limerick, Antrim and Longford to win the B title in Ballinasloe. We won promotion in the League and had nothing in our heads but a win when we met Meath again in Ballinasloe. We finished up with thirteen men, they with fourteen in a very physical game. Very low scoring 0-8 to 0-6 and we were bitterly disappointed to lose. We had trained very hard and we carried that on to the Championship in 1992, when we knew from the Open Draw of the previous September that Tipperary were our first round opponents in the semi-final. Our goal had been to reach Division 1 of the League and this we accomplished as our first objective."

The reshuffling of the National Football League format for 1992-1993 must have disappointed Clare?

"In a major way, yes. We had worked hard to get to Division 1 and though the new format worked well for us and for the G.A.A., it was no reward for hard work at the time."

The Munster Final against Kerry in 1992?

"A marvellous occasion for every Clare person. John had us in tip-top shape. We played out of our skins. No player on the team played a bad game. We weren't afraid of Kerry. Didn't worry about certain Kerry players but instead worried about our own performance."

When did you realise that you had it won?

"At the final whistle! But when Gerry Killeen got the insurance point with a minute to go, I said to myself they can't beat us now."

What were your thoughts at the final whistle?

"It was absolutely shell shock. I can remember the crowd running on to the field. Strange faces and ones you knew trying to get a hold of you. Being breathless. Carried off the field in a sea of emotion."

Did you hear the Clare F.M. radio report of the final stages?

"I did and Matthew McMahon the commentator gave a tremendous performance on the day. We were in the dressing-room for ages doing interviews. Matthew is a tremendous character and he expressed the feelings of a lot of Clare people on that day."

Were the celebrations great for the following week?

"John let us run loose for about a week. I remember in the West County Hotel after the game people were so shocked. It took twenty-four hours for the achievement to sink in. The Monday morning papers told it all. I think it was the reception we got on Monday morning when we gathered at the West County Hotel for the 'procession' through Clare because it was ten times better than even the night before."

Your greatest moment from that procession through Clare on the Monday?

"Your grassroots are your own club and your own town. When we reached Kilkee on Monday evening at around 8p.m., there was a lorry there to meet us to parade the team through the town. Gerry Kelly and myself were given pride of place at the front and I remember the two of us holding the Cup as we went down O'Connell Street and O'Curry Street and all the streets in between with about five thousand people present from Kilkee, The Loop, Doonaha."

The Croke Park occasion itself?

"That particular day in Croke Park was incredible. Winning the Munster final was one thing. Running out onto Croke Park in the All-Ireland semi-final and the roar of the Clare crowd which quite outnumbered Dublin was brilliant. Again we were very disappointed to lose and no consolation at all to have supporters say we did well etc. and thanks for the memories."

You did very well in the League too?

"Soon after the Dublin game the draw for the 1993 Munster Senior Football Championship was made and we found ourselves pitted against Cork in Ennis and Kerry in the semi-final if we won. So all our attention was geared to May 30th, 1993 and the Championship game against Cork in Ennis."

That all-ticket live telecast occasion saw Clare fight hard to retain the crown?

"That was a personal disappointment for me for after nine months solid training for that goal, I had to leave the field with injury at half-time. I never had to leave the field before. I was really down after the game but we did fight hard at the start of the second half before bowing to a better Cork team."

Whither Clare football now?

"The League is next now. We must give it another shot next year as we await the draw for the 1994 Munster Senior Football Championship patiently. We have Dublin, Kildare, Down, Donegal, Derry, Mayo in our League Group. We will be competing with the very best."

Most difficult opponent?

"The one man I always found very hard to mark was Pat Spillane."

Is he the greatest player you ever saw?

"Jack O'Shea fits that bill. You'd have to go back to that Kerry team of the 1970's. They were a magnificent bunch who complemented each other. The Bomber Liston, Ger Power, Mikey Sheehy.... Jacko was the king of them all. I played with him for Ireland against Australia in 1986 and 1990 and his leadership qualities, football ability and sportsmanship were second to none."

The Australian experience?

"1984 was a great year for me. First we won the Clare title, then a month later I was selected for Ireland to play against the Australians in Croke Park. In 1986 I travelled to Australia under Kevin Heffernan, one of the shrewdest operators I've come across. He masterminded a very successful tour down under after losing the First Test."

You have great admiration for Peter McDermott, don't you Noel?

"He generated great enthusiasm for the Compromise Rules game. The people in charge in 1984 were Liam Sammon, Peter, Eamonn Young and Jody O'Neill. I loved the Compromise Rules game. There seems to be a lull in the relationship now and financially it may not be viable as the support didn't materialise in Australia. I thought the game was fluent, very tough, with a lot of running."

Your biggest thrill from the game of Gaelic football?

"It's the love of playing the game. I like the physical aspect of it but some of the things developing into the game at the moment have to be sorted out. Like the tackle, for instance. There has to be a penalisation of a team constantly fouling. Like basketball where a team is given a free shot or bringing the ball forward fifty metres as they are doing now in Australian Rules."

Would you favour the yellow card scheme operated in soccer?

"Anything that would cut out this persistent fouling which is ruining the game. To have sixty or seventy frees in a game is unacceptable."

Your opinion of the behind the ball shenanigans?

"Cameras covering the whole field on important occasions would sort out this problem. Players will go as far as they are let and there is no doubt they are encouraged to try anything to win."

The game of your life?

"The 19th July 1992 when we beat Kerry. A fantastic occasion for me who had played for Clare for nearly fifteen years."

Did you cry that day?

"I did cry. I met my father going down the tunnel. He embraced me and it nearly brings a lump to my throat even now. He gave me such a hug. It wasn't the best game of my life but the achievement, the occasion and the atmosphere made it my greatest day in football."

Family and final thoughts?

"I got married at the age of twenty-one to Kathleen from Doonbeg. We have four children, Noelle nine, Colm seven, Edel three and Clare just a year old. They have a lot to endure. I'm gone a lot of the time."

Railway Cup record?

"One man I forgot to mention is our club Secretary John Lynch, an extraordinary, enthusiastic man. In charge of affairs for twenty-two years. I played nine years for Munster but never won a medal. I was selected first in 1983 and we were beaten in three finals."

An action shot of Noel Roche from the 1991 All-Ireland B final in Navan with John Maughan, the team manager, on his left.

Chapter 26

Denis Coughlan (Cork)

Dual All-Ireland Medalist

Denis Coughlan of Cork, The Glen and St. Nick's is one of the rare breed of Irishmen to have won All-Ireland senior medals in both codes. Mostly Corkmen, men like Jimmy Barry Murphy, Brian Murphy, Ray Cummins, Jack Lynch and Teddy McCarthy, who in 1990 won both medals. In his home in Carrigtwohill, Denis showed me his collection of medals which is awesome. Denis now likes a game of golf but is still keen on the games he graced, particularly hurling.

How many people have won All-Ireland senior medals in both codes?

"I think there are about fourteen or fifteen. Whenever anyone of us meet we don't relate to that."

How many Munster Senior medals have you?

"Five in football and all hard won against Kerry, 1966, 1967, 1971, 1973 and 1974. It was never easy to beat them and you certainly remember the years you did."

Were the two games complementary or was it a problem?

"I found it a problem because of the position I played in. I played at centrefield for most of my career in both games. In the early years, the first two Sundays in July were set aside for the two Munster finals, being switched in order in alternate years. Let's say the hurling was first, the ball would be dropping in the middle of the field and you could judge it fairly well. Then you had only two nights training for the football final and it used to take me ten or fifteen minutes in the game to adjust to the kickout which would be shorter than the sliothar."

The game you preferred most?

"Hurling was in my blood. I was born and reared in Blackpool, home of Glen Rovers. I had the good fortune of walking up to the Glen field every evening in the summer and watching the likes of Christy Ring, Vincie Twomey, and Josie Hartnett from behind the goal. Getting the ball for those and hitting it back to them. So from a very early age I was very much influenced by hurling."

Did they impress the young Coughlan?

"They could literally do anything with a ball. Unlike nowadays they had only two or three balls to train with and each had to fight hard to get that ball. The whole emphasis was on hurling skill."

Those who started you off?

"My father, who played hurling with a club called St. Mary's, who were part of the north side of the city, was a very big influence on me. So also was Séamus O'Brien."

Your juvenile days with the Glen?

"I played U-15 and minor for five years. I also went to the North Monastery which was close to my home and for my entire under-age career I never won anything of any description. My first medals were Munster and All-Ireland junior football medals in 1964. So I was well used to being beaten before I became an adult. It shaped my character no end."

The spirit of the Glen?

"The spirit is best defined by the fact that the Glen had great teams though they didn't always have the best hurlers. The standard of hurling in Cork in the 1940's, 1950's and 1960's was extremely high and the Glen won an awful lot of county titles."

How did they accomplish this?

"We were a very united section of the community and everybody knew everybody.

There were no cars. People walked to work. Many of them to Gouldings, Sunbeam Wolsey and Fords. Hurling was part of the fabric of society."

Where did Gaelic football and St. Nick's come in?

"St. Nick's, even though it was there before the Glen (formed in 1916) just had the hurlers playing football for that club. Still they won five Cork County titles. The spirit of the hurling overflowed into the football. Within St. Nick's you had men like Doney Donovan for whom football was first though Doney too, captained the Glen in County finals. But he was primarily a footballer and represented Cork and Munster with distinction. There was a John Joe Kelly and, of course, Jack Lynch, but very few of them were pure footballers."

How did you cope with training for the two games?

"There was for and against training for the two together and it didn't occur to me until I retired from one of them. I played football for Cork for ten years (1964-1974) and from 1965-1980 for the Cork hurlers. So the ten years almost coincided. In that time if you lost in one, you always had the other, it seemed, and it made you less determined to win. When I retired from football in 1974, I was playing hurling only then and I suddenly realised I was now in one game and I had to win every game."

Did the variety counterbalance the pressure?

"I had a very simple philosophy which I devised myself early on and came to terms with. Whichever was the most important next game I trained with that team be it club or county, championship getting first priority and I never encountered any problems."

How to compare the two games?

"I found the training for hurling was tremendously exciting and had great variety. You were less likely to get tired. With the hurling the ball was moving up and down the field and you could do a lot of things with it. In football, I got tremendous delight out of catching a high ball, bringing it down and giving a thirty yards pass. In hurling it was keeping the ball going on the ground. Pulling on it. I'll give you an example.

Whenever I was training for hurling I always tried to do the hardest thing. Playing as a wingback rather than stop it I always tried to keep it going."

Please illustrate.

"If someone were to ask me to pick out a thing out of my hurling career, it happened in the 1977 All-Ireland semi-final against Galway and I was playing left half back on Bernie Forde. P. J. Molloy was on the other wing and playing very well and they asked me to mark him. So I went over and it was very close and the ball came out of our goal at a crucial stage along the ground and it came fairly quickly to me and without any hesitation I pulled on it straightaway up the Hogan Stand side of the field and it travelled seventy or eighty yards along the ground. Nobody ever recalled it for me. That to me was pure hurling."

Anything you'd remember like that from a football game?

"One of the greatest fetches I ever had the pleasure of effecting was in the County final in 1969, the same year as the Glen had beaten U.C.C. in a great County hurling final. Two Sundays later it was against yet another great U.C.C. team in the County football final. They had a lot of great Kerry lads, Paudie and Brendan Lynch and Dan Kavanagh. The match was a draw with two minutes to go and there was a kickout from the U.C.C. goal and it was the highest leap I ever took to catch the ball. When I came down with it I was surrounded by two or three players and the referee, Jimmy Dennigan, blew the whistle and gave a free to U.C.C. for no obvious foul by me. They took it quickly and Brendan Lynch picked it up and put it over the bar. My greatest ever catch led ultimately to a win for the opposition in a County final."

Career achievements?

"Thirteen Munster Senior medals (I've already listed the five football ones), one Junior Football, one U-21 Hurling in 1966 having beaten Wexford after two replays, two Senior club (Hurling) All-Irelands with Glen Rovers in 1973 and 1977 and five All-Ireland Senior medals (one in Football in 1973), one Railway Cup (Football) in 1972, and four All Stars in hurling."

The status of an All Star?

"It's absolutely fantastic to be selected as an All Star. It's like being selected for Ireland. It gives us an international status. I also won the Texaco award for hurling in 1977."

Were you worried when Ireland did so well in the World Cup that the G.A.A. would take a backseat?

"I was delighted for the Irish soccer team and watched all their games. But I had certainly no fears that it would affect the popularity of hurling and football. I do think though that both games have been affected by the varied participation by the youth in a wide range of sporting activities as they grow up today. An awful lot of them play golf, squash, tennis, soccer, rugby, basketball, hurling and football and they can be proficient at all of them but my main concern is that by the time they arrive at seventeen when they have to decide which game they must choose, that they have lost the vital years in Gaelic games where you develop the skills and you never get those back."

Are the games of hurling and football being affected by the cynicism of modern life?

"The honesty has gone out of them. It's win at all costs now. Managers have taken the limelight from the team. There is more excitement generated by who is going to manage than who is going to be on the team."

Are managers responsible for the disappearance of the honesty thing?

"I don't honestly know the answer. An awful lot rests on the player himself. Football is the least honest absolutely. First of all the man to man marking is gone. The pride of beating your own man by outfielding him, outmarking him, being first to the ball has all gone. Individualism has died. We now have athletes instead of footballers. Far too much emphasis on physical fitness."

Have you gone off football?

"Certainly in the last four years. The amount of fouls in every game. The average is about sixty fouls in every seventy minute game. Players are pure lazy, even though that may seem a contradiction as they were never fitter. Just too lazy to try and legally dispossess an opponent."

Could refereeing handle that?

"Referees are getting the thin edge of the wedge. I don't know what year the personal foul rule was introduced but if you remember it was decided to enforce it, three personal fouls and you were off. Séamus Aldridge carried out the letter of the law, sent about four off and didn't get the backup from the G.A.A. O.K. John O'Keeffe and one or two other clean players were sent off. By and large, if they persevered with that and if we went for six months with only seven or eight or nine players on a side, eventually, players and managers would get the message. You'd revert back to the skills of the game."

Anecdotes?

"On the Friday before the 1972 Munster hurling final against Clare I pulled into a garage for petrol and Christy Ring pulled in behind me. Christy started talking to me about the game. We were talking about hurleys and he asked to see mine which I happened to have in the car. He looked at it and he had a massive pair of wrists. Whatever he did with it he snapped it in two and he got an awful fright realising straightaway what it meant. He said, 'Don't tell anybody', but brought me to his car - a Red Cortina - and took a hurley from the boot and gave it to me. 'There' he said, 'Will that do you on Sunday?' and it was the hurley he had used in the 1952, 1953 and 1954 finals. Now I couldn't use it as it was very heavy. I used to get my hurleys handmade by Mick McCarthy in Riverstown. 'Look,' says Christy, 'I'll get you a hurley for Sunday'. He went off and he arrived in my office later with a hurley that was exactly like the one he had broken. 'Look that will bring you luck on Sunday', was his parting comment. We played Clare and were leading very comfortably in the middle of the second half when there was a clash with my direct opponent who went down injured and the referee panicked and said 'You'll have to go off'. So I took the lonely march to the line with the 'Lucky' hurley Ring gave me. The only time I was ever sent off."

Any other anecdote?

"Oh yes, it was the 1976 All-Ireland Final against Wexford and I was under the Cusack Stand standing to attention for the National Anthem. Next thing I got a tap on the shoulder during the Anthem. You know your feelings during a National Anthem. You're wondering why am I here and it is so moving and you're responding to being Irish, the shiver up the back feeling and I get this shoulder tap from John Quigley my opponent saying 'A fiver you won't last the match today., Denis'."

Greatest opponents?

"Mick Roche of Tipperary in hurling. To me he was the consummate hurler. Frank Cummins - a great player in terms of strength and very difficult to mark. Jimmy Doyle, too, absolute gentleman and great friend. Very fortunate to have played with the Glen for three years with Christy Ring at the end of his career 1964 to 1967. Unbelievable to play with him because he had won four All-Ireland medals before I was born."

Did you ever speak to him then?

"Strangely enough he never spoke to me prior to the hurley incident and we became extremely good friends after that. He used to call to my house and office regularly. Then in 1979 I got seriously ill and was in hospital for quite a long time. On one particular occasion Christy came in to see me as I was going for an operation the following day. He had been to Lourdes the week before and gave me a bottle of Lourdes water and said, 'Ring will pray for you tonight' and he put his hand on my head and started to cry. I'll never forget that. I went for the operation the following day and two days later Christy himself died suddenly."

Football opponents?

"Certainly Mick O'Connell. During those ten years I often played on Mick. On one occasion in Killarney we went 2-2 up within ten minutes of a Munster final and by half-time Kerry had gone two points ahead purely from Mick's boot. His frees particularly impressed me. Anything from sixty yards in over the bar but he never placed the ball. Just threw it down, stood back and kicked it over the bar. I had the pleasure of playing with him on a Railway Cup team and it was like being on a different level altogether. I came across Jimmy Duggan first in an U-21 semi-final against Galway (1965). I played on him often subsequently. He was an absolute gentleman, always wished you well before a game and relied purely on football skill. Pat Griffin from Kerry was my opponent in four Munster finals when I played centre half back and he was always too clever for me."

The greatest players ever?

"Mikey Sheehy in football. Had literally everything. Control, skill, anticipation and could score with either foot. In hurling Tony O'Sullivan had all the skills, Michael Cleary is a very balanced player today - like poetry in motion. Justin McCarthy and Gerald McCarthy too whom I opposed at club level. But Mick Roche was the king."

The Cork jersey?

"An extraordinary feeling to be selected for Cork for the first time. You're aware particularly in hurling, of the tradition created for you by the great men that played in the same jersey - men like Eudie Coughlan, Jim Hurley, Jack Lynch, Jim Young, Christy Ring... Now you have the chance of doing the same."

The game of your life?

"Football first. The 1971 Munster final against Kerry. They had won out in 1970 and then won the National League and I had been moved from centre field to corner forward that year. I was actually the top scorer in the charts coming up to that game and for some inexplicable reason, I was dropped. The game was for eighty minutes then and after fifteen or twenty minutes Cork found themselves five points down and I was called in. Everything went right for me from the moment I came in. First ball - a point and I ended up scoring 0-10. Played on John O'Keeffe and we won the game 0-25 to 0-15. Since I was knee high my ambition was always to play against Tipperary in hurling in a Munster final. So often was I brought by my father to Limerick as a youngster to these great Cork against Tipperary games. In 1968 that ambition was fulfilled but they beat us well. But in 1969 the same again. Cork hadn't beaten Tipperary in the Championship since 1956 and I was marking Mick Roche. We beat them and I had an absolute blinder of a game at midfield in the first half. I went to sleep for a time and Cork didn't score in the second half until eight minutes before full-time when I landed a point from midfield with the left hand and straightaway scored another point with the right hand. I played well, scored two crucial points before fifty thousand in Limerick. We beat Tipperary and to me it was the perfect fulfilment of a childhood ambition."

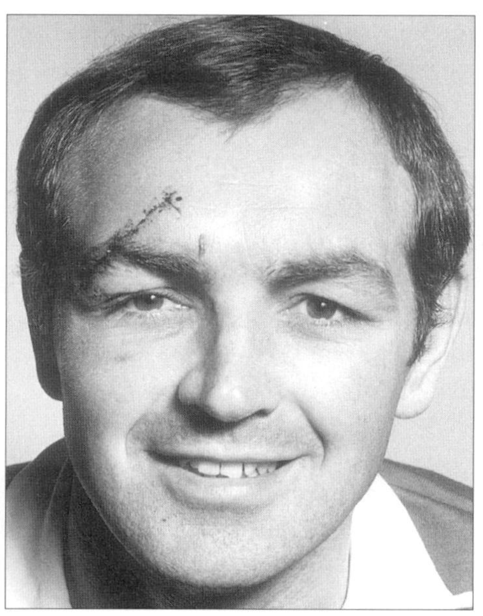

Above, left: Denis Coughlan, complete with stitches, from his All Star days.
right: Frank Cummins of Kilkenny, -'very difficult to mark'....

Chapter 27

Mikey Sheehy

Of Kerry

Kerry, popularly known as "The Kingdom", is widely acknowledged as the greatest of all Gaelic football counties. Beating Kerry in an All-Ireland Final is the ultimate as Peter McDermott of Meath said before raising the Sam Maguire Cup aloft in 1954. Football in Kerry is variously described as a religion, a passion, an all-consuming interest. Denis Moran, father of the current Kerry team-manager Ogie and a larger than life aficionado, always used to stop outside the Tralee graveyard to say a wee prayer for the All-Ireland men buried inside. In Kerry they have had their stars over the illustrious years, men like Dick Fitzgerald, John Joe Sheehy, Paddy Kennedy, Mick O'Connell, Jack O'Shea, Paddy Bawn Brosnan.... Into that category add the name Mikey Sheehy, a forward of immense stature, great feet, uncanny scoring ability, perfect gentleman and really the players' player. Mikey had this unassuming walking gait. Never flamboyant.

Did anyone describe you as a waddler?

"Páidí Ó Sé often did. In fact he'd often do it inside in a pub after a few jars and has been known to give a demonstration inside an old cowshed near Dingle."

Did you practise much as a youngster?

"I did and my mother would verify that. I'd have spent hours and hours with a ball. It started with my father being so interested and he used to bring me to every game. I'd be imagining I'd be Mick O'Connell or any of the heroes of those days. Sometimes we'd be in Killorglin out at my grandparents and we'd be glued to the radio listening to Micheál O'Hehir."

Describe that training as a youngster?

"We used to live in a gable house in St. Brendan's Park. As you go around to the back section there was a backdoor which I used to open. I used to practise frees and shots in that very narrow backdoor. That certainly helped my accuracy and various things. On the gable side of the house, there was a little section of it on top up towards the chimney that used to be my scoring shot. To claim a score you had to hit that."

Did you realise at that early age that you were developing a great kicking proficiency?

"Some people say that such and such a one has a lot of natural skill but I always feel that whether you have or you haven't you certainly can develop it over a period of time if you keep practising as I did."

Why did you choose Austin Stacks as your club?

"Like any town there is intense rivalry between Austin Stack's, John Mitchel's and Strand Road (Kerins-O'Rahilly), three senior clubs in Tralee. Funnily enough there are no boundaries really, mostly historic ones. Brothers within a family play with different clubs. We were living in the Stack's area and we had a tremendous juvenile committee at the time. Men like Micheál Hayes, Joe Mulchinock R.I.P., James Hobbert who trained me and is now looking after my young fellows. He is a clinker, at it for thirty-two years and I'm convinced that man should be paid by our club for keeping it going. Jack Parker was another. Micheál Hayes was the first man to bring us to Dublin on football trips. The earliest competition then was U-14 which we won at county level. U-16 too but we lost at minor level. We swept the board at U-16 level in 1968-1969. The club developed into a great senior team mainly through the work of those men."

The lads of your own age group?

"Teddy Brick, the goalkeeper, was my era. Ger Power, John O'Keeffe, Ger and Tony O'Keeffe were all two or three years older than me. Fintan Lawlor, Fionán Ryan were of my time but we were all relatively young and we grew up more or less together. We won our first County senior title for thirty-seven years in 1973. A fantastic occasion. Very special for me as I was the youngest player on the team. Just nineteen."

The Kerry jersey?

"Since I was out of the cradle, it was my ambition to play with Kerry and you'd always have this fear in the back of your head 'Would you be good enough to make the team'. I can remember the first time with the Kerry minors going up for trials and the start of the long process. I played minor for two years, we were beaten well the first year but only lost by a point the second year. We threw it away, we were leading by five points with ten minutes to go, yet lost. That was 1971 and Jimmy Barry Murphy had a big hand in it. When I went out onto the pitch the first day before thirty thousand people almost I didn't know where I was for about ten minutes. I got a goal that day and it was a clinker by all accounts and I don't even remember it. Actually when I got the ball into my chest, I just turned on my left leg and lashed it and it went into the top corner."

You grew up in the era of Jimmy Barry Murphy?

"He was by far a better footballer than he was a hurler in my opinion and look what he achieved in hurling after he gave up the football. I played with him in a few Railway Cup games and it was a pleasure to play with him."

The first senior games with Kerry?

"I played a few challenge games but the first real game was coming on in Killarney in 1973 in a National Football League game against Cork who were All-Ireland Champions. I remember the substitutes were kicking around on the field at half time. Mick O'Dwyer was playing and he was like myself on my last day in Killarney in 1987. He couldn't kick the ball over the bar. Missed some desperate frees. I played quite well in the second half because my entry was so unexpected. Andy Molyneaux R.I.P. gave me a slip as I was going to the dugout and told me I was on at corner forward and Johnny Cullotty who was in charge told me to kick all the frees. The first ball I got, I managed to turn and score and that gave me confidence. In all I got three or four points from play. We got a free and the roars from the line were for Mikey Sheehy to kick it. O'Dwyer came over. 'Twas about twenty-one yards out and said 'I'll kick it'. So I wasn't going to insist. He wasn't going to let the young fellow take over. That was I think his very last game for Kerry."

Did he point that twenty-one yards free?

"He did but my mother would have pointed it. The man I replaced that day was Éamonn O'Donoghoe who got injured. Eamonn was a brilliant footballer who played with his head always."

Were you always a purist?

"It's hard for me to answer that one! All of this comes from constant practice. When I was training with Stack's, I often kicked off my weak foot - the left - for an entire period say ten minutes."

Your thoughts on your first Senior All-Ireland win of 1975?

"Mick O'Dwyer is a great trainer, coach and everything but he is a thundering rogue! He conned people into thinking we were too young and not good enough. We were a very young team. But the training we went through was incredible. We went up to win and would have been disgusted to lose. The Mickey Sullivan incident probably helped us too as it got us fired up an extra bit. We started well too. I hit a weak free and John Egan got a brilliant goal out of it."

The feelings when the final whistle blew?

"Unbelievable feeling of elation, very hard to describe. We won the U-21 title that year too in Tipperary Town. I was twenty years old. All the practice I had done all came through my mind. The sidedoor."

Was Mick O'Dwyer special?

"I played in the Munster Final of 1974 in which we were well beaten by Cork in Killarney. I was corner forward and got about two kicks. The first ball that came into me I kicked it straight over the bar and didn't get a kick after and to this day I think the team that went out that day was about 50% fit. We were destroyed by Meath in the quarter final of the League early in 1975 in Croke Park and O'Dwyer took over then. I remember him taking us into Killarney and getting us started. I had been very fit up until minor age but I then picked up a bad groin injury and I had put on a good bit of weight being about fourteen stone and I remember O'Dwyer saying to me that I was in terrible shape. He told me I had to shed that weight or he didn't want me. He laid out this programme of training and you did that or he didn't want you. You had to give him the commitment his way. The reason he was special was that he was a great reader of player's needs in different years. He'd pick out different guys for special treatment, harder punishment if you like. You'd hate him at times. In your own mind you'd eff and blind him. But you never questioned anything he ever said. He had so many P.E. teachers in that team, six or seven of them. He never once asked any of them for advice or none of them ever attemped to offer it."

The Dublin Kerry rivalry?

"Nothing better than to see the Hill packed with the light blue and the navy. The atmosphere at those All-Ireland finals between Dublin and Kerry couldn't be beaten. Even taking frees and the Hill jeering you. It would help you to concentrate. And you'd say to yourself I'll quieten them now."

Did you get a special jeer after the famous Paddy Cullen goal?

"In fairness no, but that was at the other end and when I faced them they were shell-shocked as much as the Dublin team were. Dublin that day led by 0-6 to 0-1 after fifteen minutes and thought they had the game won. Then John Egan got a great goal. I was playing on Robbie Kelleher. Robbie was up at the other end of the field and I was with him. He passed the ball to Bobby Doyle who overplayed it. We were still running back in the middle of the field when John Egan goaled. That was the start of Dublin's downfall. Then came my goal, the freak goal as Micheál O'Hehir called it. The next goal straight after half-time came in this way. Jack O'Shea won a ball at midfield and was going for a point but it dropped short. It looked like a perfect pass to 'The Bomber' who buried it. It's things like that that win All-Irelands."

The Cullen goal?

"It was a chance that clicked. It comes back to training. You know you'd try these things in training and you'd say to yourself you'd love a similar situation to arise in a game. It was just instinct. The gap was there. I didn't think about missing it. If I missed it O'Dwyer would have blown a fuse. When the free was given, I was very close to Robbie Kelleher. Paddy Cullen had passed the ball out to Robbie who shook his head. At that stage Dublin were playing with heads down a little bit. Next thing Robbie handed the ball to me rather than me pulling it from him. Paddy was still arguing the toss and I had a quick look and there was a ferocious gap there. A lot of people still blame Paddy for arguing. Robbie handed me the ball. No other back lined the goal. I just put it down and had a go at it. Lucky enough it went in."

Is the game deteriorating?

"Much over emphasis on physical fitness to the detriment of the skills of the game. We did a pile of fitness exercise early on in training. But O'Dwyer had it structured that way. After that it was all ball once you got to the required level of fitness. Even at U-16 I see them running these youngsters around. These should be naturally fit. Skills and exercises with the ball for them. Maybe I'm being a wee bit unfair to label all counties thus, for to be fair Donegal played lovely football last year."

Is it sliding in Kerry?

"Kerry teams are still winning at U-age and Vocational School level but at the end of the day the Kerry football supporter wants the Sam Maguire Cup. After all very successful eras you will get valley periods. But it isn't as pessimistic an outlook as it looked at Killarney against Cork last June."

Your greatest opponent?

"The best player I marked has gone over the water to soccer, Kevin Moran. I was unfortunate to be on him in 1976. If he had stayed, he would have become one of the all-time greats."

The great players from Kerry?

"A man I had great time for was Paudie Lynch. He always used the ball very well. John O'Keeffe was a super player too. Another man who was an unsung hero in the middle of the field was Seanie Walsh. He was always 'Minding the house'. Great fielder. Páidí O'Sé another super player. I suppose of the forward line, individually or as a unit they were all as good as each other but if I was to pick out a favourite it would have to be John Egan. Spillane won many games for us. Ger Power pound for pound couldn't be better. And the Bomber created so much for us all."

And then Jacko?

"Mick O'Connell was my idol growing up and maybe I didn't see enough of him. But I would have to say Jack O'Shea was the best footballer I have seen and played with. Others who impressed me were Sean O'Neill of Down and Mickey Kearins of Sligo. Mickey for his free-taking. Lovely all round footballer. I remember O'Neill from 1968. He was going off at that stage but still tremendous. And Matt Connor of Offaly. How could I ever forget his 2-9 against us in 1980? It was one of the greatest individual displays I have ever seen."

Your greatest score?

"It was in the Munster final of 1981. The Cullen goal is the most talked about one. But this one engineered by Liston and Egan is the more memorable. It was an instinctive thing. We'd have done it in backs and forwards in training often. Nobody shouted or called. But Jacko kicked in this long ball. The dressing-room end of Killarney where we always played and our scoring goal really. We always like to play into that goal in the second half and it was the second half too in this game. We were leading by a point or two. I was top of the right, Bomber full forward and Egan in the left corner. Bomber and Egan moved out challenging for the ball and I was out looking for the break. But about half way out I turned sharply and took off in, leaving the back behind me and there was this ferocious gap inside. I knew Egan would get the break and at full speed I turned and the ball was there in my chest from Egan. I rattled it home. Couldn't miss it. All so instinctive. He'd put it on the top of a needle. I didn't have to catch it at all."

Did you ever get fed up of the training slog?

"No. You'd look forward to it. What made O'Dwyer so special was he kept everything very simple. A lot of people get bogged down with charts. None of that rubbish."

Best players today?

"Tony Boyle is the best full forward in the game. Vinny Murphy is a good footballer too. Martin McHugh had a great year last year but he is pushing on. Cork's new man Colin Corkerry is something special."

Will he be the new Tompkins?

"I'd say he'll be the new Colin Corkerry! I feel sorry for Tompkins who has got too many injuries. As fit a man as you'll ever see. A super athlete and brilliant footballer. He is a big loss to Cork. Another Tír na n-Óg player and brilliant footballer is Colm O'Rourke an amazing man. Here in Kerry, Maurice Fitzgerald has tremendous ability."

Can the game be improved?

"To me there is definitely a levelling off of standards now and the level of fitness has improved all round. I'd bring back the handpass except for scores. In the handpass days of our early successes you had plenty of scores and good entertainment."

Game of your life?

"All the All-Irelands were tremendous (Mikey won eight in all) but everything went right for me in 1979. I scored 2-6. I got a goal early on from a pass from Ogie. He could nearly have had a cut himself but afterwards said he was glad to see me alongside him. Bomber was involved in the move as well from a Páidí O'Sé free. Early in the second half I rattled one off the crossbar with my left which should have been another goal."

That 2-6 is still a record All-Ireland Final score?

"It is but you never think of a record score. You'd be told about it after the game."

You are still involved as a Kerry minor selector.

"I'm still very keen and go to as many games as possible. Tonight I saw the club juniors in action. A lot of players turn off it. Not me."

Above, left: Mikey Sheehy right: John Egan
Below, left: Sean Walsh right: The Bomber Liston

Chapter 28

James MacCartan

Of Down

When I visited him at his home in Donacloney near Lurgan, he travelled out the road to meet me, something Tony Doran had done for me in Monamolin. And boy did I receive a céad míle fáilte. In centenary year 1984 Micheál O'Hehir, oft mentioned in this book, when asked for the 'Game of his Life' or outstanding memory stated that Down's winning of the All-Ireland in 1960 and the ecstatic aftermath of that success was his. No one did more to create that, than King James, as he is oft referred to. He had this peculiar gait as he tore through opposing defences, cap on head, like a tank and nothing embodied the spirit of resurgent Down more than this. It was their clarion call. He was their king and he led them to the summit. An outspoken and very honest man always, he is one of my favourite people.

Your young days?

"My father was an utter out-and-out Downman. His whole life was Gaelic football and he just drilled it into us all. His name was Brian, known as Briney. He played for Down himself in the 1938-1940 era."

The Sundays of your youth?

"Every Sunday we were at a match someplace. If it wasn't a club match, it was a county game or a 7-a-side. Football was our life. My first All-Ireland Final was Galway against Cork in 1956 and the first semi-final was Armagh against Roscommon in 1953."

Your first Senior Football Championship game for Down?

"Against Armagh in Newry in 1956. I was marking Jack Bratten. I wasn't too long in the game until I got a dead leg and didn't perform too well. I remember laughing when Jack said 'You were too sharp for me' and I said 'I slowed you up'. We were just codding. We laugh about that everytime we meet."

The coming of the Down team as a football force?

"Maurice Hayes, the Down County Secretary, had this dream. He got the players together and organised challenge games with the big teams of the time, Galway and Dublin for instance. We became familiar with them, realised they were no better than us. It was just a matter of getting the confidence in our own ability and going ahead and doing it. He opened all the doors, organised proper training facilities, made everything ready for us. So much so, that at the end of the day he got ousted as Down County Secretary. He was the man that really started it. In this county there is a mentality that club comes first. It's my belief that the county senior team is the shop window and if it is doing well the G.A.A. in the county thrives."

From the word go then there was hype about that Down team. The team wore a lovely strip. You stayed in Butlin's for your first semi-final with Galway in 1959?

"Red and black was always the Down strip. Staying in Butlin's then was a major mistake. I'll give you my own experience of it. Usually before a big game we always had a steak breakfast after Mass. We left to go to Butlin's that Saturday evening at 3 o'clock and reached there at six. Our tea was beans on toast. No supper. They told us next morning, if we went to second Mass we'd get breakfast. Breakfast was over when we returned. I went on to play against Galway in Croke Park weak from the hunger, not having eaten since 12 noon the previous day. It was also one of the warmest nights I ever remember and the chalets in Butlin's were like ovens."

The winning of the All-Ireland in 1960?

"In my book the winning of an All-Ireland is an anti-climax. It is easier to play in Croke Park than any other pitch. If you can't play football there, you can play nowhere. It is in perfect condition. It separates the men from the boys. There is no hiding place. In Ulster you play on tight pitches. Players have no room. When you beat one man there is another man to get by. A lot of spoiling tactics. In Croke Park you're exposed."

You were never afraid of Croke Park?

"It's a matter of believing in yourself. The first day you went out on a bicycle. You fell off it. You cut your knees. In a week's time you could ride it without hands. It is all about confidence."

You were a wee bit of a rebel even in your mode of play. Scoring goals from centre half back?

"I played my best football at centre half back. But the people in charge of the team thought that the way I played was crazy. An attacking centre half back. They had to get me out of it. I still feel you should attack from the half-backline. It was my favourite position."

Your memories of 1960 when the final whistle blew?

"The first thing I thought of was my father. We met on Jones's Road and we both cried with joy. He had said if Down ever won the All-Ireland he'd get drunk. Now he never drank and neither do I and I said, 'Come on, you're going to get drunk to-night' and he said 'No'. He wouldn't do it."

Coming back to Down with the Cup must have been very special?

"It was a hectic journey. I came home with no trousers. I lost them in a lorry in Newcastle about 2 o'clock in the morning. Someone grabbing me tore the leg off my pants. It was hectic but dangerous and somebody could have been killed."

Schooldays?

"I went to the village school in Donacloney. They played no Gaelic. I played soccer and cricket with them until I went to St. Colman's, Newry. I never had any success with Colman's but played for the College in all the competitions. Fr. John Trainor had a big influence on me. He is my P.P. now and a great friend all my life."

Beating Kerry in your first final was special too?

"It was. Kerry had done the grand slam the year before and were hyped up as a super team. When I was a young lad listening to the wireless, I used to think these Kerry men were something special but we all got the belief we were as good as them. They had only two hands, two feet, one head same as everybody else. You had to go out and get into them, get the first ball and let them see you weren't going to fall down before them. The first time we played them was in a *Gaelic Weekly* Tournament in 1959 and they were full of tricks, pulling the jersey, pushing in the back and we learnt from them. When we met them next time we did these things. Kerry were the finest sportsmen I ever met. Galway were great opponents too. Frank Evers was a great footballer. To me he was the ideal midfielder. He caught the ball, delivered it and still kept running. The number of scores he got after running in to a move he started was staggering. Most underestimated and he'd be on my best ever fifteen."

I'd suggest still that that Down team was the best ever?

"The older generation might think that. But the younger people may not. Everything has improved in all walks of life. The four minute mile. Soon it will be down to three and a half minutes. The game has got faster. It's a different game. Whether it's better now, is something else. I've seen great teams Kerry, Galway, Dublin....What makes good teams is good forward lines. You can win matches with a mediocre defence, good midfielders as long as you have forwards who can score."

Derry at the moment may be short of scoring forwards?

"Derry have a great team. For the amount of possession they win their forwards don't punish the opposition enough. I hope by the time this book is printed that they have won the All-Ireland."

The great footballers of Down?

"The greatest Down player in my time was Sean O'Neill. He played with his head. He took up good positions, passed when he should pass, shot when he should shoot. He had the will to win. Footballers must want to win the ball and win the match. The O'Neills are our first cousins and in the summertime all these cousins came down to the farm on holidays to another home from home for them. They drove tractors, made hay and when we came home from work there was a match in the yard every night. We just played in our clothes. I saw my father not getting a dinner until eleven or twelve o'clock at night. He'd have been fifty then and it was dead serious. He'd kill you! At that time I worked on the farm at home and the ball would bounce in the meadow when the millers quit work for lunch. The bounce of the ball was like a magnet to me. When that ball bounced I had to go."

Other great Down players?

"Colm McAlarney was a great player but at times he tried to do too much. He held it that bit too long. But he served Down well. Leo Murphy played some fantastic games at full back. Greg Blaney is a fantastic footballer. His father Sean was a colleges star but he fell out with the Armagh County Board at an early stage after captaining Armagh to an All-Ireland minor title in 1949 and didn't play afterwards. Greg has vision. This is what makes football special. He sees the man in the loose space and gives him the ball at the right time. The timing is all important."

What's it like to be the father of an All-Ireland star - wee James as he is called?

"I got a bigger thrill out of him winning it. He played well on the day too but I thought he had a great Ulster final that year. I go to matches and come home and listen to the wireless and read the papers and I don't think it is the same game I saw. The press write to sell papers. They don't write to tell the truth."

Can you remember meeting James after his star All-Ireland display?

"I met him at the function in the Burlington that night. We were all thrilled. I knew we'd win because we had played Meath in the League final the year before and they had great bother in beating us by two points. We took a lot of punishment early on that day."

Are players getting enough protection from referees when negative tactics abound so much?

"I go to a match every Sunday to see the Tohills being allowed to play and show their skills. I don't want to see them pulled and punched out of the game. Peter Canavan of Tyrone is a beautiful footballer but he is not allowed to play. There are people out there to stop him and the referees ignore this."

Has the game improved?

"More cynical now. Players were more honest in my day. It was hard, tough and fair. Today you stop somebody no matter how you do it. The G.A.A. has got it all wrong in the refereeing and I don't know the answer to it. I'd pick a pool of referees for inter-county games and grade them on performance. I'd pay them well. A pool of club referees too with promotion and relegation from one to the other."

Achievements?

"Six Ulster medals, two All-Irelands, four Railway Cups and two Caltex Awards."

Did you regard the Caltex Footballer of the Year Award as a superb honour?

"Yes and no. Looking back on it a lot of these awards are given out by the press. Take the All Star Awards. I lost all credibility in them, when they didn't give Mickey Linden an All Star in 1991. Anybody who watched football and was honest would know that Mickey was the most consistent player in the country that year."

Anecdotes?

"In 1960 when we won the All-Ireland the club leagues were pushed aside. Around Christmas we were playing Clonduff in the League and both of us were around the top of the table after about three games. Anyhow I got involved with this Clonduff opponent and was put off, unjustly I thought. This great supporter of the Glen club, Mrs. Kerr, known locally as Winnie Sands, went on to the field, put her foot on top of the ball and nobody dared take it off her and the match was abandoned. I was suspended but the League was abandoned. So Winnie Sands stopped the Down Senior Football League with one touch of her foot. Something like what happened in 'The Mountains of Mourne' song. She was a great character and I have fond memories of her. I won three Down Senior Football titles with Glen. Where I live is a very Unionist area with no Gaelic football at all. The nearest club was Tullylish but I had difficulty in getting to and from training. My cousin, Séamus collected me regularly to play for Glen as he had a motor car at the time. I played for Glen until I got married and for Tullylish after that."

Would you have considered yourself a rebel?

"I spoke my mind and some people didn't like that. When Down got successful, people wanted the team and the officials didn't like that. Things were done that shouldn't have been done. And the team got broken up."

Greatest opponent?

"The man who gave me the hardest time was Paddy Holden of Dublin. He marked very tight and left very little space. At that time I liked the ball released fast. If a midfielder delayed on a ball he'd give the back the advantage. I couldn't master him playing for Down."

Did you ever favour dirty play?

"No. I don't mind strong play but everybody must go to work on Monday morning. Once when wee James was playing in an under-age game, the mother of his opponent kept urging her son to 'sew the boot in him'. I went to her and asked her how she would like if somebody did that to her son and she got the message."

Your greatest thrill from the game itself?

"I loved playing the game. Once I went on holidays to Salthill after beating Kerry in an All-Ireland semi-final and we went to Dunmore for a 7-a-side competition under assumed names etc. Nowadays it has got too serious. We did it for fun and there was no harm in it. Officialdom dictates that everything now has to be written down and recorded. Too much paper. Spontaneity has gone."

Other footballers in the family?

"To me, Brian my eldest son, lived in the shadow of James. James was scoring but Brian was making scores from the middle of the field. He won two Hogan Cup medals with Colman's and an All-Ireland minor medal in 1987 and he has been dogged by injuries, having had four operations. It is breaking his heart. He trains every day. I'd love to see him get there, because he wants it so much. Charlie Pat, now eighteen, is on the verge of Down seniors. The two young lads, Owen and Daniel, are football mad."

They couldn't but be?

"On an average Sunday we go to a game say in Croke Park. I'd rush out to get the comments on the radio going down the road. Then at 6.15 p.m. we'd turn on Radio Ulster to get their reports. Back to Radio 1 at 6.40p.m. for their reports. Then rush home for 'The Sunday Game' or in some hotel if we couldn't make it. Then 'The Championship' on B.B.C. later that night."

Do you talk much to wee James about his game?

"He relates to me. I'd be honest with him. I'd tell him when he played well or when he did wrong. We'd discuss his views too. Sometimes we'd agree to differ. We'd always sort of half agree."

Do you see much of yourself in him?

"Yes, I see the heart in him. He wants to win. I see the workrate in him. He works hard at the game even when Down are down."

Why is Gaelic football so popular now?

"Television. You see plenty of scores and excitement. Television has sold Gaelic football. Sponsorship has helped too. Clones this year was a debacle. Clones should not have been developed. The road structures into it and out of it are chaotic. If I go to Clones with the family on a wet day they get wet to the bum."

Greatest players you ever saw?

"Sean Purcell of Galway the most complete of them all and close behind him Eoin Liston. Liston was the hub of the Kerry attack. Egan, Sheehy, Spillane were brilliant but he was the hub. Purcell played full back, centre half back, midfield, centre half forward and full forward and became the best in the land in all positions. That's some player in my book."

The game of your life?

"If you enjoy the game, every game is the game of your life. For the two All-Irelands I played in, I worked in the bar at home until 12 o'clock and travelled up on the Sunday. But if I had to pick one game, it would be the All-Ireland semi-final against Kerry in 1961. We had to prove ourselves. They had won the National League. We met them over in Wembley and gave them a walloping. But I told them it was nothing to what they'd get in the All-Ireland semi-final! I remember Kevin Coffey, Tom Long and myself went off to buy Kevin a pair of football boots in London. He wanted to buy Hotspur boots. It was before the game and he said to Long, 'Tom, do you think I should wear them today, or break them in at home first?' To which I interjected, 'Wear them today, you won't get too many kicks at it'!"

Your greatest legacy from the G.A.A?

"The friendships. I go to Kerry today and I'm taken by the hand. Once we went to a Munster final in Cork. Fourteen of us left after the bar closed on a Saturday night without a ticket in the world. I arrived in Cork, rang up a friend, told him my story. He said, 'Be at Gate B at half one', and at half one there were fourteen Downmen with 'Maor' on their chests in on the sideline at a Munster final."

George Glynn, your Galway brother-in-law?

"Lovely fellow but we are total opposites in so many ways. George's wife Gay, is as keen on football as myself. But where would she leave it? I remember coming home in the car with my father after Galway beat us in the All-Ireland semi-final of 1959. He blasted me the whole way home. I got out of the car in the yard and said, 'Daddy, I'll bring it home next year, should I steal it'. I met him in Jones's road the following year, after the game and he said, 'You kept your promise'."

Above: James McCartan working on the family farm during his Down playing days.
Below: This photograph was taken on All-Ireland day 1991, after 'wee James' won his All-Ireland medal. From left, Dan his uncle, the star of the '91 final and proud father, 'King James'.

Chapter 29

Paddy Mo

Of Armagh

Paddy Moriarty became the national focus of attention in 1972 when out of the blue, so to speak, he gained an All Star Award. Subsequently the Lurgan based solicitor from Derrymacash convinced all the 1972 doubters that here was a footballer of great commitment, versatility and ability. By the time he won his second All Star, in an altogether different position from 1972, there was no hue and cry. Paddy Mo, as he is affectionately known in Ulster carved for himself a cherished place in Ulster football folklore.

The people who influenced you towards football?

"Initially I would have got my love of football from my father who was a Kerryman with a keen interest. He was a greyhound trainer who farmed as well on a small holding. He hailed from just outside Killarney and he often spoke about Dee Connor, a friend of his who was right back on Kerry's first ever 4-in-a-row team. I'd have been hearing about Kerry footballers always."

Were you brought to Kerry in your youth?

"Practically every summer until the early 1960's. In 1961 I remember travelling by train from Killarney to see Kerry play Down in the All-Ireland semi-final, won by Down, and sitting on Dee Connor's knee. At home in Armagh my father didn't go to too many matches being involved in farming but come 3 o'clock on a Sunday, the radio was on and Micheál O'Hehir told it all. My big hero then was Mick O'Connell. O'Hehir painted the picture so well. He is missed sorely still. One of the nicest things ever to happen to me in my career, was in the aftermath of the 1977 All-Ireland Final, as I walked away from Croke Park with my girlfriend Una (now my wife) to have Micheál O'Hehir tap me on the shoulder from behind and say the kind words 'It wasn't your fault' which meant so much at the time."

Others from Armagh?

"The Principal of the local primary school in Derrymacash was Peter Murray, brother of Alf, a man involved in the G.A.A. all his life and practically every footballer who played for the local Wolfe Tone's club for years came through Peter's hands at schoolboy level. In my time Pat McCann, a strong no-nonsense footballer, was there and we played for Armagh together. Before that in the Wolfe Tone's club, the big names were Bill McCorry, who died a few weeks ago and John McCarron who played together at midfield for Armagh before John got hurt. They were the Terrible Twins of Armagh football."

A pity Bill McCorry's name was always linked with the missed penalty of 1953 against Kerry?

"Very unfair and there were times when people mentioned it to him when they shouldn't. He played senior club football at twelve or thirteen. Strong man and a gentleman. Funnily enough I was standing in the graveyard at Bill's funeral and this solicitor friend said to me, 'Well Paddy, how does it feel to be the only Armagh man alive to have missed a penalty in an All-Ireland Final?!'."

Why is Ulster football so dominant now?

"The move to the Open Draw in the other provinces certainly hasn't helped some of the traditional counties like Kerry, Cork, Dublin or Meath. The counties in Ulster studied Kerry and Dublin and put an awful lot more thought and preparation in. Kerry used to talk about training for twenty-eight nights in a row. Here in Ulster, the teams have planned well, they have good men on the line and have enough good players at the one time."

College days?

"The C.B.S. in Armagh, as distinct from St. Patrick's College (they have since amalgamated). We were never strong, we played in secondary competitions. In our last year we prevailed on the P.T. teacher Jimmy McKeown to enter us in the McRory Cup, the major one. We didn't cut any ice in it. I played minor for Armagh in 1969 and 1970. It was enjoyable but we didn't win anything. I played three years in U-21 and we were beaten by Fermanagh in one of the finals."

Your first senior game with Armagh?

"A National Football League game against Fermanagh in Irvinestown in 1980. A bit of interest had crept into the Armagh team. Tom McCreesh was the big Armagh star of the 1960's and was still on the team. Tom always had the knack of arriving on the field just in time for the throw-in having driven from Virginia or wherever he was living. Tom McCreesh and Larry Kearns who also played in 1977, were very encouraging to me, the eighteen year old making his debut."

The great Armagh players besides Tom McCreesh and Bill McCorry?

"Jimmy Whan was another. Jimmy lived in Dublin but never let down Armagh. Jimmy was Armagh's star for years and like Tom McCreesh won a number of Railway Cup medals. Sean Quinn, the captain of the 1953 team and the first to pass away, is a much talked about footballer in Armagh, John McKnight, Jack Bratten... The only thing that team didn't do was win the All-Ireland. It was the first of the six counties teams to come up and put up a great show and against Kerry too. They were treated as if they won the All-Ireland. The names are still recalled, Pat Campbell, Joe Cunningham, Art O'Hagan, Mal McEvoy. The early part of the 1970's were fairly lean. Peter Makem started to organise things. At one stage we went through a few years without winning a game. Something had to be done."

Who changed all that?

"Peter Makem came along and travelled round the county to get enthusiasm going again. This was 1972 and Peter got Gerry O'Neill back in again to train the team (he had left after a stint in the late 1960's). I remember well Peter Makem's first game and the poor man got a fit of the jitters and took ill. The game was against Leitrim and we won it on home ground in Armagh. I remember going to see him with the team after the game and after that we started to move forward again. Tom McCreesh was still the father figure. Others playing well were Jimmy Smyth, Peter Loughran and Joe Kiernan."

Your achievements to date, Paddy?

"I have very few medals. Twenty in all would be the height of it. Three Ulster Senior Football Championship, four Railway Cups (three with Ulster, one with the Combined Universities), a few Dr. McKenna Cups, some first year University medals. No county Senior Football Club medals. Twenty years ago Wolfe Tones reached the Armagh Senior Football Final but were well beaten by Clan na Gael. Colm McKinstry, one of their star players got married the day before and left for his honeymoon. They still won handily. I'd love to have won a County medal but if I can mould a team to do so, that will make amends."

Your two All Star Awards?

"I got my first in 1972 at corner forward. A lot of criticism of my selection at the time. I didn't ask to be picked. Mickey Kearins was left out and so was Mick O'Dwyer. I hadn't a particularly good year that year but had played very well the previous year before losing to Derry in the Ulster semi-final. Somebody saw me and liked me and fought their corner for me. I got my second in 1977 at centre half back. Some criticism then as well because I hadn't played the position that much that year having started at right half back, then at full forward before holding centre half back down for the rest of the year. On that occasion they were pressing for Kevin Moran. The only football trophies on display in my house are these two awards and I was thrilled by them. For someone coming from a small rural club in County Armagh, a county with not too much by way of achievement, I was proud of them and of being the first All Star from the county."

Anecdotes?

"In 1982 we travelled to the U.S. on a thank you trip after winning three Ulster titles. With great help from John O'Reilly who organised the fundraising and organisation, we headed off in September and our great rivals over those years, Roscommon, decided they'd organise a trip for themselves to coincide with ours. We played Roscommon in New York, San Francisco and Los Angeles and at the end of the three games the aggregate scores were level. When we arrived in New York some of the boys went on the beer and for the first game at Gaelic Park some were still affected by their imbibing. The game was played in a fine spirit and this ball was heading for the Armagh goal when Jim McKerr, our full back went out to meet it, followed by a Roscommon forward. Jim went through the motions of catching the football, toe-tapping it and clearing it but it was an imaginary ball because while he was involved in this double vision, the Roscommon forward had the ball in the back of the net. Jim's explanation was quite simple. He got the ball he went for!"

Greatest opponent?

"I had two careers basically. The first seven years in attack or at midfield. The latter years mostly in defence. The players I enjoyed most playing against were Mikey Sheehy, Jimmy Barry Murphy, Ogie Moran or Brian Mullins. As a back the player who gave me most trouble and who was extremely difficult to mark was Charlie Mulgrew of Donegal."

Any regrets from the playing days?

"I think we missed the boat in 1980. Roscommon, who lost the final probably say the same thing. Our team in 1980 was probably better than our 1977 side for the experience level and a few new players like Brian Hughes and Martin Murphy had come along to bolster the team. Hughes had an inspired year. We lost Colm McKinstry at a crucial stage in the semi-final against Roscommon. Martin McDermott came on at midfield for them and caught a lot of ball and swung the game their way."

1977?

"That was like a fairytale. Great crack. If anybody had told Tom McCreesh in 1971 that he'd play in an All-Ireland Final before he'd finish, he would not believe it. He had played from the early 1960's and had won a Railway Cup medal as far back as 1963."

How many years did you play for Armagh?

"From November 1970 to July 15th, 1984. That latter date is special as I'll tell you later."

Was it a great thrill to walk out for Armagh in an All-Ireland Final?

"I always got a thrill, took the jersey, turned it around and there was a number between two and fifteen on it. I wouldn't have wanted to pull on any other jersey but an Armagh one. I remember the whole 1977 thing vividly. We stayed out in Trinity Halls. Got up in the morning, got breakfast, went to Mass, then togged and went for a kickaround in the grounds and the first thing I noticed was that the place was patrolled by the Gardaí because of our presence. Then we had the Gardaí motor cycle escort to Croke Park which was totally new to us. We had a team outfit, blazer and slacks. We went across to the dressing-rooms while Down were playing the minor final. I remember sitting in the dressing-room alone for about fifteen or twenty minutes while the other lads watched the minor game. I was focussing my mind on the game and on my immediate opponent Tony Hanahoe. I didn't for one minute think it would be my last All-Ireland Final being twenty-four at the time. I wanted to do well and the minor game wasn't going to distract me. In hindsight people tell us we went out too early and got soaked in the rain, whereas Dublin stayed in and were dry. The Dublin team at that time were too good for us. Simple as that. The problem in Ulster, then as now, was that no team could get out of the province two years running though that doesn't present a problem to Down, Donegal and Derry now it seems. The final itself was over in a flash. I watched it on video again for the first time a few months ago and it was great."

What will it be like when Armagh eventually win out?

"It will be like what it was in Donegal, in Down and in Derry. It will come but it would need to come fairly soon unless another crop of players appears. At the moment we have ten or eleven players capable of playing to that level, but we don't have enough of them. A lot depends on how quickly some of the minors of 1992 come through and how well they mature."

Your greatest thrill from the game itself?

"If the ball broke in a crowd of players I used to get a great kick out of zooming onto it and getting straight out and away."

The game today?

"In 1977 we got sheer enjoyment out of it because we played just 'off the cuff'. Some of the best crack we had in training was when we split into two teams of eleven and played up and down the field. Everything is down to possession. Short ball, hold it, don't give it away. Tactics much more prevalent. Negative tactics too. Certainly I like to win but the win at all costs bothers me. I suppose if you win a major competition and you've done it all tactically you'll get a great kick out of it at the time. I don't think you'll get the same enjoyment out of playing that game. Players could end up their career having gone through eight or ten seasons of grind without being able to remember enjoying it."

Your favourite position?

"Centre half back. I liked to get the odd burst up the field. You'd get the opportunity to take a pass from the midfielder and go forward, knowing there were men behind you to cover for you. The central avenue behind you was closed. From wing half the gap behind might not be covered if the move broke down. If I could finish off the move for a score all the better."

Your greatest score?

"I got one like that in a Railway Cup game. A few points against Roscommon in a National League game in the Athletic Grounds from a massive distance out. Way back in 1970-1971, I scored a couple of goals against Down in a McKenna Cup game very early in my career and there was a fair thrill in that too."

Greatest player ever seen?

"Mick O'Connell was my idol. I played with him in an All Star trip and that was a great joy. The Down half forward line of the 1960's O'Neill, McCartan and Doherty was class. O'Connell had great mystique. Mikey Sheehy, John Egan, Jack O'Shea of my own era. Frank McGuigan, Colm O'Rourke. I'd hate to say one man but O'Connell would be the boy I was brought up on. Frank McGuigan was a lovely footballer. I remember the day - 15th July 1984 when he scored the eleven points in the Ulster final against us. I never made any formal announcement that I was retiring from football but after that game, I sat in the dressing-room in Clones alone and I knew that it was time to go. That's why I remember that date so well."

The game of your life?

"There were three games one after the other that gave me tremendous satisfaction. The Ulster final of 1977 and the draw and replay with Roscommon later. In the Ulster final we got a couple of goals just before half-time. Early in the second half Jimmy Smyth hit this long ball in and Larry Kearns came on to the ball about twenty-one yards out and put it in the net. That won that game. Coming back for a draw after being seven points behind in the first game against Roscommon was thrilling too. And the replay would have to be number one. I think it finished 0-15 to 0-14 same as Dublin against Derry this year. The noise in Croke Park that day is a great memory."

Greatest legacy from your time in the G.A.A?

"You can walk down the street in Galway, Tralee, Dublin, Cork or Killarney and you'll meet somebody that you played on for an hour and you've met a friend."

Your hurling interests?

"The townland I was brought up in is called Aughacommon - The Plain of the Hurler. Listening to Micheál O'Hehir bred an interest in hurling in me and I played the game for Armagh up until 1977. I was a keen supporter of the Tipperary team of the 1960's John Doyle, Mick Maher, Tony Wall, Mick Roche, Jimmy Doyle, Mackey McKenna, John McLaughlin, Liam Devanney. Jimmy Doyle was the one hurler who really appealed to me. He was a real artist. I won an Ulster junior medal for hurling in 1973. Kerry beat us in Armagh in the semi-final. One interesting thing from that game. The present trainer of the Armagh Camogie team Tom Monaghan, really Mr. Camogie in Armagh, was one of our players and he wore glasses while playing. Just as the game against Kerry started there was a heavy drizzle and Tom had to quit the scene. No wipers on the glasses!."

Above, left: Paddy Mo in his All Star days. right: Jimmy Doyle - 'a real artist'.
Below, left: Mick O'Connell - 'my idol'. right: Jimmy Barry Murphy.

Chapter 30

Jim McKeever

Of Derry

He was one of the classiest fielders of all time. There was a photo of Jim in classical pose outreaching Johnny Joyce from behind in the 1958 final. There is no better photographic production of this great art. In the Derry G.A.A. History published in 1984 that photo appears under the simple title 'The Catch'. Jim has now retired from lecturing at St. Mary's Training College, Belfast where his influence in moulding the G.A.A. interests of the Northern Counties primary teachers will be missed. I saw him play for the first time in Tuam for Ulster Colleges way back in 1948. Though Ulster lost that day I remember the young Derry lad scoring an immaculate point from the left wing.

It must be great to be a Derryman now?

"After the game against Dublin in Croke Park, the Derry people just wouldn't leave. They had won a match that was worth winning."

Did you sit in the Hogan Stand?

"In the Derry section, directly behind Johnny Mc Gurk, as he kicked his final point. All of us knew if he got that one, we'd have won it. If he missed it, Dublin might break and win. It was so important."

Did you visit the Derry dressing-room afterwards?

"I did indeed. About five minutes after the players got in. They came in in dribs and drabs. Some guys half dressed, some guys hadn't even started undressing. All obviously pleased and lots of press people and old Derry players. No over-exultation. Quiet enough."

You would have coached many of these players, Jim?

"About half the squad were on the team coached by me for the 1987 semi-final against Meath. Tony Scullion, Danny Quinn, Brian McGilligan, Enda Gormley, Damien Barton, Damien McCusker, Damien Cassidy, Kieran McKeever, Dermot McNicholl, and Seamus Downey. I know all the rest of the lads, many of them coming through from the minor All-Ireland winning team of 1989."

Any premonitions in 1987 of the greater successes later?

"Those of us in charge then - Tom Scullion, Phil Stuart and myself - took it for three years. We realised that it would need five years to develop a team of greater potential. I'm still in touch as the present manager Eamonn Coleman is a clubmate of mine and I talk to him occasionally."

That club was Ballymaguigan?

"Yes and the year of our only title win was 1962. Eamonn scored a goal in that game after coming on. He grew up about four or five fields from where I grew up. I know his people."

That Ballymaguigan triumph?

"I grew up in Ballymaguigan. It is about half the Newbridge end of Magherafelt parish. What you might call the countryside of Magherafelt parish. Originally there was one team, Newbridge. Eventually there was a difference of opinion and Ballymaguigan decided to have a team of their own. There was a great rivalry between Newbridge and Ballymaguigan. I was in St. Malachy's College in Belfast and Newbridge minors asked me to play for them. So I was then attached to them and played for them for about five or six years much to the disappointment and maybe annoyance of the Ballymaguigan club. Only one chapel for the two areas but I always knew I'd go back and play for Ballymaguigan some day. I won two Senior Football titles with Newbridge, then I went to England and when I returned, I taught in Downpatrick and played club football with them then. So I was four years away from Newbridge. I then got a post in Derry and lived at home in Ballymaguigan and decided to play for the home club. My brother Denis decided to do the same thing around the same time having previously played for Newbridge. It was a team that was growing in strength and for the next five years we played in four Senior Football Championship finals, the last one in 1962 which we won. I was about thirty-one at the time. Four McKeevers shared the triumph Denis, Eddie, Frank and myself. A cousin Sean played too. It's a small place so you would have sets of brothers and family relatives involved."

How do you rate this achievement?

"One of the things I really loved and wanted to be part of. We knew it was a team nearing its end and once it would go it would be hard to replace. In fact the club has just won its way back to the Senior Division this year."

The people who influenced you in your youth, Jim?

"The only sport people in Ballymaguigan were interested in was Gaelic football in my young days. My father was interested and he used to bring me to games on the bar of his bicycle in the country. The early heroes were the lads who played for Newbridge - big Barney Murphy, a tall blond-haired man who played at midfield and at centre half back, a county and Ulster player, the McGroggan brothers, Mickey McPeake - all heroes to me."

Schooldays?

"We didn't have an official team in the school. Sean Young's father, Master Young, was very keen on the game. We got a ball at one stage and went to the local field and played a bit but there was no primary school competition as such. Of course, we went to the local field in the evenings and stayed behind the goals to get a kick as we said when the seniors were playing. I think my father bought me a football once and eight or ten of us used to get together in one of the fields and often play away for four hours at a time."

Secondary schooldays?

"I boarded in St. Malachy's in Belfast where we had a lot of internal football. We didn't play competitive games until my second last year. We hadn't been in the McRory Cup for the previous twenty-five years. We reached the final in 1948 in Breffni Park and they beat us by a big score that first year of entry. They had Jim McCabe, Tom Hardy and Joe Lennon, a Leitrim lad. The following year we got to the final again but lost to Violet Hill in Newry who had Kevin Mussen and Sean Blaney, their first ever McRory Cup winning team in St. Colman's. I played for Ulster Colleges both of those years. The first year in Tuam we had Malachy McEvoy, the Devlins of Tyrone, the Leitrim Joe Lennon. We had very little tactics then. I remember that day in Tuam being given one simple instruction. Every ball I got, I was to play it to the right corner forward. No solo. The point you remember was an instinctive one where I had this space, soloed and shot over totally against my instructions."

The first day with Derry?

"I remember seeing Derry play in plain red jersey. By the time I started they had the white with the red band. I've always liked it. My first game was a friendly game against Antrim at The Glens Feis before going back to St. Malachy's for the final year. I knew some of the players like Roddy Gribben of Newbridge, Sonny McCarr and others."

1958? How did Derry get there?

"It didn't happen in 1958 - began in 1950 virtually. In 1950 we reached a junior All-Ireland Final to be beaten by Mayo but many of that team stayed the course to 1958. We were knocking at the door in Ulster from 1953. Armagh beat us in 1953 en route to their All-Ireland Final appearance. We kept on building - lost to Cavan in the Ulster final of 1955 in a close game. Peter Donoghoe scored points from all angles after coming back. Back in the Ulster final again in 1957 when we lost to Tyrone. So as you can see it was gradual. Against Cavan in those days I was opposed often to 'The Gunner' Brady and Victor Sherlock, two great players. I was very friendly with 'The Gunner' and Victor. 'The Gunner' was an honest player. He didn't do anything treacherous or devious. If he hit you, you saw him coming. We beat them easily enough in the 1958 semi-final but they were over the hill then. In the 1958 Ulster final we beat Down in the start of their golden era."

Kerry in your first ever semi-final?

"We knew we were a pretty good team. In the old days we thought Micheál O'Hehir would never ever have to comment on a Derry against Kerry game. Wild dreams! The match itself was on a very wet day and we went out to give it our damndest from beginning to end and at the final whistle Owen Gribben was the nearest player to me and he said 'We're in a final'. Sean O'Connell scored the crucial goals. He made a habit of that."

Memories of the buildup to the final of 1958?

"We trained in Newbridge. Very little experience of training teams then. We didn't import people in. Roddy Gribben managed the team and generally organised the training himself, sharing the duty with me betimes. Simpler times. We travelled to training under our own steam. We didn't have showers. Nor did we expect such facilities. We stayed out in Malahide or Portmarnock for the Kerry game. Getting back to that semi-final I remember the entire Kerry team coming into our hotel on the morning of the game and we never knew whether it was a ploy to upset us or a pure accident. For the final we stayed at the Hollybrook in Clontarf."

Were Dublin as big a force then? Was the Hill then a Dublin preserve?

"No. I don't remember a mass of Dublin support. We were not fearful of them. They were just another team to be played in Croke Park. Kerry would have been a bigger obstacle mentally."

The great Derry footballers?

"The players I envied as I grew up were Barney Murphy, 'Sticky' Maguire of Magherafelt, Harry Owens a smashing full back, Mickey McPeake, John McGroggan, Mick McGuckian, Matt Regan and then just before my time Roddy Gribben, Larry Higgins, Pat Keenan, Jack Converry, Francie Niblock, Jimmy Cassidy, 'Scutcher' McCloskey, Séamus Keenan. I could reel off every name of the team of 1947."

Your own time?

"I still have a great grá for the 1958 team. Patsy Gormley in goal, Patsy McLarnon,

Hugh Francis Gribben.... Patsy Breen, Colm Smith, Colm Mulholland, Phil Stuart I liked playing with him at midfield..."

Which of them all?

"Sean O'Connell had the coolness to put away scores. Freetaker, good goalscorer. Peter Smith and Patsy Breen were very reliable wing half backs."

Which of your coaching involvements gave you greatest satisfaction? Club, county or college?

"I'd have to say the college team because I have coached it much longer. There were three or four college teams which were almost perfect. Within the capabilities of the players they played perfectly. That for a coach is the best and most rewarding of all. We are talking of St. Mary's Training College where I worked. I'm now retired but I can remember a team which won the Ryan Cup in two successive years with a smashing team beating U.C.D. in both finals."

Did you see some players flower to greatness under your guidance literally?

"Some of them were good players before they came in like Peter Rooney of Down in 1968. Lads like James Morgan, Colm McAlarney, Jimmy Smyth, Séamus Lagan, Ray McConville. About four years later we had another great team. Once against Maynooth this latter team scored something like 2-12 in one half. Absolute perfection. Never missed a chance, never gave a bad pass, never failed to contest a ball. I remember Paddy Purcell (Irish Press) raving about the performance and Tony O'Keeffe the Kerry County Secretary who played for Maynooth that day always talks about it to this day. Another team which won the Sigerson in 1989 was very good. Nearly all of that team are county players now, John Rafferty (Armagh), Jarlath Burns (Armagh), John Reihill (Fermanagh), Séamus Downey (Derry), Ollie Reel. In that Sigerson team again almost perfection."

The player in St. Mary's who gave Jim the greatest satisfaction?

"McAlarney, McGinnitty but the one of all I would pick is Peter Canavan of Tyrone. Simply because he has the best scoring record I know. He is the best scorer from play that I have ever seen. Kicks with both feet with tremendous accuracy. Frees as well. He doesn't need time. He can make space. Opponents sit on him as much as they can and if he gets the ball in his hands he is dynamite. Marvellous talent. I would like to see him on a team with a few big men who could give him the ball, knock the ball into space for him and just let him score. Unfortunately, Tyrone don't have the big men to feed him now. I've seen him score some of the most marvellous goals."

Have the managers of today got too much say?

"I don't think so. If the game is even to hold the position it has now, Gaelic has to compete with all the other sports in a much more competitive and hyped up sphere for the interest and involvement of young players. The kind of shop window we have now, we have to have managers. I don't think they have too much power but I do think they get too much publicity and they have attributed to them power they don't have. The publicity ought to swing back to the players."

Is refereeing keeping pace with the game?

"It is not. It has been a problem since we played. Bad decisions, lack of uniformity in interpretation has always been a problem. Refereeing has improved because they have put some effort into it. But mainly in the externals. They are fitter, they look better, give good signals. The right interpretation is not as good as it should be. They are influenced by instructions sent down to them from Croke Park. Watch out for this particular kind of foul and then they go baldheaded for that foul for the next six months and think they have mastered refereeing when they can interpret that one thing well like the late tackle or the sliding tackle."

Any referee you like particularly?

"I like Tommy Sugrue. He has a style that all referees should study. He does not antagonise players. He respects them and doesn't treat them as juvenile delinquents. Some referees antagonise players by ticking them off repeatedly."

The game today?

"As good if not better than ever before. I know the Ulster scene better. The players are fitter. In many ways they have honed their skills better. Freetaking is a good example.

Better than it ever was. More people kicking with both feet now. It hasn't changed that much except in skill development at the top level."

Has the skill level in catching and kicking deteriorated?

"The catching is not as good as it used to be. In our day the catch was contested in all positions. They went up for the ball in every position then. Didn't counteract the catch as much. You need a few good fielders but apart from the middle of the field now you seldom see a Paddy Prendergast type fellow who soars up and fields the ball."

Why is the game so popular now?

"In the 1958 Ulster Semi-final between ourselves and Cavan in Clones I noted recently from an old cutting the attendance was given as six thousand. No Ulster semi-final now would have less than double that. But take the Railway Cup now. Once very well attended now attracting very few fans. The inter-county scene has become very popular especially the Championship. Television has helped, focussing on personalities and clashes. The B.B.C's coverage here in the North is outstanding."

The all ticket craze?

"People who go to the ordinary games should be able to get tickets for the big game but how do you arrange it? That's the problem. Being practical. Nothing wrong with the all ticket system provided there is a fair distribution system."

Does the lack of an international outlet other than the Australian Rules experiment hamper the game?

"In my professional life being involved in sport and a member of the Ulster Sports Council and meeting a lot of sportspeople, I'm often questioned in relation to international sport and why these non-international G.A.A. games are so popular. I keep pointing out that two other sports American Football and Australian Rules manage to maintain tremendous popularity within their own countries without being international. Just like the G.A.A. here in Ireland. I think there is something to be said for a sport that is just national because people feel closer to it. The Derry folk feel close to the Derry team. There is an empathy that other sports don't have. There is a big distance between the international star and the ordinary spectator. There is no distance between the Derry team and the Derry supporters. Absolute love. That's why it would be terrible if they start to pay players for playing. It would erode that lovely relationship."

Any regrets from your playing days?

"The big regret is that we didn't win the 1958 All-Ireland. It isn't a sore point. Simply because it would have meant so much to Derry over the years."

Greatest thrill from the game itself?

"A day when you're completely on form and you're catching the ball really well. I remember John D. Hickey interviewing me for a series he did for the *Irish Independent* called 'This Game I will Remember' and I took a colleges game where everything took off. The timing was right, you reach and you get the ball, you come down and you get your space. I still can feel that beautiful feeling if you're completely stretched looking up at the ball and nothing above you only the ball and the sky and you knew you were going to get it."

Greatest opponent?

"Mick O'Connell has to be rated as the greatest footballer I played against. But the one for many reasons I would opt for is Eddie Devlin of Tyrone. There is nothing you got easy from Eddie. If you won the ball from Mick O'Connell you could easily get away with it. He didn't hassle you. The problem was to catch the ball with O'Connell. Eddie was a man of great spring, good tackler, fine reader of the game, great kicker. I couldn't relax when playing on Eddie. The last time I met him was at Iggy Jones's funeral."

Greatest score?

"In my first season playing against Tyrone in Coalisland I got the ball soloed towards goal and people just kept opening out leaving me tons of space and I couldn't believe my luck. I ran straight through and placed it in the corner of the net. If only that continued to happen for me! Probably my first goal for Derry."

Greatest player ever seen?

"How do you judge? The greatest fielder and the most stylish footballer was O'Connell without a doubt. The hardest guy to play against was Frank Evers. He was just so bloody massive. You couldn't get near the ball with him standing there beside you. Another very complete player would have to be Pat Spillane - a scorer, a runner, a worker, he could turn games, a good if not great fielder, I'd have him on my team."

The game of your life?

"One is a McRory Cup game against St. Patrick's Cavan in Belfast in my final year. They beat us well the year before but this time we beat them by a point in this semi-final. I think I scored 1-10 in McRory Park. One of these games where you did things like a man possessed and went on automatic pilot almost."

Greatest legacy?

"Friendship. Almost any part of Ireland I go to there is somebody there I can say hello to or will say hello to me. A feeling of respect and so on which is mutual. It is recognition although I wouldn't be looking for that."

Thoughts on the G.A.A. itself?

"This is the area I have most misgivings about. The games have developed beyond the structures catering for them. The development of teams, the massive interest with fans, the media hype. It seems to me the counties do all the work now and I wonder if you simply wiped out all the Provincial Councils and the Central Council and anything above the county structure, would it make any difference? The work done by the counties and the clubs is quite spectacular. I'm not sure what the higher Councils are doing. It seems to me that any big business has to occasionally review itself and make changes. Change or die. The G.A.A. hasn't the capacity to do that. People at Provincial and Central Council level almost have to make a career of it. But they are not close enough or involved enough at the grassroots. Good management has the minimum number of tiers. There is no way at the moment where radical views can get into the G.A.A. currency. Not enough players involved. To get in you have to be a careerist. The G.A.A. is a great organisation but if it is to hold its place then it has to make room for radical views, to allow the hierarchy to be challenged."

Anecdote?

"Ballymaguigan were playing Coleraine in a club game in Coleraine. The pitch was not very well marked. No nets. The crossbar a kind of a rope. The ball was bobbing around and somebody pulled on it. One umpire gave it a goal, the other a point. Our umpire gave the decision against his own team. Similarly with the other. The referee realised they were honest decisions. So he used commonsense and split the difference and awarded two points. Both teams accepted it without question."

Above, left : Jim McKeever in his playing days.
right: Peter Canavan - 'the best scorer from play I have ever seen'.

Chapter 31

Martin McHugh

Of Donegal

In the glorious history of the G.A.A. now into its second century, there have been few more fairytale stories than Donegal's winning of their first All-Ireland football title in 1992. They first won out in Ulster in 1972 and subsequently won three more titles (1973, 1983 and 1990) before eventually getting past the penultimate hurdle. Máirtín Beag McHugh, as he is known in his native county, has been part of the latter three Ulster triumphs of Donegal. In their marvellous journey to the Sam Maguire summit of 1992, no man did more to inspire his county. Against Derry in the Ulster final and when faced by Keith Barr in the All-Ireland Final against Dublin, he led by inspiration and his name will always be heralded in the Hills of his beloved Donegal.

Did Donegal really believe in 1992 that they'd beat Dublin in the final?

"We really believed that we'd win. You saw the same confidence and belief in Derry this year. Our biggest trouble was to get over the semi-final. Dublin being in their own backyard and being hot favourites suited us. We knew we had very good footballers and we believed if we got ahead of them we'd win. A doubt crept in when Dublin got the penalty and if they had scored that we might have been in trouble. Our heads might have dropped."

Great memories of 1992?

"Some magical memories that we won't really appreciate for twenty or thirty years. My great memories are putting my arms around referee Tommy Sugrue after catching the ball and it was all over and the first person out on the field to me was my own wife. The linesman tried to stop her when she anticipated the final whistle but my father intervened and insisted she be allowed in. Bringing the Sam Maguire Cup into the county for the first time was full of hype. Being on that bus was special and we had never been through anything like that. But the greatest memory was waking up the following morning and realising that we were champions of Ireland. You lie in the bed on your own, waking up at 7 o'clock in the morning in the Grand Hotel, Malahide. I had gone to bed reasonably early and it was the first time I got the chance to think about it. Another memory is the word coming into the dressing-room that Joyce McMullen's brother (who was ill) had died. From being a happy dressing-room scene, all the players felt as if we had lost the game. It was just a mistake and a pity such a rumour spread. I'll never forget going over to Joyce and saying that a person is better off not suffering as words of consolation and his answer to me was 'It's a hard life isn't it?' Then his sister came into the dressing-room to tell us that it was all lies and we went from one extreme to the other, back to tears of happiness again. The last memory is coming into the Diamond in Donegal Town to more than twenty-five thousand very proud Donegal people who were simply ecstatic. And when the whole crowd sang 'Simply The Best' it was the first time a tear came into my eye."

You got some stick from supporters after the semi-final against Meath in 1990.

"I'm a stubborn kind of individual and can take that but I have a family and my mother and father lived for football and they couldn't understand that kind of stuff. It hurt them and by hurting them it hurt me. I don't believe any amateur footballer deserves that. You do your best and you have to work. My son was born the Wednesday after that game and that changed my attitude. Priorities were placed in proper order. I remember a friend of mine, Ian Hegarty from Kilcar, saying to me that it was a long road that had no turning. Two years later it all turned out well."

The hype that is All-Ireland Day now?

"It's massive. For an amateur footballer not to be affected is difficult. We got police escorts for the whole weekend. Some players take it in their stride. It makes you into a kind of celebrity when you're up there and a lot of ordinary individuals cannot cope with that but that's up to the manager to protect his players. If Croke Park could hold one hundred and twenty thousand for a football final it would be full. That interest has made it very big. So has T.V. The B.B.C. and U.T.V. must get a lot of credit for the upsurge in Ulster football. The B.B.C's programme on Sunday nights called 'The

Championship' is brilliant. As good as 'Match of the Day' and all the kids are watching it."

Was there too high an expectancy that Donegal should win the League afterwards?

"A lot of people are saying different things. The fact is we have never won a National League and still have not done so. We never contested a league final until 1993. We contested an All-Ireland Final and a league final in the same year both for the first time ever. League titles don't grow on trees either and we went within a kick of the ball of winning it. What took its toll really was the list of injuries and we couldn't shake them off."

Your achievements to date Martin?

"I started playing on the senior team in 1980. My first game was against Tipperary in the National League in Ballyshannon. I was nineteen then. I never played for the county minors at all but played on the Kilcar senior team and in the county final a few weeks before the National League. I scored ten points in all, from frees and play. We won that final and I joined the panel in October 1980. Three Ulster Senior Football titles, contesting six finals, losing three, four Railway Cup, four County Senior Football Championship medals 1980, 1985, 1989 and 1993, one U-21 All-Ireland, one Senior All-Ireland, two All Stars 1983 and 1992, one B. and I. and one National Irish award."

The status of the All Star Award?

"I think it is a great award. When a team wins an All-Ireland it puts the achievement back a bit. It is difficult to select such a team and the Award means an awful lot to those who have never won an All-Ireland. It gives a kind of international status to those selected. I'm not so sure if the sending off of a player should preclude him from being selected. I suppose there is for and against."

The tradition in Kilcar?

"As a young fellow it was all Gaelic we played. A very good bunch of players came along together in Kilcar in my age group. We contested six Donegal Senior Football

Championship finals in the 1980's, winning five Leagues. Great for the town which lived for the G.A.A. and our social life was wrapped around football. My parents were great supporters and my next door neighbour Hugh Shovlin had me out with a ball at about four or five years of age. He coached me in all the skills and I owe him a lot. He taught me how to sell dummies etc. and when I came into a field to play I had all these skills perfected beforehand. We perfected a different skill every week on the road or beside the house. Along the road there was Barry Campbell, the biggest single reason why four All-Ireland medals were won in this area by Noel Hegarty, John Joe Doherty, James and myself. He is the man looking after the football in Carrick Vocational School. We had a great school team there winning everything up the ranks first year, U-14, U-15, U-16 and senior (I won two Donegal Senior Vocational School medals). Got on the County Vocational Schools team once but I was even smaller then. The year I played on it, Packie Bonner was at midfield."

Was winning the All-Ireland always an ambition?

"Totally and utterly. I was a bit obsessed by it all. I believed we always had the team to do it. We didn't know what it took to win one and that worried us. I always thought maybe we weren't doing enough. Then all of a sudden last year we trained harder than ever before."

Is Donegal football safe now?

"I'd be worried about it as I believe the under-age structure is not good in the county. More money should be pumped into the under-age sector. The appointment of full time coaches should be considered. Men who would go around schools to advise school coaches, also to lend a helping hand. Even if a levy had to be adopted by clubs for this purpose it would be money well spent. There is a big hype now amongst the youngsters in the county. Instead of a Manchester United or Liverpool jersey they wear the Donegal strip proudly. That hype will run off if it isn't tapped."

How has the game changed in your time with Donegal, Martin?

"The basic change I've noticed is that county fitness level has evened off. No such thing now as an unfit county team. Kerry and Dublin used to dominate in this area.

The game itself hasn't changed much. The catch has gone out of it a bit. Nowadays it is all tactics, preventing opponents from getting the ball."

How do you see the game ten years on?

"It cannot get much more tactical. A lot of coaches have it off to an art. The organisation behind an inter-county team is every bit as good as the Irish soccer team. I'd like to see it go professional. I think there is a place for it. I believe we will lose the good talented players to other codes. The pressure on life now is a lot worse than in 1980 when I could leave school and walk into a job. That is not there now. We have lost a good player this year in Declan Boyle who is gone to play soccer with Sligo Rovers. I'd like to see him stay with Gaelic. I believe that down the line it has to come. We have massive gates now. And yet we have players who may be out of work. If you took the top ten teams in Ireland and made them professional I don't see how they wouldn't survive. Maybe a lot of people would not see that line but I think if we want to keep the standard high, to sell the game abroad, it has to go that way. The clubs would reap well on the whole thing as they would be supplying players who would graduate to being professionals. I'd be worried that we'd lose out because of the pressures of life today."

Are the pressures becoming too great for a top G.A.A. star?

"Since I left the house this morning I have signed at least ten autographs and we went out of the race this year. If you go out at night there are always people chatting to you. Now that's a good thing but you need a certain amount of privacy as well. The biggest pressures in Gaelic at the moment are on free-takers. A definite skill and it takes practise. Now the free-taker has a day's work to do like everybody else. He is expected to score every free inside fifty yards on the pitch. If he doesn't supporters are on his back. He cannot train too often. He isn't getting paid. It's not his job. Often he has to go out and train on his own."

How are you enjoying the **Sunday Independent** *weekly slot and the T.V. analysis?*

"I enjoy the writing. I'm not claiming to be a top journalist or that but sometimes you are able to articulate how players think in the field of play. I'd know how other players think. You get a bit of ragging but if you're honest and tell the truth you're O.K. I was a bit nervous on the telly at the start but it wore off. I'd prefer to add my comments during the actual game than the analysis afterwards or at intervals."

Brian McEniff's strengths?

"His great understanding of players. Very close to us. His organisation for the 1992 All-Ireland Final was unbelievable for a man never there before as a player or manager. He shepherded and shielded us in every way. He was on top of the situation and we knew exactly what was happening at all times. He phoned us all regularly beforehand and roomed us all together with a purpose, goalkeeper roomed with the full back etc. If he has a weakness then it is that he gets too close to players and cannot distance himself from them. But he is very human."

Are managers getting too much of the limelight?

"I suppose they are but it has become a big pressure job. If a team is beaten, the manager is always on the mat. Down the line it too may have to be professional as there is now too much pressure on them in their jobs, families, their lives. I'd like to get involved in that capacity myself sometime but that will depend on how long I will keep playing myself. I don't know yet when that will be, but I'll know when the legs are done and it's time to say goodbye."

Is a modern day successful forward subject to much physical abuse?

"The man to man marking is more prevalent now than ever. I don't enjoy football as much now. Even club football which used to be more open and free. You're marked from the word go especially when you're small. There isn't much you can do about it."

The Clones fiasco? How did Donegal feel on that very wet day?

"We have to look at it logically. We arrived a wee bit late at the pitch, at about 2.35p.m. When we saw it I thought it was unplayable. When we assembled in the dressing-room we felt if we asked for it to be called off Derry would consider we were using a ploy to give us Noel Hegarty back and those dogged by injuries would be given a better chance. In the end I think it was down to the Ulster Council and the referee to decide on it. A junior football game would not have been played in similar circumstances."

Clones as an Ulster final venue?

"I always liked the surface on the Clones pitch. Other Ulster players like it too but we must look further afield. The biggest problem with the venue is getting in and out of it. Parking, driving. We got away this year about 8p.m. and there were still car-queues down the roads. They should have opted for Cavan. So central and on the main Dublin-Northern road."

Improvements you'd suggest in the game?

"I'd get rid of the square ball. I'd allow the pick up off the ground, not a skill anymore. Take the fisted pass now. Teams barring Cork don't use it to success much but the Australians came over here and in a short time perfected it. With their level of fitness and physique they showed that maybe this was the way to play our games. They ran in fours up the field fistpassing the ball over and back and nobody could stop them. A lot of the handpasses of the moment are doubtful so we may have to go back to the fisted pass only again. Another thing I have recommended is that after five personal fouls from one team a point should be awarded to the opposing team. The emphasis would be placed then on the tackle which would then be made on the ball rather than on the man. Maybe the solo-run should be limited to one solo and a hop of the ball, although I should be the last to recommend this!"

Favourite referee?

"Tommy Sugrue of Kerry. Players are very hyped up in a game. He has control and is nice to players. He is absolutely fit and is always up with play. He talks to players during a game. He often plays the advantage but will always return afterwards and let transgressors know he has seen the foul. Tends to ignore players' comments if they are not abusive. Players respect his honesty and commonsense."

Most difficult opponent?

"Henry Downey over the years. From the point of view of tough battles. Tony Davis and D.J. O'Kane too."

Greatest Donegal players past and present?

"Of our own team Anthony Molloy would be the best leader in determination and spirit we have ever had. He always sweated blood for Donegal. I played with him all my life. The Donegal player who impressed me most that I've seen as a spectator would have been Martin Carney. Sean Ferritter as a midfielder is talked about still today."

Greatest player you have seen?

"Matt Connor of Offaly. He had everything it took to be a footballer. Big, strong, a ball-winner, could kick with either foot. His close control in a solo-run was unreal. Had speed and accuracy too. And he could look lazy through it all with the hands on his hips. The greatest footballer I have ever seen. I remember being at a 7-a-side in Dublin and seeing his club Walsh Island play six men at the back with Matt on his own up front and every team put two men on him. But it didn't matter. He got the ball, beat the two men and stuck it in the net. He scored a point from a free that day - the finest I have ever seen. It was on the fifty yards line, on the right hand side of the field which was off his foot about two feet in from the sideline. As a free-taker myself I looked at him and considered it impossible. Just stepped back and struck it perfectly, landing it on top of the net. Brian Mullins in his own way was a great footballer. For natural talent there was Mikey Sheehy."

Greatest score?

"The most important score would have to be the free-kick against Cavan to draw the first game which kept us in the All-Ireland race. I wasn't a wild man to get goals. Used to lay them on more! Another was a penalty against Down in the Ulster Championship in 1985 in Ballybofey with five minutes left and the sides level. It was an important kick as I had missed a penalty the week before and as I stepped to take it a man in the crowd shouted 'Don't let McHugh take it'. I just had the confidence, had practised it all week, didn't even look at McEniff, knew where I was sticking it and had my mind made up."

Martin McHugh

Game of your life?

"Winning the first of anything is great. In my first County title win I scored ten points in a great match. Then the U-21 final our first ever All-Ireland title and now the All-Ireland Final of 1992 would have to be the game of my life in a Donegal jersey. There was a lot of talk about Keith Barr before the game and I remember standing up in the Donegal dressing-room and saying 'We'll see who is the main man at 5 o'clock this evening'. I had the confidence to say that then as I felt good. I would have to class it as the greatest moment in sport."

A final idea got from John O'Keeffe of Kerry in relation to juvenile coaching?

"In Kerry they take in one hundred and fifty U-15 footballers (three from each club) and coach them for a week with fifteen or so top coaches in the county involved and all paid by the G.A.A. in Kerry. Then they cut that down to fifty and they coach the elite fifty from that stage up to minor level. That's the way they produce their minor team in Kerry. In Meath they have a similar system building from U-16 up with a close relationship to the minor management."

Your greatest thrill from the game itself?

"Being in a very tight situation and kicking a great point, like the one I got in the final minutes of the Ulster final in Clones in 1992. Coming in from the right corner, beating three Derrymen and kicking it over my right shoulder. Maybe it appeared a fluke to some but I would have done that often in training. It put us a point up. In a case where defenders thought they had you covered and you still managed a point. Maybe I should have given you that as my greatest score!"

Martin McHugh solos through against Antrim in Ballybofey in June 1993.
Photo - Ann McManus (Irish News)

Previous books by the author:

1. Twelve Glorious Years (Published 1965)
2. Three in a Row (1966)
3. Gaelic Games Quiz Book 1 (1975)
4. Gaelic Games Quiz Book 2 (1978)
5. Action Replay (1983) - Cost £3.95.*
   A G.A.A. Centenary Year production of the author's life and times in the G.A.A.
6. Gaelic Games Quiz Book 3 - two editions (1984 and 1985)
7. Only the Teachers Grow Old -Cost £4.95.*

* All the above titles are out of print except *Action Replay* and *Only the Teachers Grow Old.*